Extracts from the minutes of the Epping and Ongar Highway Trust from ... 1769 to ... 1870. With ... illustrations, etc.

Benjamin Winstone

Extracts from the minutes of the Epping and Ongar Highway Trust from ... 1769 to ... 1870.
With ... illustrations, etc.
Winstone, Benjamin
British Library, Historical Print Editions
British Library
1891
vi. 303 p. ; 8°.
10368.h.29.

The BiblioLife Network

This project was made possible in part by the BiblioLife Network (BLN), a project aimed at addressing some of the huge challenges facing book preservationists around the world. The BLN includes libraries, library networks, archives, subject matter experts, online communities and library service providers. We believe every book ever published should be available as a high-quality print reproduction; printed on- demand anywhere in the world. This insures the ongoing accessibility of the content and helps generate sustainable revenue for the libraries and organizations that work to preserve these important materials.

The following book is in the "public domain" and represents an authentic reproduction of the text as printed by the original publisher. While we have attempted to accurately maintain the integrity of the original work, there are sometimes problems with the original book or micro-film from which the books were digitized. This can result in minor errors in reproduction. Possible imperfections include missing and blurred pages, poor pictures, markings and other reproduction issues beyond our control. Because this work is culturally important, we have made it available as part of our commitment to protecting, preserving, and promoting the world's literature.

GUIDE TO FOLD-OUTS, MAPS and OVERSIZED IMAGES

In an online database, page images do not need to conform to the size restrictions found in a printed book. When converting these images back into a printed bound book, the page sizes are standardized in ways that maintain the detail of the original. For large images, such as fold-out maps, the original page image is split into two or more pages.

Guidelines used to determine the split of oversize pages:

• Some images are split vertically; large images require vertical and horizontal splits.
• For horizontal splits, the content is split left to right.
• For vertical splits, the content is split from top to bottom.
• For both vertical and horizontal splits, the image is processed from top left to bottom right.

WAKE ARMS.

NEW PIECE OF ROAD.

BEGINNING OF OLD ROAD.

Road from Wake Arms to Epping.

EXTRACTS FROM THE MINUTES

OF THE

EPPING AND ONGAR

HIGHWAY TRUST.

FROM ITS COMMENCEMENT IN 1769 TO ITS TERMINATION
IN 1870.

———

With Maps and Illustrations.

———

A CONTRIBUTION TO LOCAL HISTORY

BY

BENJ. WINSTONE.

London:
HARRISON AND SONS, ST. MARTIN'S LANE,
Printers in Ordinary to Her Majesty

1891.

(For Private Circulation.)

PREFACE.

One of the concluding clauses in the Act of Parliament which established the Epping Highway Trust ordered that the transactions of the Trustees should be entered in a book or books, kept for that purpose. Mr. John Windus having been clerk to the Trustees when the Trust terminated in 1870, the books have been retained in the office of Messrs. Windus and Trotter, Epping.

The entries made in the Minute Book the first half of the hundred years during which the Trust existed have in many places perished, and in others have become almost obliterated. The mildew, which has been at work for some time, will no doubt continue its work of destruction; and in a few years the records of the earlier transactions of the Trustees will be obliterated, and the information they contain lost.

On the establishment of the Trust, it at once proceeded to take measures for lessening the gradients of Golden's and Buckhurst Hills; a little later on the Trustees undertook the formation of a road suitable for coaches as far as Writtle, on the way to Chelmsford, and in 1830 they commenced making the new road through the heart of the Forest from the "Wake Arms" to Woodford.

These matters have at least a local interest. I have, therefore, thought it advisable, by printing the records of transactions of the Trustees, to preserve the history or accounts of the work carried on for the improvement of the important high road through Epping into the eastern counties. Until 1769 the road was under the management of local Justices and County Justices of the Peace, assembled at Quarter Session.

From the Acts of Parliament passed in the last century some knowledge may be obtained of the opposition against which they had to contend, and also the powers with which they were entrusted to enable them to meet difficulties as they arose. The objection to the payment of tolls gave rise to riots, leading to the destruction of turnpikes, toll-houses, &c. So serious were the disturbances that laws had to be made inflicting severe punishments on offenders. The accounts of riots in Herefordshire and in Bristol are copied from the "Gentleman's Magazine," as they illustrate the lawless proceedings which the Acts were passed to suppress.

The construction of vehicles, waggons, carts, &c., appears to have obtained more attention from the framers of Highway Acts of Parliament than the best manner of making roads suitable for the traffic passing over them. The width of the fellies of the wheels of carts and waggons, the weight of their loads, and the number of horses to draw them, as well as their position when harnessed, were all regulated by Acts of Parliament, and the Justices of the Peace at Quarter Sessions were empowered to impose fines and penalties on delinquents. Occasionally Highway Acts are noticed in the "Gentleman's Magazine." Abstracts of some of the comments have been made, as they show the state of the roads at the time the Acts were passed, and the opinions formed of the measures taken to improve them.

Many of the Acts of Parliament and other matters mentioned are anterior to the formation of the Epping Highway Trust—when the road was under the management of the Justices of the Peace—the Act, however, which created the Trust, did little more than transfer to the Trustees the duties and powers exercised by their predecessors, so that the references to Acts of Parliament, and extracts from the "Gentleman's Magazine," are not perhaps out of place, although the sole object of this publication is to preserve records of the proceedings of the Epping and Ongar Highway Trusts.

The desire shown by Archæological Societies, established in Essex as well as in most other counties, to obtain information respecting pre-historic remains, affords the explanation of my having devoted a few pages to the grass roads at Epping Long Green, Rye Hill, and Wintry Wood, and supplying what information has come under my notice relating to British roads, supporting the supposition of their having been ancient British track ways.

Anthropologists have pointed out that there are characteristic differences between the English people and the Teutonic tribes from which they derive their origin. It is believed that these are due to the mingling of the blood of the Britons with that of their Saxon conquerors. The formation of their head and features, and the colours of the hair and complexion, differing from those of their kinsmen in North Germany, are adduced as evidence of the admixture of the blood of a race not Teutonic.

The people, more especially the children inhabiting the district through which the roads passed, differing so much by their dark blue eyes, rich brown wavy hair, graceful figures, and elastic step from the North German, favour the supposition that the Saxons amalgamated by marriage with the Britons, whose lands, as conquerors, they occupied. The presence of Ambresbury Bank and Cowpers Camp in the Forest—British enclosures—indicate by their extent that at one time there was a large number of the native race living in the neighbourhood of Epping. Dr. Beddoe says that, although there is little information respecting Essex, it is quite possible that in certain parts small British States, or Roman-British towns, may have allied themselves with the invaders; and also, that he believes the people, except near the coast, are more usually dark-haired than those of Kent, Norfolk, and Suffolk.[*]

The Minutes relating to the work done at Golden's Hill and Buckhurst Hill, the road to Chelmsford as far as Writtle, and making the new road through the Forest from the "Wake Arms" to Woodford have been arranged under separate headings, in order that the account of the alterations and improvements might appear as a continuous narrative.

In accordance with an article by a writer in the "Athenæum," when reviewing a county archæological journal, in which he suggests that as opportunities arose ancient deeds, not previously

---

[*] "Races of Britain," page 64.

printed, relating to property in the county should be noticed, and abstracts made; there is, in an Appendix, copy of a deed relating to North Weald; also abstracts of deeds relating to Wintry Wood, Latton Priory, &c. The former I obtained by purchase; but I am indebted to my friend, Walter de Grey Birch, for the translation; and for abstracts of the other deeds, which are in the British Museum. He also kindly procured for me a copy of the Act of 1769, appointing Trustees of the Epping Highway, and an abstract of a deed relating to the Forest (page 89). I have to thank Mr. Walter Metcalfe, F.S.A., for the drawing of Winchelsea House, which he copied from an old deed relating to the property, and so procured valuable information, as it shows that in 1634 the road from Loughton into Epping was in use. I have also to thank Mr. Cecil Harrison for his advice and assistance whilst the pages were passing through the press; and my daughters, Bertha, Jessie, and Flora, the former for copying the portion of Chapman and André's Map of Essex, showing the old road up Buckhurst Hill, running in front of the "Bald Face Stag Inn," and the two latter for the use of their young eyes when endeavouring to read the almost obliterated entries in the earlier Minute Book, and for assistance rendered in reading proofs, &c.

Mr. Henry A. Cole, of Buckhurst Hill, has made the sketches showing some of the work done on Golden's and Buckhurst Hills; and on the new road from the "Wake Arms" to Woodford.

There may perhaps be errors in dates, and in the figures copied out of the accounts, which extend over many years, although care has been taken to ensure accuracy; but the Minutes may be accepted as correctly copied or abstracted, and I trust, therefore, that the compilation will be useful as a contribution to local history.

BENJ. WINSTONE,
Ockeridge, Epping,
Essex.

May, 1891.

LIST OF ILLUSTRATIONS.

CHAPTER I.

OME REMARKS ON THE REMAINS OF ANCIENT ROADS, ETC.,
IN EPPING AND THE ADJOINING PARISHES.

a country becoming inhabited communications have to be
aintained between the settlements which are formed, as the
ulation increases, at a less or greater distance from each
er, and from the land occupied by the first immigrants.

For this purpose paths or trackways are cut through the
neval forest, or in some way marked out over moorland or
n country, where the higher ground is selected, on account of
being, from the natural drainage dryer and firmer than in
valleys, where heavy rains and floods might render the track
assable.

In England these trackways, leading merely from one
lement to another, are in many instances the origin of parish
ds; so that until more direct, and therefore shorter roads
e made, communications between distant places had to be
ntained by long and circuitous routes. In some localities
re high roads have been constructed, portions, nevertheless,
he primitive track or road remain; and, when they have not
n gravelled by the authorities, they are known as grass
ds.

In the Parish of Epping are the remains of two ancient
ds, and, as reason can be adduced for believing them to be
-Roman, they are deserving of notice when speaking of the
ds over which the trustees of the highways had the control,
ough they have long since ceased to be recognised as roads
the parish authorities—excepting the small portion from the
age in the uplands to the top of the hill leading to Parndon,
ch has been partially gravelled. But the continuation of the

road to Rye Hill in one direction, and in the other to Harrold's Farm, exists in its primitive state. The remains of the other ancient road is a cart track, through the portion of the Forest marked in the ordnance map Wintry Wood.* It runs from the corner of Thornwood Common and Duck Lane to the Ongar Road, and was at one time the high road to London, through Coopersale Common and Abridge.

Britain is said to have been well inhabited at the time of the Roman invasion by Julius Cæsar; and the cause of his interference in the affairs of the Island makes it evident that means of communication existed between distant places.

The counties, Essex and Hertfordshire, have the credit of commencing the history of England. Essex was inhabited by the Trinobantes, and part of Hertfordshire by the Cassii, two powerful tribes. The chief of the latter, Cassivellaunus, whose aggressive policy had deprived several petty princes of their territories, overcame and slew Imanuentius, Prince of the Trinobantes, and, by taking possession of his country, drove his son Mandubratius into exile. It appears that Mandubratius and the other deposed chieftains applied to Cæsar, then in Gaul, for assistance to oppose Cassivellaunus, who, like Napoleon the First, was ever anxious to extend the boundaries of his kingdom.

Cæsar's disciplined army speedily overcame the irregular troops of Cassivellaunus. He, however, being anxious to leave a country where he had experienced much opposition and hard fighting, proposed or accepted terms of peace. One of the conditions was that Mandubratius should be restored to, and remain in undisturbed possession of, his father's kingdom.

Historians have taken very little notice of the internal affairs of Britain during nearly the hundred years following Cæsar's invasion, when its history commences again with the

---

* Wintry Wood and Wintry Park are placed on the north side of the Harlow Road in Messrs. Chapman & André's map, and also in that drawn for the use of the Trustees of the Ongar and Epping turnpike road. In the Appendix is a deed relating to Wintry Wood.

domestic troubles of the kingdom of which Essex formed the chief portion.

At that time Tasciovanus ruled over the Cassii, and his son Cunobeline was the chief of the Trinobantes. Arminus, the son of the latter, having been banished the country on account of his rebellious conduct, went to Rome, where he gave such an account of the political state of the country, as induced the Emperor Claudius to assume, that a favourable opportunity was afforded the Romans for again invading Britain. The natives fought with their usual bravery; but the discipline of the Roman troops, and the facilities Gaul afforded for re-filling their ranks when thinned by fighting, enabled them to overcome the armies of the Trinobantes and Cassii, and to take possession of their countries: so that Essex, Hertfordshire, and part of Middlesex, including what is now London, became a Roman province. It extended from the sea-coast to Verulamium, the capital of the Cassii, which the conquerors fortified and made their stronghold on the inland boundary of their conquest. The site of the capital of the Trinobantes became a colony immediately under Roman Government. Maldon is supposed by some writers to have been the site of Cunobeline's residence, and Colchester a Colony, "Colonia," formed by the Romans; but it is generally believed that Colchester was the capital town. Maldon, however, must have been a place of great importance, as there is, close to it, the remains of an extensive British encampment.

Cæsar, when speaking of his invasion of Britain, mentions war chariots as a formidable portion of the armies opposed to him. There must, therefore, have been tracks or pathways traversing the country of a sufficient width, and in a suitable condition for the passage over them of wheel carriages,—both those used in war and those employed for domestic purposes.

The conveyances were, no doubt, very light. The war chariots were probably made of wicker-work, and covered with hides, like the boats used by the Picts when they crossed the river or arm of the sea to invade England, and constructed in the same manner as the coracles used in the shallow rivers in

Wales at the present day. Had they not been very light, the drivers could not have turned the horses or stopped them when at full speed, as they are said to have done, in the description of the mode of fighting given by Cæsar and Tacitus.

Waggons of some kind were also in use; for Tacitus mentions them drawn up in the rear of the famous battle in which the Queen Boadicea was defeated, and the rebellion she headed crushed. There is no description given of these waggons. It may, however, be supposed that they were somewhat like those used at the present time in some parts of the Continent, made of very light framework, and having wattle-like hurdles for their sides.

The two capitals which have been mentioned, Camulodunum (Maldon or Colchester) and Verulamium (St. Albans), as having been permanently occupied by the Romans were important places, the former being the capital of the Trinobantes and the latter the capital of the Cassii ; it may be therefore assumed that for many generations they had been the strongholds of the respective petty kingdoms, and that at the period under consideration, as Tasciovanus occupied Verulamium, and his son, the celebrated Cunobelinus or Cunobeline,[*] Camulodunum, these places were connected by trackways, roads suitable for the use of wheel carriages; over which intercourse between the inhabitants of the two towns and the district surrounding them could be carried on. As the vehicles were very light, roads such as those now known as grass roads would be sufficiently hard or firm for that purpose.

On referring to a map of England it will be seen that the most direct road from Verulamium (St. Albans) to the east coast of Essex, would run by way of Hadley, through Enfield Chase into the valley of the River Lea; and crossing the ancient road—the Ermine Way—be continued over the Lea marshes and by a ford through the river, to the land on which stands Waltham, or as it is generally called Waltham Abbey. Then by the now village of Epping Uplands, over Rye Hill,

---

* Thomas Wright—"The Celts, the Roman and the Saxon," page 40.

running past where at the present time are the remains of Latton Priory, into the Harlow Road. But it is most likely the ancient road turned to the left and passed by the mound (supposed to be British) to join the road over Hazlewood Common a little nearer to Harlow.

From Verulamium (St. Albans), and also from Brockly Hill, near Elstree, the Roman Station of Sulloniaceæ, which Dr. Stukeley believes was once an oppidum or stronghold of Cassivelaunus, are roads which run through Hadley and Enfield Chase, into the Lea Valley. The Rev. Mr. Newcome, in his history of St. Albans, states : "There is still visible, besides Watling Way, or road from London to Veralam, another original Roman road through the forest of Enfield Chase, called to this day Camlet Way, and which seems to have been the road from Verulam to Camulodunum or Canonum." The Rev. Mr. Cass, however, doubts the road having been the road from Verulam to Camulodunum. He thinks it went by Hertford and Bishop Stortford, and supposes the Camlet Way probably ran from Sulloniaceæ. He, however, mentions that in Gunter and Rolfe's map, 1658, Camlet or Camelot is distinctly laid down as the road between Hadley Church, and the elevated ground known as Ridgway. And that it is certain from early times one of the most direct communications between the villages of Hadley and Enfield, through the heart of the intervening Chase, was thus designated." Ridge is but a few miles from St. Albans, and there seems to be no room for doubting that there was a communication between Ridge and St. Albans; and, consequently, that the Camlet Way commenced at St. Albans, and was continued through Enfield Chase, to the valley of the River Lea.

Across the marsh on both sides of the river there was probably a natural causeway, banking up the river on the Hertfordshire side, and forming there a sheet of water. Farmer says, in his history of Waltham Abbey, that when

---

* Cass' "Monken Hadly," page 5.

King Alfred, in the year 876, cut the Dykes, the marshes and meadows were under water, "which great water was then navigable." Sir H. Chauncy, in his history of Hertfordshire, speaking of Ware, says when the Danes sailed up the river (894),* the tides flowed as far as Hertford, and that the Danes erected a fort there and raised the water with a great bank or dam round the same, by which means they made a "great Weare,"† and so secured themselves from the hurt of King Alfred's army. King Alfred, by making a great wall, now Blackwall, stopped the flow of the tide in great measure up the River Lea.

It is admitted by historians of Essex that King Alfred cut the dykes which now exist at Waltham, and so, by draining off the water, left the Danish ships dry, and useless. As it is evident that the water on one side must have stood at a much higher level than it did on the other, or the dykes could not have run it off, it is not assuming much to say that there must have been raised ground to bank up the river to form the weir, or sheet of water, and this bank forming a natural causeway was, when the tide was not at its full height, the continuation of the Camlet Way, into Essex.

How early Waltham became inhabited cannot be determined. Its name is first introduced into history at the time the manor was granted to Tovi. But it is not likely fertile land bordering on a river or sheet of water would have been left unoccupied by the ancient Britons, who depended so much upon their cattle for subsistence; as the ground between the hills and the river would have afforded them land for cultivation, and the marshes food for their cattle. County historians derive its

---

* There is a discrepancy in dates; the dates given by the respective authors are, however, correctly quoted.

† In J. O. Halliwell's "Dictionary of Archaic and Provincial Words," weir is said to mean either a pool or dam. At Epping there was a large pond called Butler's Weir. In the title deeds of Spriggs Oak it is described as being situate on Butler's Weir Hill. Bailey's dictionary, 1742, spells the word "ware," and gives its meaning, "dam."

name from Weald-ham, Saxon words meaning a manor or congregation of houses in or near a wood. Tovi seems to have valued the manor on account of the quantity of game to be found in its vicinity; for (by Camden) it is stated that he placed on the land 66 men to guard his possessions; these were probably freemen, holding their land by military tenure, and unlike the villeins who cultivated the soil for the benefit of the lord of the manor. So there must, at the time, have been a population, against whose depredation the property had to be protected.

Through the extravagance of Athelstan's son, the property became vested in the Crown, when it was given by Edward the Confessor to Earl Harold, on the condition that he built a monastery on the manor in place of the little convent, with two priests, which had been established by Tovi. The establishment consisted of a Dean and eleven secular Canons. "Secular" Canons did not, like "regulars," live always in communities. But they found their duties in the villages and hamlets around their abbeys, living amongst the congregations entrusted to their care. The inhabitants were, no doubt, a mixed race, having for their ancestors the Saxon conquerors and the daughters of the Britons, whose lives had been sacrificed in repeated battles, leaving their homes and children to become the property of the victors. If, as is supposed, the population around Waltham Abbey was numerous, it is not perhaps assuming much when suggesting, that where Waltham Abbey now stands there was at one time a British settlement.

Although it is stated in county histories that the name Waltham is derived from Weald Wood and Ham, signifying a manor, or the dwellings constituting the village or hamlet situate in or near to woods, there are grounds for the supposition that it, and also Walthamstow and other places, were originally British settlements, deriving their name from Wealh, Wealas, or Wala, stranger. It is known that Wealas, or Whealas, and Wala, were names the Saxons gave to a people not belonging to their own race, and it was so applied to the ancient Britons, who were a large population at the time of the Saxon invasion.* Although conquered in the southern and eastern portion of England they still remained, for the most part, as a servile race, cultivating the soil for the benefit of the Saxon owners of the land, as they had previously done for the Romans.

In the west of England there were in existence communities of Cymry (Britons), using their own language and observing their own usages, 500 years after the invasion of Hengist. Beddoe† mentions that in a considerable portion of Wessex, of which Berkshire and Hampshire were the nucleus, it may be admitted that as late as A.D. 700, Welshmen and Englishmen (Britons and Saxons) lived intermixed under English law; the former, however, as the conquered race were subjected to some derogatory legal provision, but they were not altogether deprived of their land, and they remained too numerous and powerful to be treated without some consideration. The Weregilds, or value of a life of a Wealas (British) churl was at a lower rate than that of a Saxon churl, whose life was valued at 200s., but that of the former, though he held a hide of land, was only 120s.; if he had none he was rated at 60s., the price of a slave. About A.D. 530 the kingdom of the East Saxons (Essex) was founded, after 12 years' hard fighting. It consisted of modern Essex, Middlesex, and part of Herts.

Union of the two races was probably completed in Essex at a much earlier period than in other parts of the country, owing to the large infusion of Teutonic blood that had been introduced by the Romans; who, 200 years before the Saxon invasion, had made settlements of captives, in accordance with their practice of breaking up to some extent nationalities. It is stated that in England many settlements of Alamanni, South Germans, were made in the time of Probus, Emperor of Rome,‡

---

* Dr. Nicholas' "Pedigree of the English People," page 208.

† Beddoe—"Races of Britain," page 65.

‡ Gibbons' "Decline and Fall of the Roman Empire," second edition, Vol. II, page 83.

and that manors having their place names ending in "ing," and ingas for the plural, were settlements of South Germans.* As there are many places in Essex having such a termination to their names, as Epping, Nazing, Matching, Shering, Rodings, Mountnessing, &c., it may be inferred that the German colonies were numerous. It is also stated that these settlements were made amongst a conquered people for military purposes, in order that there might be at hand men, having no national feeling, who could be relied on, to put down an outbreak of the natives. When the Saxons overran Essex, they must, in consequence of these German settlements, have found in many parts of the land people of their own stock, and also a mixed race, as well as the Britons, so that the complete union of the two races would naturally have taken place more rapidly in Essex than in most other parts of England.

The Wealas (Britons), having at a very early period ceased to be known as an alien race, their name would not be so familiar, as applicable to the derivation of the names of places, as the household word Weald (Wood). The monks would therefore readily adopt the idea that the first syllable in Waltham, Walthamstow, and other places, was derived from Weald, and signified the position of the place, when entering the names of the various manors bestowed on the monastery whose property they were enumerating. The name Wealtham occurs in Saxon Chronicles as late as the 10th century, in a Chronicle A.D. 909, which was a confirmation of King Edward to Tridistan, Bishop of Winchester, of land at Veranburn, Wealtham, Bramleage, or Overton with Tadly Waltham, and Bradley, co. Hants; also in a grant by King Edward to the Thegn Alphage, of land in White Waltham, co. Berks, entitled "Carta Regis Eadmundi de Wealtham." (*See* de Grey Birch, "Cartularium Saxonicum," pp. 297 and 490.) One of the manors granted to Waltham Abbey is spelt Wealtham and West Wealtham, and they had also Walafar

---

* Seebohm—"Village Community," page 358.

in Boreham.* Besides Walthamstow and Waltham Abbey, in the vicinity of Epping there are North† and South Weald, whose names are supposed to have been derived from the fact that they are situated in the forest. As Essex abounded in woodland it is difficult to see why the places should have been denominated Weald by the Saxon, as characteristic of their situation, when so many other places must also have been surrounded by woodland. But, if the land was occupied by the ancient Britons, whom they called Wealas, it follows that in time the places would derive their name, Weald, from the earlier owners. Some support is afforded to this suggestion by North Weald being situated on a road which ran from the British oppidum, in the forest, known as Ambresbury Camp, and perhaps from Cowper's Camp, by Loughton to Fyfield, supposed by Gough to have been a British settlement. He states : "At Fyfield by Ongar, in 1749, were found a great number of celts, with a large quantity of metal for casting them, 50 lbs. of which, with several of the instruments, the late Earl Tilney gave to Mr. Lethieullier."†

At South Weald there is a circular camp. Although it is said by some to be Roman, its form favours the idea that it was originally a British oppidum, and supports the suggestion that South Weald was also a dwelling place of Wealas, or Britons. In Nordon's "History of Essex," 1594, the name is spelt Walde, and in the "Gentleman's History of Essex," vol. 5, page 6, when speaking of the Manor, it is said, " This church was given by Earl Harold to his Abbey of Waltham under the general name of Walde. The gift was confirmed by Richard the 1st under the name Walda."‡ Walde has the

---

* Walafar was a small manor in Boreham. It gave the name to a family —De Walafar, or Walkfare ; which bestowed it on Waltham Abbey. (*Vide* Morant's "History of Essex," by Meggy and Chalk, Chelmsford, under " Walkfare," page 13 ; and also "The Gentleman's History of Essex," page 131.)

† Gough's " 'Camden' Britannia."

‡ Doomsday Book relating to Essex, translated by T. T. Chisenhale Marsh. —"Walda is held by Richard of Raneilfus ; it was held by Godwin, a freeman in the time of King Edward, for a manor and half for a hide and xv

same meaning as Wood or Weald but it has been already pointed out that during the several hundred years which had passed since the Saxon conquest the origin of the name might have been lost; for the Wealas had long ceased to be a distinct race.

Between Bishop Stortford and Sawbridgeworth, and not far from the river Stort, is a large encampment named "Walbury." It has been called a Roman Encampment. But the name Walbury leads to the suggestion that it was British, and designated by their Saxon neighbours Wala Berg, or the "Dwelling of the Strangers."

Roach Smith, a great authority on Roman Antiquities, mentions in an article in the "Gentleman's Magazine" for 1865, part 2, having visited the place; and he gives it as his opinion that it was not a Roman Encampment but a British oppidum, and in Camden's "Britannia," edited by Gough, it is stated that "it was anciently termed 'Walla.'"

At Walton-on-the-Naze there have been found flint flakes, knives, and scrapers which afford evidence of its having been a British settlement; thus favouring the idea that its name may have been derived from "Wala" and "ton"—Strangers' settlement. There is also in Essex Wallasea Island. These names lead to the conclusion that for many years after the settlement of the Saxons in the county, there existed localities inhabited by the Britons, who were alluded to as "strangers" under the names of Wealas, Whealas, or Wala, by their Saxon neighbours.

It cannot but be admitted that the derivations of the names

---

acres. Always one team on the demesne, and half a team of the homagers manor of Weld or Sewells in Harlow (and North Weald)." Bowen, in his map of Essex, 1717, spells it North Wald. It has been suggested that the Waldenses, who were Christians driven by persecution from Italy into the nearly inaccessible mountains of the Alps on the north side of Italy, derive their name from Walda=strangers. But Bosworth, in his Anglo Saxon Dictionary, gives the English word "ruler" as the equivalent of the Saxon word "Walda."

of places are undeterminable with certainty, and that they must remain debateable ground. There is, however, as good a foundation in the word Wala, Wealas, Wealhas, as in Weald, for the names Waltham, and Walthamstow, which at the time of the Norman survey was spelt Welanneston,* the first syllable apparently derived from the Saxon word "Wala," "stranger"; also for the supposition that North† and South Weald derived their names from Wealhas or Wealas or Wala, signifying stranger, i.e., Britons, as from Weald or Walde, a forest. The suggestion therefore can be permitted, that Waltham may at one time have been a British settlement, situated in an ancient British road, running from Verulamium to Camulodunum. For the road which runs from it through Epping Uplands, apparently the continuation of the road through the marsh, over the river Lea, presents the characteristics of an ancient British road, as described by the author of the Commentary attached to the Itinerary of Richard of Cirencester, in the following extract.

"By the early account of the Britons it appears that they maintained a considerable foreign commerce, and that they formed towns, or large communities, and raised chariots for warlike, and undoubtedly for civil, purposes. Hence it is evident these internal communications must have been free and numerous. We need not therefore be surprised, if after the lapse of so many centuries marks of such British roads appear at present to an observer, differing in many respects from the roads subsequently made by the Romans and traversing the Island in every direction.

"These ancient ways may be distinguished from those made by the Romans by unequivocal marks.

"1st.—They are not raised nor paved, nor always straight; but often wind along the top or sides of the chain of hills which lie in their course.

---

* Lewis' "Topographical Dictionary."

† In North Weald there is marked, in Smith's map of Essex, "Whealas," which is much nearer to "Wealas" than "Weald."

MOUND IN THE FIELD BY LATTEN PRIORY

"2nd.—They do not lead to Roman towns of note, or notice such towns except when placed on the site of British fortresses.

"3rd.—They are attended by tumuli, like those of the Romans; but usually throw out branches; which after running parallel for some miles are united to the original stem."

The road soon after leaving Waltham divides into two branches; [as did an ancient British road] one branch runs up Gally Hill on the left hand side and the other branch on the right hand side of Gally Wood. These two roads are nearly parallel, Harold's farm separating them; they run along a ridge of hills; one over Nazing Common the other by the village of Epping in the Uplands (marked in the map Nazing Green and Epping Long Green respectively), and at the present time the latter continues as a grass road to Rye Common, and through several gates, passes by Latton Priory, running into the Harlow Road. Near to Latton Priory on the left hand side, a short distance from the Harlow Road, is a moated mound or tumulus, which is a distinctive feature of a British or Roman road. The road which runs by Nazing Long Green has been gravelled by the parish authorities, and no doubt its direction has been altered to suit the requirements of landowners in its vicinity, but it joins the primitive road at Rye Hill.

It has been mentioned that formerly roads were made only to connect hamlets or villages, so that in many instances distant places were reached by very circuitous routes.

The old road from Harlow and the neighbouring villages to London, which town is believed to have been a stronghold of the Trinobantes, ran over Rye Hill, to the village of Epping Uplands. This portion of the road has been previously mentioned as the King's Highroad from Rye Hill to Waltham Abbey. From the village it ran along the ridge of hills to the parish church, where it divided, as did the British roads, into two branches, one passing through Wintry Wood, so named in the ordnance map, across the forest, where a remnant still

remains, now used as a cart track,* and continued through the
forest to Coopersale Common, passing on the left hand side
of Coopersale Hall, the property of the Houblon family, to the
bottom of the hill. At the back of the brick fields, close to
which the road or trackway may have originally run, is a
moated mound, the existence of which is known as one of the
characteristics of a British road.

The other branch of the road, that divided at Epping
Church, known as Lindsey Street, crosses the present high road
at Epping, and passing between the Grove and Mr. Pearson's
house, joins at the bottom of the hill, in Coopersale, the other
division of the road, which ran by Wintry Wood and
Coopersale Common. On the brow of the hill, by the railway
cutting, in the grounds of the Grove, is another tumulus or
mound, said to be evidence of the existence of a British road.
These two roads, running on each side of Coopersale House,
uniting at the bottom of the hill, formed the ancient road to
London, passing by Stewart's Green, Theydon Garnon Church,
and Abridge.

When speaking of Lindsey Street as having been, perhaps,
an ancient British trackway, it may be pointed out that Lindsey
is the name given to the country round Lincoln. The name
Lincoln is said by the Reverend Edmund Venables to be "taken
from the leading characteristic of the place;"† the whole low-
lying land was one wide mere or pool. "Llyn is the British
name for a pool of water," so that Lindsey Street seems to
have some connection with a pool of water. The idea derives
support in the name of the lane which connects the Bury Lane
with Lindsey Street—"Bolsover Lane"; for, as "over"‡ is a
Saxon name for shore, it too, apparently, has some relation to a
large sheet of water. *Meres* are mentioned in the boundaries of
Tippendene, a Manor belonging to Waltham Abbey. Epping
is not mentioned in the list of manors belonging to it, entered

---

* See map, Epping Ongar Trust.

† "Walks through Lincoln," page 10.

‡ "Over" appears in the names Dover and Andover, &c. In Derbyshire
there is a place called Bolsover, and a Bolsover Street in London.

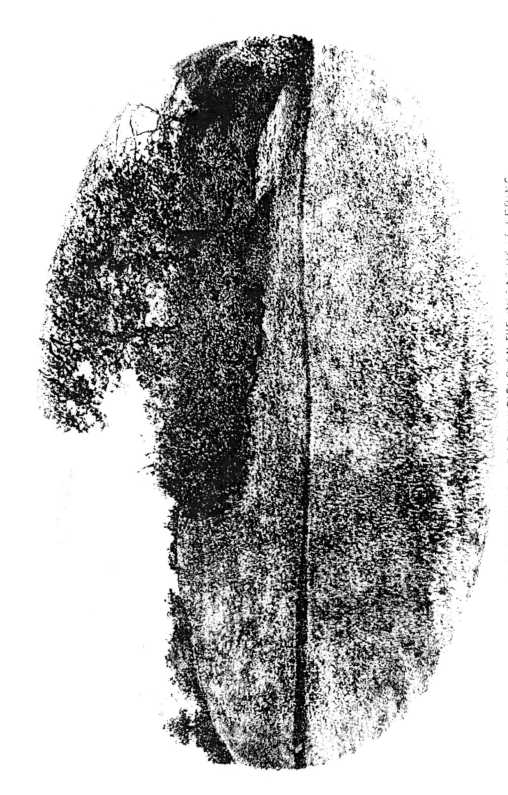

MOUND AT THE BACK OF THE BRICKFIELD ON THE ONGAR ROAD EPPING

MOUND IN THE GROVE BY THE SIDE OF THE LANE LEADING TO COOPERSALE.

in Doomsday Book; but it is supposed, owing to an error in putting Ti instead of E, that Tippendene appears in the place of Epping. Morant, in his "History of Essex," writes "these are the *meres*, lands, or bounds of Tippendene —Tippeburne, or brook; from the brook up to the heath or plain; thence to the bounds of the valley, with its back enclosure, so to the *water* and along that till you come again to Tippenburne."* The boundaries, however, cannot be, at the present time, followed; they appear not to relate to the whole parish of Epping. At the time of Edward the Confessor, when the boundaries were defined, only a small portion of the land was, probably, under cultivation, and the boundaries may have related to it. A brook called Cobbin Brook runs along the valley between the Bury Lane and Lindsey Street, and across Bolsover Lane. If, and it is not unlikely, there was a natural dam or obstruction to the flow of Cobbin Brook, a sheet of water would be formed in the valley. And if a British trackway at one time ran in the direction of the church path through the fields, from the ridge of hills on which the church now stands, and skirted the sheet of water, or mere, "Lindsey" may have, and probably did, like Lindsey in Lincolnshire, derive its name from the British word "Llyn"—a pool of water.

The ancient roads will perhaps soon yield to the requirements of the parish; but the mounds, which denote their antiquity, and are characteristic of their origin, are in private grounds, and consequently private property. Their preservation will cause neither trouble nor expense. They can be preserved on the negative plan, that is by the owners not allowing them to be destroyed. The requirements of the Union Workhouse caused the one which, half a century ago, used to be on the plain, to be levelled. Work had to be found for the paupers, when the levelling of the mound afforded the guardians the opportunity wanted of employing task labour, and lost to the parish an interesting memorial of the early inhabitants.

---

* The boundaries are taken from the Monasticon.

When the Romans had, by conquest, extended their possessions throughout Britain, they made, for military purposes, roads in a direct line from one military station to another. But for a long time the native roads or trackways were used. The one from Verulam, over the River Lea, by Waltham into Essex must have been at high tides impassable and, therefore, very inconvenient, and often from floods impassable for many days; whilst the road by Bishop Stortford into Essex would be open for traffic at all times. It is not therefore surprising that they gave the preference to the road through Hallingbury, Dunmow, &c., which they made a perfectly straight road, now known as Stane Way.* But, nevertheless, the road through Epping Uplands seems to have been, for some time after the country was occupied by the Romans, a road of importance, as the settlements, which they formed of South Germans, having their names terminating in "ing" have been placed either on, or near to it, viz., Epping, Nasing, Sherring, Matching. In the title-deeds of property situated on it, it is termed "King's Highway from Ryehill to Waltham." The King's Highway was free to all men, leading either to the market or from town to town; or any cart, horse, or foot-way common to all people is the King's Highway, whether it directly leads to any market town or not.† It was evidently once a highway, although now only a grass road, and thrown out of use as a highway, owing to other roads having been gravelled and made passable.

---

* Stane Way, see Map of the Roman Roads.

† See "Parish Law," by Joseph Shaw, 1743, pages 261 and 262.

London Road

Winchelsea House

go. Wintry wood Common

Sketch from an old map drawn in the year 1634

CHAPTER II.

ABSTRACTS OF ACTS OF PARLIAMENT, AND OBSERVATIONS CONCERNING THEM.

DURING the greater part of the 17th century the country was in a very unsettled state, brought about by many causes. The rapid political changes and the devastating civil war left but little opportunity for attention being given to matters domestic or parochial. Amongst these must be included roads.

There can be no doubt, the movements of troops during the war between King Charles and the Parliament, brought the state of the roads, in all parts of the country, under the notice of those who were leaders in the contests. It can readily be believed the soldiers suffered greatly; and that the fatigues experienced during the long marches they had to make, brought the condition of the highways they traversed painfully before them. It is not, therefore, surprising that in 1655 a Turnpike Act was passed.

There had been, by an Act passed 2 and 3 of Philip and Mary, a local office created, that of surveyor of highways. The appointment of the surveyor was to be made by the Justices of the Peace; he was to be under their control, and had to carry out their instructions.

The Statute rendered every one liable to contribute towards the repairs of the roads. For this purpose they were divided into two classes :—

1st.—Such as occupied a plough land, or kept a draught or plough.

2nd.—Householders, cottagers, and labourers, not hired servants by the year.

Those of the first class were required, each of them, to send, four times in a year, one wain or cart, with oxen, horses,

C

or other cattle, and two men, or to forfeit for every draught making default, 10s.

Those of the second class were required, by himself or his substitute, to work on such days, in mending the highway or to forfeit 12d.; every individual of each class was taxed the same without regard being paid to his means.

The Act seemed to be unfair; it was, therefore, altered in the 18th year of Queen Elizabeth's reign by subjecting those cottagers who had 5l. in goods or 40s. in land to additional service. They had to send two men instead of one; and the number of days' labour was increased from four to six.

The laws relating to "statute" duty or labour remained in force until the year 1835-6, when they were repealed by Parliament, 5 and 6 William IV, as the work done by Statute labour had shown itself to be insufficient for the purpose for which it was instituted.

In 1653 the first turnpike was erected.

The contributor of the article on roads in the "Penny Cyclopædia" writes as follows :—

"The inefficiency of the system of maintenance by parish and statute labour was proved before the passing of the first Turnpike Act in 1653; yet the necessity of improvement, and obvious justice of maintaining roads by the produce of tolls, did not lead to the extensive adoption of the turnpike system for about a century after that time. In the latter half of the last century turnpike roads multiplied rapidly, and superior principles of construction also made some progress."

William and Mary, in the first year of their reign, passed an Act for repairing and amending the road from Harlow Bush Common to Woodford. It did not, however, have the result anticipated.

An Act was passed in the reign of Queen Anne limiting the number of horses allowed for drawing waggons, carts, &c., to six, except up hill. They were to be harnessed in pairs, the two wheel-horses to have a pole between them or to be in double shafts.

In the first year of George I, 1714, there was passed an Act to "Restrain waggoners, carriers, and others from drawing any carriage with more than five horses in length," stating that great injury was done to the roads by the excessive weight, or loads, drawn by the six horses allowed by the previous Act.

In the following year, 1715, an Act was passed for enforcing the laws for repairing the highway in accordance with the Act 3rd and 4th of William and Mary for amending and repairing the highways, and to settle the rates of carriage of goods. The surveyors were ordered to view the roads every four months, and report on oath their condition, and also any encroachment, &c., on them, to the Justices of the Peace at a Special Session held for that purpose.

In the 10th of George I., 1723, another Act was passed for "Repairing and amending the highway from the north part of Harlow Bush Common, in the parish of Harlow, to Woodford in the county of Essex," commencing :—

"Whereas the highways or roads leading from Woodford in the county of Essex, to the north part of Harlow Bush Common, in the parish of Harlow in the said county, notwithstanding the provision made by an Act made and passed in the first year of her late Majesty's reign, intituled 'An Act for the better repairing and amending the highways from the north end of Thornwood Common, to Woodford in the county of Essex' are become so bad, and in such a ruinous condition, that the same cannot be effectually mended and kept in repair by the ordinary course appointed by the Laws and Statutes of the realm, without some further provision being made by Parliament for raising of money to be applied for that purpose; [material for repairing the same being at a great distance from the said road] for remedying whereof, and to the intent of the said highways may, with all convenient speed be effectually amended, and hereafter kept in good and sufficient repair; may it please your Most Excellent Majesty that it may be enacted," &c.

"That for the better surveying, ordering, repairing and keeping in repair the said highways or roads, the Justices of the Peace at some special sessions to be holden for the county of Essex, in accordance with an Act passed in the reign of William and Mary, for the better repairing and amending of the highway, shall appoint every year two or more persons to be surveyors of the parishes in which they reside, and in default of such suitable person, any other persons willing to accept the office."

The surveyors, or any three of them, were required, within one week of their appointment, respectively to meet within their several parishes or divisions, to view and survey the highways or roads, and to report at the following special sessions their defects, the best means of repairing them, and an estimate of the cost, to the Justices of the Peace, who were then to make such orders as may appear to them to be required.

The surveyors were by the Act empowered to "appoint and require such carts, carriages and persons who are liable to work on the highways by the Statutes already in force" to work on the highways when they thought needful, and to pay the labourers and owners of the teams or carts according to the usual rates paid for such services in the county. But no person was by the Act compelled to travel above four miles from his dwelling house, nor to work above two days in any one week, nor at any time in seed time, hay time, or corn harvest.

The Act also gives to the Justices of the Peace power to authorise the erection of turnpike gates across the highways or roads, and to take for every coach, chariot, chaise, or caleche, drawn by one or more horses, before they shall be permitted to pass through the same, the sum of sixpence. For every waggon the sum of one shilling; for every cart or carriage the sum of eightpence; for every horse, mule, or ass, laden or unladen, and not drawing, the sum of one penny; for every drove of oxen, or neat cattle, the sum of tenpence per score, and in proportion for any greater or lesser number; for every drove of calves, hogs, sheep, &c., the sum of twopence halfpenny per score, and so in proportion for any greater or lesser number.

The money received for tolls was by the Act to be vested in the Justices of the Peace for each division of the county. Power was given to them to distrain for non-payment of tolls, and also to levy a fine of 10s. on any person having land near to turnpike gates and bars, who allowed any coach, cart, &c., to pass on his land, with the object of avoiding payment of the toll. But as all the gates were to be toll free on election days for knights of the shire, this clause was not to be in force at that time.

The Act also gave to the justices power to appoint receivers of the tolls, who, with the surveyors, had on the first Monday in every month to give in a " true, exact, and perfect account in writing, under their respective hands, of all monies which he and they had" received, paid, and disbursed. The surplus money was to be given to the Justices of the Peace, who were by the Act directed to make such allowances to the receivers and surveyors and other persons employed on the roads, as they should think good.

The surveyors, in addition to the power given to them to make use of labourers and carts as provided by a previous Act, were authorised as follows : —

" To dig, gather, take and carry away gravel, furze, heath, sand, stones, chalk, or other materials, out of any waste or common of any parish, town, village, or hamlet, in or near which any foundrous* or ruinous places of the same highway or roads do lie, and for want of sufficient gravel, furze, heath, sand, stones, chalk, or other materials there, to dig, gather, take, and carry away the same out of the waste or common of any neighbouring parish, town, village, or hamlet, in the same county, without paying for the same."

It was also lawful for the surveyors to take gravel, &c., from private grounds, excepting pleasure grounds, when they could not obtain it off the waste, compensating the owners by paying to them such an amount as the Justices of the Peace thought reasonable. The Act in addition gave power to the surveyors to remove all obstructions, such as dirt of every kind, to make or alter drains, clean ditches, remove bushes, and cut

---

* So in Act.

down branches of trees where they interfered with the maintenance of the roads in good condition, and to charge their expenses on the owners of the property occasioning the nuisance, and if after removal of annoyances persons again offended they were liable to a penalty of 10s.

As capital would be required to put high roads in a thorough state of repair before they could be made available for traffic; the Act gave the Justices power to assign over the tolls, to repay any loan which may have been made to the trustees for that purpose.

Tolls were not to be taken more than once in the day from any person passing through the turnpikes, or any gates on the trust. He was, however, to show, when required to do so, the ticket he had taken at the first gate where he paid the toll.

The following were exempt from paying toll :—persons carrying stones, gravel, or materials for repairing the roads in the parish or neighbouring parishes ; or any cart or waggon carrying chalk or any kind of manure, for manuring gardens or lands ; carts or waggons carrying hay or corn in the straw, to be laid in the barns or houses of the inhabitants of the several parishes in which the roads lie, or in any neighbouring parishes; any agricultural instruments ; or horses, or cattle going to and from water or pasture ; post horse carrying mails or packet, or any person riding post; also the horse ridden by a waggoner, and passing through the turnpike with waggon, &c. ; horses of soldiers on the march, also the carts and waggons attending them and waggons travelling with vagrants sent by " passes." Disputes must have arisen respecting the intention of the clause as to the liability of paying toll for cattle going to "water or pasturage," as in Act passed in the 17th year of George III there is a clause exempting their owners from payment of toll.

The Act, although it gave power to erect turnpikes and gates or turnpikes across any roads leading from the highway, did not exempt persons liable to do "statute" work from their engagements, but directed that they " shall still remain chargeable and do their respective works in the parishes in which the said highways or roads do lie." Authority, however, was given to the Justices of the Peace to compound or agree with any parish to whom the high road belonged for a certain sum of money, in lieu of the statute work to be done.

By the erection of turnpikes and the demand made for toll, it was supposed that a burden had been laid upon the inhabitants of parishes, who had hitherto found the roads in the condition in which they had existed for many years sufficiently good for their requirements. In order to lessen the effect of the tolls, the Justices could " compound or agree by year, or otherwise, with any person or persons using the road to travel through the said turnpike or turnpikes either with any waggon, cart, coach, horse, chaise, or any other carriage for any sum or sums of money to be paid quarterly, from time to time, after such agreement shall be made." The Bill was to continue in force for 21 years, but it was provided " that if at any time before the expiration of the term of 21 years, the highways or roads were sufficiently amended and repaired, the Justices might, at a Quarter Session, if all liabilities on account of the roads had been satisfied, order that the tolls and duties should terminate."

The Justices of the Peace " authorised and empowered to put this Act in force " were ordered to meet together at the sign of the Crown* in Epping on or before the 25th day of March, 1724, and then adjourn themselves, and afterwards meet there or at any other place, near the highway or roads to be repaired as often as necessary for carrying out the provisions of the Act.

The Act is further stated to be a public one in the concluding paragraph as follows :—

"And be it further enacted by the authority aforesaid, that this Act should be deemed and judged and taken to be a public Act, and judicially taken notice of as such by all Judges, Justices, and other persons whatsoever."

The Act conferred upon the magistrates at Quarter Sessions the whole management of the roads or highways ; the

* The ground where the "Crown," burnt down in 1827, stood is now occupied by Messrs. Cottis' and Mr. Butcher's shops.

parishes had, however, to continue to supply labour as ordered by Philip and Mary. But the money required to defray the expense of making the roads, keeping them in repair, and erecting the turnpikes, toll-bars, and gate-houses, was not procured by making a rate, which is, at the present day, the mode of providing money for every purpose. But those persons who used the roads, and for whose benefit they were to be made, and repaired, had themselves to pay by a toll, for the benefit they obtained ; and the burden, if any, was lessened as much as possible to the inhabitants of the parishes in which turnpikes were erected, by allowing them to make a yearly payment of a small sum, and so annually compound for their tolls.*

Although great care appears to have been taken to avoid injustice being done to anyone, by putting in force the Highway Acts of Parliament, the turnpike gates and the tolls were a cause of much, and probably widespread, dissatisfaction, giving rise to disorderly meetings, and even serious riots. In places where the population was large, the rioters pulled down and burnt the gates and the toll-houses. The injuries done were so serious that special Acts had to be passed to enable the authorities, by severely punishing the offenders, to put a stop to illegal behaviour.

In the first year of the reign of George II was passed " An Act for punishing such persons as shall wilfully and maliciously pull down, or destroy turnpikes for repairing highways, or locks, or other works, erected by authority of Parliament, for making rivers navigable."

The preamble runs as follows, and indicates that when the law was made, local feeling must have been roused to a serious extent, by the interference in the course of rivers by locks, and the obstruction occasioned by the erection of turnpikes.

" Whereas several ill designing and disorderly persons have, in several parts of this kingdom, associated themselves

---

* See further on the amounts paid by the compounders with the Epping Road Trustees.

together, both by day and night, and cut down, burnt and otherwise destroyed several turnpike gates and houses, which have been erected by the authority of several Acts of Parliament, made for repairing divers roads within the kingdom by tolls taken, or to be taken at such turnpikes, and thereby preventing the tolls from being received, which has lessened the security of divers of His Majesty's good subjects, for considerable sums of money which they have advanced or lent, on the credit of the said Acts, and deterred others from tendering any money on the same, and thereby the said Acts are become ineffectual, the laws now in force not inflicting any punishment on such offenders, suitable to their offences; and whereas other evil disposed persons have threatened the pulling down and destroying of locks, sluices, and floodgates erected to preserve and secure the navigation of rivers made navigable, pursuant to Acts of Parliament for that purpose."

In order to put a stop to the disorderly conduct above mentioned, it was enacted that from and after the 24th of June, 1728, any person so offending should be sent to the common gaol or house of correction for three months with hard labour, without bail or mainprize; and that the "Justice should also order and adjudge that the offender or offenders shall be by the master or keeper of the gaol or house of correction on the first convenient market-day once publicly and openly whipped in the city, town or borough next to which the offence was committed, at the market-cross or market-place, between the hours of 11 and 2 o'clock."

If a person was guilty a second time of wilfully demolishing any locks, floodgates, or turnpikes, and convicted, he was to be adjudged guilty of felony, and be subjected to the pains and penalties as in the cases of felony, and be liable to transportation for seven years.

The Act was to be publicly read at every Quarter Sessions during the five years in which it was to remain in force.

In 1731, fifth year of George II, an Act was passed to "Explain and amend the previous Act." The preamble, after reciting the object of the previous Act, commences: "And whereas the provisions of the said Act made for punishing such offenders have by experience been found to be insufficient; for remedying thereof and for rendering the said Act more effectual; be it enacted by the King's Most Excellent Majesty," &c., &c., that any person after the 24th day of June, 1732, convicted of injury done by them to turnpike gates, and locks or floodgates, shall be adjudged guilty of felony, a felon, and be liable to like pains and penalties as in cases of felony, and power and authority was given to the Courts where the case was tried to transport the culprit for seven years.

The Act further ordered that if the offender returned to England before the expiration of seven years he should suffer death as a felon, and have execution awarded against him as persons attainted of felony, without benefit of clergy. This Act provided that the charges of the prosecutions should be paid out of the proceeds of the tolls.

A very lawless spirit for some time after the Acts were passed appears to have prevailed in many parts of the country. The following accounts of the destruction of turnpikes in Herefordshire evinces, besides a lawlessness amongst the people, a want of power on the part of the magistrates to suppress assemblies, only 150 years ago, quite astonishing at the present day; and it is hardly credible that a magistrate should be besieged in his own house and have to exchange shots with the besieging mob.

Turnpike Riots.

("Gentleman's Magazine," Vol. 5, October, 1735.)

"The Commissioners of the turnpikes at Ledbury, in Herefordshire, being informed that an attempt would be made to pull them down, about 8 in the evening repaired, with their attendants well armed, to that which leads towards Hereford, where a great number of persons provided with guns, axes, &c., advanced against them, upon which the proclamation

against riots was read aloud, by candle-light. Some of the
rioters notwithstanding, began to assault the townsmen who
endeavoured to apprehend them, and an engagement immediately ensued, till two of the rioters in women's apparel, with
their faces blacked, and axes in their hands, were seized; the
rest, after firing several guns on each side, were put to flight.
The gentlemen, imagining all over, left the place, bringing the
prisoners to Justice Skyp's house, in order to be committed to
gaol; but the rioters, having intelligence of persons coming to
their assistance, re-assembled in a body of about 200, and cut
down six several turnpikes, then went to the Justice's house,
about 1 o'clock in the morning, and threatened to fire it, if
the prisoners were not released. They discharged several guns
at the windows, loaded with ball, which were returned from the
house; but one of the rioters being killed, and several wounded,
they retired, carrying off the dead body, and next day the
prisoners were carried to Hereford Gaol" (sic).

On Friday, 9th of April, two of the rioters were hanged at
Worcester, and a party of soldiers attended the execution, as
the turnpike levellers had been very tumultuous at the trial; but
no further disturbance took place." Another rioter was hanged
at Tyburn.

In the account[*] it is stated that he was cut down by
the executioner as usual, but as the coffin was being fastened
he thrust back the lid. The executioner would have hanged
him again, but the mob prevented it, and carried him to a
house and gave him a glass of wine, when he died immediately
from hæmorrhage.

At Bristol, 1749, August 1st, at 8 o'clock in the morning,
about 400 Somersetshire people cut down a third time the
turnpike gates on the Ashton Road, and burnt the timber;
afterwards they destroyed the Dundry turnpike, and thence
went to Bedminster, headed by two chiefs on horseback, one

* Vol. VI, page 229
† Vol. VI, page 422.

with his face blacked, and the other, a young gentleman farmer,
carried the standard, being a silk handkerchief on a long staff.
The rest were on foot, armed with rusty swords, pitchforks,
axes, guns, pistols, clubs, &c., calling themselves Jack-a'-Lents,
having the letters J. L. on their hats and caps.

They arranged themselves in the main street, before the
George Inn, a hunting horn and three drums attending them.
The outbreak assumed the character of a dangerous riot. The
mob having drank freely proceeded, with much noise, to break
the windows of a house of a "tything man of the hundred."
He had, in obedience to the order of the Commissioners,
carried three persons, accused of destroying turnpikes, before
two Justices of the Peace, who committed them to prison. The
chief ringleader, not satisfied with the mischief already done,
directed the rioters to pull down the house itself; the order was
readily complied with, and the house speedily destroyed. The
levellers, as they were called, then made their way to Totten-
down, and destroyed the turnpike gate and buildings. But
before they could complete the work of destruction the Commissioners armed, constables with their staffs, and seamen with
cutlasses, appeared on the heights and charged down upon the
crowd, which, in spite of the declaration they had made " that
they were afraid of no man," made off as fast as they could to
Knowle Hill. Many of them were knocked down, and a farmer
had his skull cut open by a cutlass, a few others were wounded,
and about 30 taken prisoners and lodged in gaol.

The Riot Act was read, and all business operations suspended. A report was given out that large numbers of persons
were flocking into the city to release the three prisoners. From
Hannum and Kingswood a great body of countrymen made
their way to the city. They obliged the workmen to join
them, and compelled the miners to do so by threatening to cut
the ropes whilst they were in the pits. The Kingswood people
continued their work of destruction, so that almost all the
turnpikes, and turnpike houses about the city, were demolished.
The colliers, with much huzzaing and hooting, made their way
to Stoker Cross, and partly cut down that turnpike; but not

caring to wait for the attack of an armed force of gentlemen, citizens, and a few soldiers and sailors which unexpectedly came on the scene, they made off as fast as they could. On the 5th, five days after the outbreak, six troops of dragoon guards arrived. On their appearance the country people immediately dispersed, when chains were again erected, and tolls levied, but the turnpikes were fixed nearer the town.

The gatherings in other parts of the country were probably not so serious. The two Acts of Parliament, however, indicate that the opposition was widespread, and that the turnpikes were frequently destroyed or injured. For the first Act, first year of George II, which inflicted imprisonment and flogging, was not sufficient to put a stop to the evil. So a more stringent Act was passed the following year, making the crime felony, and punishable by transportation for seven years.

Notwithstanding the efforts made by Parliament to put the public roads throughout the kingdom into a suitable condition for the traffic, which the prosperity of the country was fast developing, their state of repair was very unsatisfactory, and the condition of the roads throughout the County at the beginning of the last century was undoubtedly very bad. The highway from St. Leonards, Shoreditch, through the town of Hackney, to Stamford Hill, on the Great Northern Road, as also the cross road leading from Cambridge Heath over Bethnal Green to the turnpike in the Mile End Road, is described as follows, in the preamble of an Act passed 1738 for putting it in repair, "By reason of the many heavy carriages frequently passing through the same are become so very ruinous, and, some parts of the same roads in Winter season, are so bad that passengers cannot pass without danger."

The difficulty the Trustees had to contend against arose from the ruts, occasioned by the drivers of the heavy waggons and carts keeping in the same line, and the weight of the load they carried.

The Legislature therefore turned its attention to the vehicles and made a law affecting them, which came into force 14 George II, 1741. In the preamble the Act says that the laws in force for the preservation of the public roads have not answered their intentions, on account of the excessive weights carried by the waggons, caravans and carts passing over them.

In order to lessen the weight which could be carried, the Act regulated the number of horses to be used as follows :— A waggon passing on any public turnpike road, was not to be drawn by more than four horses either in length, pairs or sideways. No cart was to be drawn by more than three horses.* Every horse above those numbers was to be forfeited and also the harness. The seizure was to be made by the toll collector, and he was to receive half the money which they brought at the sale to be made by order of the Trustees, the other money to be added to the tolls collected for the repair of the roads. The Trustees of the roads, were by the Act directed to fix a weighing machine at some convenient place in every high road over which they had control, and to order the collector of tolls to weigh all waggons and carts laden with goods and to take twenty shillings for every hundredweight over and above 60 cwt. The fine to be applied to the repair of the road. That facility might be given to the collector for carrying out the orders of the Trustees the owners of waggons, carts, &c., were compelled to have their names and addresses written upon the covers or some conspicuous part. There were exceptions made in favour of noblemen and gentlemen's private carriages, also for carriages employed in husbandry. or in His Majesty's service.

For some reason not explained, Justices were empowered at Quarter Sessions to license any waggon, to be drawn with as many as six horses, and carts with four, in any roads above thirty miles from London. They had imposed on them the duty at Quarter Sessions of fixing the prices of all carriage to and from London, and any carriers presuming to take more than the rate fixed by the Justices, were liable to a penalty of 5l., payable to the party overcharged. Waggons and other

---

* Four years after carts were allowed to be drawn by four horses.

carriages having wheels bound with sheaths of iron or tire of the breadth of at least 8 inches when worn, and not set on with rose-headed nails, were exempt from the provisions of the Act.

A letter to the Editor of the "Gentleman's Magazine," 1747, by a traveller, describes the state of the road in the Midland Counties at that time. It was written, he says, with the hopes of calling the attention of County Members of Parliament to their condition, so that the description of the journey is perhaps a little more vivid than the facts warranted; but nevertheless it, and the account which follows, of a journey in a different part of the Country, may be accepted as descriptive of the difficulties attending travelling at that time.

"In my journey to London, I travelled from Harborough to Northampton, and well was it that I was in a light Berlin and six good horses (sic), or I might have been overlaid in that turnpike road. But for fear of life and limb, I walked several miles on foot; met twenty waggons tearing their goods to pieces, and the drivers cursing and swearing for being robbed on the highway by a turnpike, screened under an Act of Parliament. When I got to Northampton I ran the 'gantlop' (sic) through a number of soldiers to an obliging Landlord. I observed near twenty officers and soldiers, some learning to stitch above stairs, some cookery in the kitchen, and could not think of what use they were, till I saw a charitable box for the Infirmary, and guess they might encourage contributers when they saw their charity so well guarded. I made my complaint about the bad road, and hoped that these lusty soldiers, according to the Roman usage, and our method in Scotland, were come to repair the highways; but was told they rather staid to prevent the country rising, and cutting down the turnpikes, and to humble a rich town by living upon it." ("Gent. Mag." vol. 17, page 232) —1747.

The Editor of the Magazine writes: "These complaints we have found experimentally true in a journey to Derby, and

rather than travel the said bad and dangerous roads twice, chose
to go several miles about into another turnpike road."

The Acts of Parliament had been to a great extent
permissive, conferring great powers on the Justices of the
Peace. The local Justices were expected to attend to the
duties pointed out to them, and to see that the surveyors
were not negligent. At Quarter Sessions the Justices had
power to indict parishes and towns for not repairing their
roads; and also by the 3rd and 4th of William and Mary and
1st George I to raise money by a rate not exceeding sixpence
in the pound when it was required. But the measure was
generally hard upon the parishes, and in individual cases
oppressive.

John Shapleigh, Esq., Barrister-at-Law, writing in 1749,
says that the Legislature had given very little consideration
to the burdens and hardships many parishes were yearly obliged
to bear, in order to repair their roads, and that the numerous
laws which had been made had never met with success, as
there always had been, and was then, "great reason to complain
of the neglect of the repairs of most roads" in the country.
The fault he thought to be with the surveyors, who are, he
says, often mean persons, having no interest in the parish,
their highest qualification being, by the 3rd and 4th of William
and Mary, 10*l.* per annum real estate, or 100*l.* personal estate.
The Act, moreover, permitted tenants of 30*l.* per annum to be
appointed surveyors; and if none could be found having either
of the above qualifications, then the most efficient man in the
parish may be appointed.

Over the surveyor the parishioners had "not in themselves
any coercive power to oblige those mean persons to discharge
their duties." But the surveyor might neglect to call out the
parishioners to do their six days' statute labour, or overlook
the non-attendance of some, from inattention, "or, which is very
probable, from bribery and corruption." Mr. Shapleigh asks,
would it not be very unreasonable, and severe, for those
parishioners who had done their statute duties, to be punished
for the neglect of those cottagers and labourers who ought to

have done their statute work, and the surveyors, whose duty and power alone it was to oblige them to perform it.

The clauses of the various Acts were for the most part permissive, so far as they defined the duties of the magistrates; who were clergymen, and landed proprietors living on their estates, having a kindly feeling towards their tenants and to their neighbours, both rich and poor, so long as they did not interfere with their rights or privileges, and abstained from trespassing in their preserves and meddling with their game. It cannot, therefore, be supposed but that they would, as far as they could, avoid any action being taken at Quarter Sessions which would be unjust or oppressive to the parishes in which their estates were situated, and often, for the most part, their own property.

The leniency of Magistrates and the toll-keepers appointed by them, in not noticing any little infringement on the part of their parishioners or tenants in the matter of the breadth of the wheels or the number of horses drawing a cart or waggon has especial notice in the 6th of George III. 1756, "where it is stated that in spite of the prohibition of the previous Act respecting the breadth of wheels, etc., several trustees, or commissioners, and gate-keepers have permitted waggons having the fellies of the wheels of less breadth than 9 inches to be drawn by more than four horses or beasts of draught to pass through their turnpike."

1753.—*Anno Vicessimo Sexto Georgii II, C. 30.*

In the Act it is stated that, owing to the excessive weight carried by waggons, carts, &c., and the narrowness of the wheels, great part of the highways and roads have become ruinous and almost impassable. It therefore enacted that after 29th September, 1754, it should be unlawful for any waggon, cart, wain, or wheel carriage to be drawn on any turnpike road unless the fellies of the wheels be of the breadth of nine inches from side to side, under a penalty of £5 or the forfeiture of one horse, not being the shaft or thill horse, with all its harness.

The Act, however, did not extend to any coach, Berlin chaise, &c., nor to any waggon drawn with less than five horses, or any two-wheel carriage drawn by less than four horses, nor when drawn by oxen or neat cattle. But in order to encourage the use of broad wheels, vehicles having the fellies of their wheels nine inches broad might be drawn by any number of horses not exceeding eight.

In the same year, for the safety of passengers and cattle, it was ordered that all people digging gravel should fence round the gravel pits, and that fourteen days after they had ceased to make use of them they should either fill them up or slope down the sides.

In the "Gentleman's Magazine" for the year 1754 are the remarks on the above-mentioned Act, which was to come into force in the following September, as follows :—

" The inconveniences which the Legislature intended their regulations to remedy, arise from the great number and weight of wheel carriages, and the thinness of the wheels, which are found to render all preceding laws for amending roads ineffectual ; some having become almost impassable, and all growing every day worse, notwithstanding the perpetual expense of levelling and repairs." " To give our readers a more clear and distinct notion of a waggon with such a team, and such wheels as this Act has directed, we have exhibited two representations, figs. 1 and 2. Fig. 1 represents one of the new waggons, with the rim of the wheels nine inches broad ; it has two pair of shafts, and is drawn by four pair of horses" (as is shown in fig. 2).

" These waggons are said to move very lightly on plain, or even sandy roads, and are able to carry great loads, yet they are most certainly liable to several of the inconveniences mentioned in the following letter signed Com. Staff; and ' It is remarkable that the *Yorkshire waggon* from which our print is taken, was on Saturday last, July 27, more than an hour in turning in at the gate of the White Bear Inn, in Basinghall Street, and at last received considerable damage. The writer of the letter above referred to who signs himself Com. Staff, says that although the

Gentleman's Magazine
July 1754.

Fig. 3.

Fig. 1.

Fig. 2.

regulations to be enforced by the Act of Parliament, will undoubtedly prevent the ruts being cut so deep, and consequently keep the roads in better condition, they will be attended with many inconveniences which must in a great degree obstruct the principal purpose which roads were intended to answer ; viz., the conveyance of various commodities from one part of the Country to another; for the commodious migration of gentlemen in chaises and coaches is but very inconsiderable in the public utility of roads.' He supposes there will be a difficulty in procuring proper timber to furnish all carriages of burden with wheels 9 inches broad, for which there will be a great demand ; and that the expense of procuring them will raise the cost of carriage, and increase the price of commodities. The farmers would suffer greatly as they could not obtain an equivalent by increased charges and the wheels would wear out faster, as in numerous places, and on the sides of hills the weight of the load would rest chiefly on the outer edge of the lower wheels, which must therefore become weak in the joints, and unfit for use. He makes further objections to the construction of the waggons ; saying that in Bristol, London, and most of the old towns in this kingdom, they could not be turned, and adds that ' there are many other inconveniences, which we who live in the country foresee in the use of 9 inch wheels ; but I never think myself at liberty to complain of evils, for which I do not propose a remedy, I therefore send you a model of the carriage part of a tumbril or cart, exhibited at St. John's Gate, Clerkenwell,' (represented by fig. 3,) ' which I have long used in my own business, with great success.' The principal peculiarity in the carriage is the difference between the length of the axle of fore wheels and the hind wheels. It is proposed that the fellies of these wheels, instead of nine be only 5 inches broad, which will be sufficient to level 10 inches, on each side of the road ; that the axles of the hinder wheels be the same length as at present, and that of the fore wheels so much shorter as that they may run just in the middle of the space of ground between the course of the hinder wheels and the horses track. The position of the wheels could not fail to keep the road quite level.' The arrangement he considers, will be equivalent to a reduction of half the load in every carriage, for supposing the load to be 2,000 lbs. weight, 1,000 only will press on each track, the weight being equally divided between the two pair of wheels; and to facilitate turning it is suggested that the front wheels might be made sufficiently small to run quite under the waggon. The writer (Com. Staff) in the Magazine concludes his article as follows: 'As these wheels will be made at less expense than those directed by the late Act, so they will last longer, for the reasons mentioned above; and as by the general use of them, the road would become perfectly level, the use of oxen might again be introduced among us with great advantage. The horse indeed will toil a little more cheerfully, and will keep jogging on, without the continual attendance of the driver, but oxen will hold out much longer, and upon an emergency exert greater strength. I have often wondered that our farmers, who upon other articles, calculate with so much exactness, should never have discovered that a man who rents 60*l.* per annum must clear his whole year's rent to maintain a team of six horses, but that oxen, on the contrary, may be maintained for less than half the money, besides that they make so much better muck, and improve upon the farmer's hands, so as at the end of three years to put three-fourths of the money for which he sells them clear into his pocket. The use of oxen would also reduce the price of meat to the old standard, which is little more than half the sum at which it is now sold; so numerous and important are the advantages which I think are evidently in our power, and if by any means any of them may be secured either to the present age, or to posterity, I shall enjoy much more than my proportion of the common good; as a man looks upon a child with greater pleasure than upon a servant, from whose labour he derives ten times more profit.' Signed,—Com. Staff."

August, 1754. A contributor to the "Gentleman's Magazine" writes that "having with some pleasure inspected the cuts of waggons, and read your account of the Acts of Parliament for broad wheels, and also the letters quoted, he desires to say something in support of the proposal for horses

to go two abreast as in coaches, usually called quartering; and
for the distance between the two fore wheels, and the hind
two wheels to vary. The Act to which the letters of 1754 relate
allows waggons having broad wheels eight, and carts five horses;
other waggons only four, and other carts three horses, and does
not limit the weight or quantity of goods which may be carried
in waggons with broad wheels. He proposes that a similar
allowance of horses, and weight for all carriages quartering, with
horses as well as wheels, "as coaches do," and so treading in
very near where ruts would otherwise be made, which would
then be totally prevented. And the same regulation should
be allowed to carriages having the axles of the hind and fore
wheels of different lengths. The drivers should also keep on
their proper side of the road so as to make two tracks at least.
In many roads there was only one track.

In October of the same year it is noticed that there were
very few travelling waggons on the road with broad wheels,
most of them drawing with four horses only, which they might
do with narrow wheels, as formerly, if drawn with three
horses only. The writer goes on to give the result of his
observations, which seem to be that on hard roads the breadth
of the wheels is of no consequence, and that the broad wheels
are best for sandy and soft roads. But where the road is cut up
with ruts six inches deep, and the ground at the bottom of
the ruts is sound and the ruts filled with sludge, then the narrow
wheels would be better, because they would sink no farther than
broad wheels, viz., to the hard bottom, and the slush to be
removed by the broad wheels would be as nine inches by six,
and the sludge to be removed by the narrow wheels will only
be as three by six inches, from which he concludes that in such
a road carriages with broad wheels would be drawn with greater
difficulty than carriages with narrow wheels, and also that where
the ruts are cut by narrow wheels the difficulty to broad wheels
would be increased.

His opinion is, that if broad wheels are used the roads will
be kept in better condition; but the law being defective in
allowing vehicles to be used by carriers having narrow wheels

(which can make ruts) the broad wheels will not be used. Attention is drawn in the letter to the stage coaches, which were heavily weighted through having boots before and the baskets for luggage behind, and it is suggested that the wheels of waggons should be nine inches broad, and the wheels of stage coaches at least five inches broad.

Another correspondent, in 1754, vol. 24, page 396, writes: "In a journey from London to Bath, I saw between Marlborough and Toxfield a team of three horses, with 60 pounds in a cart, dragging only half a bushel of gravel for a load, and I was informed by the drivers, that the dragging eight of these loads about two hundred yards, was esteemed a 'statute' day's work to be performed, for a plough." The word plough was apparently the measure of the work to be performed by a team of three horses. In some County histories, " Rudder's Gloucester " for instance, "Plough Land" is a measure of land. Under the head Saperton is mentioned that in it with Frampton there "were 5 hides in each, there were 7 plow-tillage," and that Todini the Lord of the Manor, gave a "plough-tillage" to the Priory which he had founded at Belvoir in Lincolnshire. It may be concluded that the amount of statute work the horses taken from the plough had to perform in the day was calculated on the basis of the time it took them to plough the land, considered to be the quantity to be ploughed as a day's work by a plough team. It is remarkable that the term " plough " should be continued to so late a date as 1754 as a measurement of agricultural work.

The writer to the Editor of the magazine was evidently not satisfied with the management of the County business, and appears to believe that there was at Quarter Sessions, what would be termed at the present time "jobbery." He writes, " I can point out a parish which has compounded with the pike at 15l. per annum for a piece of road that before had annually expended on it 60l., and that on an appeal at Quarter Sessions they loaded the turnpike with 10l. damage for breaking up a piece of ground and carrying off stones for no other use but highways, the fee simple of the ground broken and all the stones in it was not worth 50s. at 25 years' purchase, and all this was transacted without hearing the defence the surveyors had to make." The author of the letter then proceeds to state he "knows a pike" where materials had been carted a mile to repair a road, though there had been at the time the same materials contiguous to the spot to be repaired, which a gentleman declared should not be used, because they were on his estate, and, here we may ask are there no Lords, and Dukes, who had obtained a monopoly of stones, and been commissioners and contractors for fascines. If there be a necessity of a small strip of land to make a road more convenient, sometimes it is peremptorily refused, and if you obtain it legally, it would cost twenty times as much as it is worth."

Public attention having been directed to the insufficiency of various Highway Bills which had been passed, to remedy the injury done to the roads by the narrow wheels of carts and waggons passing over them, further, in order to encourage the use of broad wheels, an Act was passed exempting waggons, &c., having wheels nine inches wide from the payment of any tolls.

1755.—Anno Vicesimo Octavo Georgii II.

The Act was passed 1755 as follows:—In the preamble to the Act it is stated, that the previous Acts, not having answered the good purposes intended; it is enacted by the King's authority, &c., that for three years, and no longer, "It shall be lawful for all waggons, wains, carts and carriages, for all goods and merchandise either loaded or unloaded, having the fellies of the wheels thereof of nine inches from side to side, at the least, to pass through all and every turnpike gate or gates, bar or bars, without paying any toll or duty." All waggons with wheels six inches broad might pass through all the gates and bars with six horses, and carts drawn by four horses "without paying any more toll than is paid for waggons now drawn by four horses, and carts drawn by three horses, or for the horses drawing the same." The Trustees of the roads were also empowered by the Act, to take an additional toll if they should believe the same necessary, not exceeding one-fourth more than the tolls then payable, from the drivers of carriages with wheels, under six inches.

In order to avoid loss of money by those who had lent it to the Trustees of the roads, on the security of tolls, it was enacted that when necessary this Act, and those previously passed, should be continued for five years longer from their respective expiration. The Act of Parliament further explains that the fellies of the wheels nine inches broad were to be flat, and that the Trustees were to make the roads level, and to keep them in good condition, in such manner as shall be most commodious for the use of travellers, and for the several sorts of carriages passing upon the same.

The penalty for offences according to the present scale of punishments were very severe. For unloading a waggon or cart, &c., at or before it came to the turnpike gate, to avoid payment of any part of the toll the penalty was 5*l.*, and the driver of the waggon so offending was to be imprisoned in the house of correction for one month. A toll collector of a gate where or near to which any weighing machine was in existence, permitting a waggon, cart, &c., not having the fellies nine inches wide, to pass through the gate without weighing it, was to be sent to the house of correction "to be there kept with hard labour for the space of one month." As there were no police in those days to press for conviction, and the necessity for supporting the police had not therefore entered into the deliberations of the County Gentlemen, who were then the magistrates, it is probable that the law was not strictly enforced; and that only determined offenders were so severely punished. It appears moreover that the previous Act had done wrong in the limit it put to the draught cattle. The present states "Whereas the allowance of oxen or neat cattle only, without an horse or horses, hath been found inconvenient and dangerous; it is therefore enacted that—waggons, &c. with narrow wheels may be drawn by six oxen in pairs and two horses, or eight oxen and one horse, and carts by six oxen and one horse, or four oxen and two horses. The horses drawing carriages with broad wheels were exempted from toll for three years. The exemption from toll in previous Acts not having been clearly defined, the clause above mentioned was put in the Act by way of explanation.

In the year 1757 there came into operation an Act passed Anno Regni Georgii II Tricesimo, having for its object the rendering "more effectual the several laws now in being for the amendment and preservation of the Publick Highways and Turnpike Roads of this Kingdom." It was to remain in force for seven years, and its principal object was to regulate the width of the tyres of wheels, the relative position in which the horses were to be harnessed to the vehicles, and also the distance or width between a pair of wheels. The preamble says :—

"Whereas it hath been found that the use of broad wheels does very much contribute to the improvement and preservation of the turnpike roads, and using heavy carriages with narrow wheels, is very ruinous and destructive to the same ; for remedy whereof be it enacted, by the King's Most Excellent Majesty, &c., &c., that the Trustees shall and may demand and take for every waggon, wain, cart, or carriage having the fellies of the wheels of less breadth than nine inches from side to side, or for the horses or beasts of draught drawing the same, one-half more than the tolls or duties which are or shall be payable by Acts of Parliament made or to be made, for making or repairing turnpike roads, before any such waggon, wain, &c., shall be permitted to pass through any turnpike gate or bars where tolls shall be payable, *except* carts or carriages drawn by one horse, or two oxen, and no more ; and carts or carriages drawn by two horses, or four oxen having the fellies of the wheels of the breadth of *six inches.*"

In several previous Acts exemptions "were allowed in particular cases from payment" of tolls on waggons, carts, &c. By this Act exemptions were confined to vehicles having the fellies of their wheels *nine* inches in breadth :—

"And whereas it will tend to the advantage and pre-

servation of turnpike roads to confine such exemptions to
carriages with wheels of the breadth of nine inches, be it
therefore enacted that during the term aforesaid (seven years)
no person shall by virtue of any of the said Acts of Parliament
have, claim, or take the benefit of any exemption from tolls,
or pay lesser tolls, for any waggon, cart, or other carriage, or
horse, or horses drawing the same, than other carriages of the
like nature ought to pay, unless such vehicles have the fellies of
its wheels nine inches broad. Excepting, when they are drawn
by one horse or two oxen, and no more. Or when they have
the fellies of the wheels six inches wide and are drawn by
two horses or four oxen."

The additional tolls were to be paid on all other vehicles,
and on the beasts of burden drawing them. But waggons with
wheels having fellies nine inches broad were to be allowed to
pass through any turnpike within one hundred miles of London
on paying not more than half the tolls payable on such waggon
and horses by previous Acts of Parliament.

The position of the horses was also regulated by this Act.
It says, "Much damage is done to turnpike roads by waggons
and wains with broad wheels drawn by horses or beasts of
draught *at length* (*i.e.*, one before the other) *and not in pairs*, for
remedying whereof be it enacted, That during the time aforesaid (seven years) it shall not be lawful for any waggon or wain,
having fellies of the wheels of the breadth of nine inches, to pass
upon any turnpike road, unless the same be drawn by horses or
beasts of draught in pairs" (an odd horse was allowed). Great
damage it is said is also done to the roads by waggons, or
wains with narrow wheels being drawn by horses in pairs, but
not when drawn by oxen. It was consequently ordered that no
waggon or wain, having the fellies of the wheels of a less breadth
than nine inches, should be allowed to pass on any turnpike road,
if drawn by horses or beasts of draught in pairs, and not by
oxen.

The Trustees of the turnpike roads were prohibited from
allowing composition for tolls to be made for any waggon, wain,
or cart having the fellies of the wheels of less breadth than nine

inches. And the clause in the Act passed 28 George II, which allowed a certain number of horses for draught as follows, was repealed by this Act.

It made it lawful for waggons or wains having the fellies of the wheels six inches broad to pass through turnpike gates or bars with six horses, and all carts or other carriages having the fellies of the wheels six inches, with four horses, without paying any more toll than is paid for waggons and wains now drawn by four horses and carts drawn by three horses, or for the horses drawing them. Also allowing other four-wheeled carriages, not being common stage waggons or carriages, although the fellies were not either nine or six inches wide, to travel on the turnpike road with any number of horses not exceeding five. It also repeated the penalty of 5*l.*, or one month's imprisonment, inflicted on any driver who "shall act contrary to the true intent and meaning thereof."

Hitherto Acts have dealt only with the width of the fellies of the wheel and the number of draught horses allowed. But in this Act attention is given to the width between a pair of wheels, as follows :—

"And be it further enacted by the authority aforesaid, that from and after the time aforesaid, no waggon having the fellies of the wheels thereof, of the breadth or gauge of nine inches at the bottom, shall pass along any turnpike road, which shall be wider than five feet six inches from the middle of the fellies of the wheels on one side of such waggon to the middle of the fellies of the wheels on the other side of such waggon ; and the surveyor or surveyors, gate-keeper or gate-keepers, of any turnpike road, is and are hereby authorised and required at any turnpike or toll-gate or at any other place upon the turnpike road, to measure every such waggon from the middle of the fellies of the wheels on one side to the middle of the fellies of the wheels on the other side thereof."

And it was unlawful for any gate-keeper to allow a driver, objecting to such measurement being made, to pass through the turnpike gate.

There appears to have been some uncertainty as to the

meaning of two of the clauses passed 28 George II, as the following clauses in this Act are explanatory :—

"Whereas some doubts have arisen concerning the meaning of the words common stage waggon, it is hereby declared that every waggon, wain, cart, or carriage, travelling with or carrying goods by hire, is and shall be deemed to be a common stage waggon within the true intent and meaning of an Act made in the 28th year of the reign of His Present Majesty (to amend an Act made in the 26th year of His Present Majesty)."

In which it is enacted that if a collector or receiver of tolls at any turnpike gate at which a weighing machine is erected shall permit any cart, waggon, or carriage within the description given to pass or repass through his turnpike gate without weighing it, he shall be liable, on conviction, to be committed to the House of Correction for one month with hard labour. Doubts also having arisen whether such collector or receiver is not by the said Act obliged to weigh all carriages, whether loaded or unloaded ; "and many difficulties having arisen thereupon ; it is hereby enacted and declared that from and after September 29th, 1757, any collector or receiver of tolls shall and may permit all persons travelling through any turnpike with an empty cart, waggon, or other carriages to pass through the same without weighing such empty cart, waggon, or carriage, and shall be obliged to weigh only those which are laden."

The clause in the Act limiting the width between the wheels at the bottom only, left it open to the builders of waggons, carts, carriages, &c., to do as they pleased concerning the distance between the wheels at the top, so long as they did not exceed the prescribed breadth of fellies and the width allowed between the wheels at the bottom.

In order to obtain a breadth for the body of vehicles, the axletrees were bent, causing the wheels to be out of the perpendicular ; there was a greater distance between the top than at the bottom of a pair of wheels, when on waggons, carts, &c.

The wheels being out of the perpendicular, the weight of the load would have been on the outer edge of the tyre ; whilst the inner edge, on broad wheels, would not have touched the

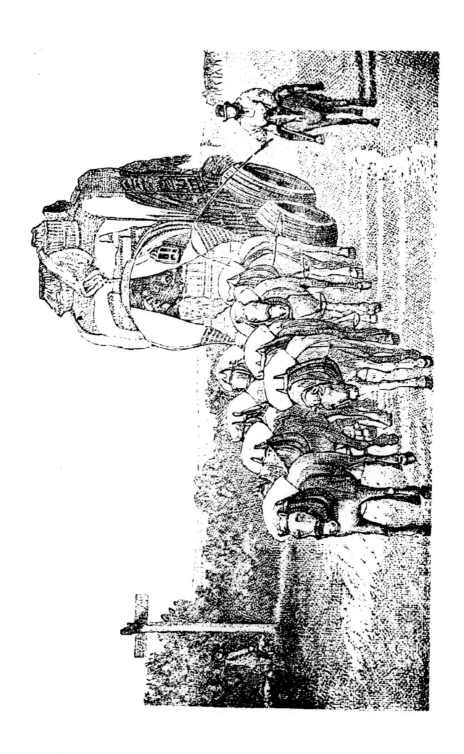

ground. But in order that the whole breadth of the wheel should run evenly on the road, the outer rim was made of less diameter than the inner: that is to say, the wheels were made conical.*

Two circles of different diameters revolving at the same speed, cover different lengths of ground at each revolution. A circle nine feet in circumference would cover a distance of nine feet, and one of eight feet circumference a distance of eight feet. A conical wheel, as shown in the representation of a road waggon, in use in the early part of the present century, has the outer rim of less diameter than the inner, and so the inner edge, each revolution of the wheel, would pass over more road than the outer, and the difference of distance would have to be made up by dragging. There would be a dragging commencing at the inner rim, and gradually increasing to the outer.

The bevelling of the wheels may not have been very great, and the difference of the diameter of the inner and outer rim of the wheels only a few inches: but there must have been a dragging of the wheels during each revolution; for each circumference or edge had to pass over the same length of road in the same time. In order to make up the difference in distance travelled by each portion of the wheels during a revolution, there was dragging; considerably increasing the labour of the horses, and giving rise to the grinding noise, which accompanied the heavily-laden stage waggons, as they slowly made their way along the high roads—a sound familiar to those who lived in the country during the early part of the present century.

The Highway Act of the 30th of George II, which came into force 1758, was to be continued seven years. It consequently expired 1765, when a new Highway Act was passed 5th George III, cap. 38. It was to remain in operation seven years.

It re-enacts the clauses in the previous Act, relating to the

---

* See plate.

tolls to be taken for waggons, having the fellies of the wheels
of less width than nine inches; and for the horses drawing
them. It also allowed the exemptions, but continued the
restrictions relating to the mode of harnessing the horses.

The clauses which in the previous Act permitted waggons
having the fellies of the wheels nine inches broad, to pass
through turnpikes on payment of half tolls, was repealed;
except the wheels should be fixed in manner hereafter
described, viz.: "having the axle-trees thereof of such different
lengths that the distance from wheel to wheel of one pair of
wheels should not be more than four feet two inches, to be
measured at the ground, and that the distance from wheel to
wheel of the other pair thereof be such that the fore and
hind wheels of such waggon and wain shall roll a surface at
least sixteen inches on each side of the said waggon or wain,
and having the fellies of the wheels thereof of the breadth of
nine inches from side to side at the bottom or sole thereof."
Waggons so constructed were allowed to be passed through
the turnpikes on paying half the toll.

This Act also repeals 26th George II, allowing waggons
drawn by eight horses, or any four-wheeled carriage having the
fellies of the wheels nine inches wide drawn by any number
of horses, not exceeding eight, and carts, or other two-wheeled
carriages, with similar wheels, drawn by five horses, to pass
through any turnpike without being weighed. And it is ordered
that they should be weighed together with their load, except
regulation waggons, "the fore and hind wheels of which shall
roll a surface of at least sixteen inches wide."

This clause must be read in connection with one further
on, commencing :—

"Providing always that nothing in an Act entituled An
Act for the preservation of the public roads in that part of
Great Britain called England, passed in the 14th year of his
late Majesty King George II; nor in an Act entituled An Act
to explain and amend an Act passed in the 14th year of his
Majesty's reign entituled An Act for the preservation of
publick roads, in that part of Great Britain called England;

and so much of the Act passed in the 3rd year of the reign of King William and Mary, entituled An Act for the better repairing and amending the highways, and for settling the rates of the carriage of goods, as relates to the settling of the rates of the carriage of goods passed in 21st year of his late Majesty, nor shall this Act be understood to compel the Trustees of any turnpike road to erect any crane or machine for weighing carts carriages, etc., having wheels of the breadth of nine inches. But if other waggons, on being weighed, exceeded six tons, or carts three tons gross weight, the Trustees were authorised to demand 20s. per ton for over weight.

In the Act there are other clauses relating to hedges and fences, and prohibiting persons ploughing within fifteen feet of the centre of the road under penalty of 40s. ; nor might any person enclose, on both sides within the distance of thirty feet from the centre of the road.

The numerous Acts which have been passed evidently did not meet the various difficulties which arose, causing impediment to the progress of the work, carried on for the improvement of the highways throughout the country. Turnpikes had been erected, and tolls taken from travellers for amending and keeping them in repair. When more than ordinary expenses were to be incurred, power was also given to borrow money on the security of the tolls.

Power, excepting where there were Trustees or commissioners of roads, was vested in the Justices of the Peace. But there was evidently a reluctance to press heavily by penalties or otherwise on those who were travellers over the roads within their jurisdiction. For 1766, 6th of George III, cap. 43, there was a Highway Act passed, and the following clause shows great dissatisfaction on the part of the Legislature at the manner in which the law had been enforced. It states, that in spite of the prohibition of a previous Act—26 of his late Majesty, in which it is prohibited for waggons having the fellies of the wheels of less breadth than nine inches, under the penalty of 5l. or the forfeiture of one horse, not being the shaft (or thill) horse, and its harness —to pass through any turnpike gate, except when drawn by less than five horses, it appears, notwithstanding the directions in the Act, several trustees or commissioners, and gate-keepers, have permitted waggons, having the fellies of the wheels of less breadth than nine inches, to be drawn by more than four horses or beasts of draught, to pass through their turnpikes.

The necessity of a comprehensive Highway Act, meeting the difficulties in the way of obtaining the effective working of the different Acts then in force, had evidently occupied the attention of the Government. In the following year, 1767, a very comprehensive Act was passed, dealing with all matters relating to the high roads.

In the seventh year of the reign of George III, chap. 42, "An Act to explain, amend and reduce into one Act of Parliament, the several statutes now [then] in being for the amendment and preservation of the publick Highways of the Kingdom," commences—*

"Whereas the several statutes now in being for the amendment and preservation of the Highways of this Kingdom are very numerous, and in some respects, ineffectual; and whereas the good purpose thereby intended might be better effected if the said statutes were entirely repealed, and reduced into one Act, Be it therefore enacted by &c. &c. &c., that from henceforth on the 22nd day of September in each year, unless it be Sunday, the constables, headborough, tythingman, churchwarden, surveyor or surveyors of the highway, and householders being assessed to any parochial or public rate of every parish &c. for which surveyors of highways have been usually appointed, shall assemble in Church or Chapel, of such parish at the hour of 11 in the forenoon."

The surveyors were by the Act required now to make every cartway leading to any market town twenty feet wide at least, and when a causeway was used, they were not to be less

---

* A writer in the "Gentleman's Magazine," who reviews the Act, says: "This Act is of such general concern that every householder should be apprised of its contents."

than three feet wide. Should there not have been sufficient width between the fences, the power was given to the Justices of the Peace to order the widening of the road, in any manner they should think fit, "so that the said highway, when enlarged, should not exceed thirty feet." But they might not pull down any house, nor take any portion of a garden, park, or paddock, court or yard, without the consent of the owner and occupier, at a price mutually agreed upon, and settled as fair by the owner, to whom the recompense or payment had to be made. Should the surveyor and tenant be unable to agree as to the price, the value was to be fixed by a jury at the Quarter Session. There was also given to the Justices power to order highways to be repaired, and direction posts to be erected where necessary, to direct wayfarers on their road to the various towns and places. They could also contract for the material for the repairing of the road, and if not obtainable in the parish, they could obtain it from private ground. Regulations were made by the Act for statute work. Every person keeping a team was obliged during six days in each year, computed from Michaelmas to Michaelmas, to find and send, on every day and at every place, to be appointed by the surveyor of the highway, one wain, cart, or carriage, furnished after the custom of the county, with horses, oxen, or other cattle, and two able-bodied men with each wain, cart, or carriage. And every person occupying land, tenements, &c., of the yearly value of 50*l.* or above, were in like manner to send a wain, cart, or carriage furnished with not less than three horses, or four oxen and one horse, or two oxen and two horses, and two able-bodied men to each vehicle, with spades, shovels, &c. An exception was made in favour of the parts of the country where carts with only single horses were used; but they had to find two such carts and tools equivalent to the above-mentioned assistance.

Fines and penalties could be enacted for the non-performance of statute duty, but liberty was given to persons to compound by money payments for their statute duty, the value of them being fixed by the Justices of the Peace. Part of the sum, where there were turnpikes, was payable to the surveyor of the

L.

Turnpike Trust.   When money was required, beyond what was
procurable by other means, for the repair of bridges, highways,
causeways, &c., an assessment might be made by order of the
Justices of the Peace, but not exceeding sixpence in the pound
sterling.   The money was not, as had been done previously to
the Act, paid into the Court of Exchequer or other Court, but
into the hands of some person or persons residing in or near
the parish.   So that by this Act a treasurer was appointed.
The surveyor of the parish was to collect the rates, forfeitures,
penalties, and compositions, which were to be entered into a
book, as well as the monies due, and a list made of the tools,
materials, implements, and other things provided for the repairing of the road.   The books were to be produced to the
Magistrates at Quarter Sessions and certified as correct by oath.

In the 38th chapter are regulations as to broad and narrow
wheels as follows: "And whereas the highways not being
turnpike roads are much prejudiced by the narrowness of the
wheels of the several carriages travelling thereon, and by the
excessive burthens loaded in such carriages, be it enacted, that
no waggon having the sole or bottom of the fellies of the wheels
of less breadth than nine inches shall go or be drawn with more
than six horses; and that no carts shall go or be drawn by
more than four horses, and that no waggon having the sole or
bottom of the fellies of the wheel of nine inches shall go or
be drawn with more than eight horses, and no cart, having the
sole or bottom of the fellies of the wheels of the breadth of
nine inches shall go or be drawn with more than five horses
upon such highways."

Supernumerary horses and their accoutrements were to
be forfeited.   Waggons shod with narrow tires or set with rose-
headed nails not to be drawn by more than three horses.

There were exceptions made when the waggons were
laden with stone, marble, metal, or timber, or when employed
in His Majesty's service, or in husbandry, until the year commencing Michaelmas, 1769.

In order to afford facilities for enforcing penalties, &c., the
owner's name and place of abode were to be painted in large

letters in a conspicuous part of the waggon or cart. This Act repealed 13th of Edward I, 14, 15, and 26 of Henry VIII, two Acts of Philip and Mary, four Acts Queen Elizabeth, two Acts Charles II, part of an Act of William and Mary so far as the power of making assessments for repairing highways, three Acts of George I, and much that was done by George II. The numerous Acts which were taken into consideration and re-pealed by the passing of the present Act made it apparent that the Government was giving great attention to the state of the roads. But the legislation respecting the breadth of the wheels and the weight of the loading shows that its attention was given to preventing injury to the roads rather than to the means of making them hard and solid and capable of bearing the traffic which the requirements of the business of the country were inducing the owners of waggons, &c., to put upon them.

The powers of the Justices of the Peace were more clearly defined, and made amply sufficient for enforcing the provisions of the Act. The duties of the surveyors were stated, and heavy penalties imposed on them for any omission or dereliction of duty. Many clauses were only the re-enacting of those pro-visions, of numerous Acts, by it repealed, which were to continue in operation, and in some instances they were modified or enlarged. The clause in the Act 5 George III, 1765, which allowed a waggon, wain, or cart having the axle-tree of different lengths, so that the wheels rolled a surface of sixteen inches, were to pay only half toll was continued, and no waggon was allowed to have the wheels so arranged that they made two ruts. 7 George III, c. 40 (1767), the Trustees of the High-ways were allowed to erect weighing machines and charge for over weight. But waggons and carts, &c., having the fellies of the wheels nine inches wide, and the axle-trees of such different lengths that they rolled sixteen inches, were not to be weighed, or charged for over weight, neither were waggons or carts employed in husbandry. The Trustees of the roads were to order the turnpike keepers to measure the fellies of the wheels when necessary, and no waggon or cart having the fellies of their wheels under nine inches were allowed to compound for their tolls.

The dimension of the waggons or carts were also limited. No waggon or cart, within twenty miles of London, were allowed to travel on the highway having the fellies of the wheels nine inches broad, unless constructed in such manner that no pair of wheels should be more than four feet six inches apart (except such as roll a surface of sixteen inches), and the distance from the centre of the fore wheel to the centre of the hind wheel was not to exceed nine feet, except timber waggons.

The number of draught horses continued to be limited. Broad wheel waggons were not to be drawn by more than eight horses, and two wheel carriages with more than four. Narrow four wheel carriages were not to be drawn with more than four horses, and two wheel carriages with narrow fellies with more than three horses, under a penalty of twenty shillings or forfeiture of the extra horse. And there was also a penalty for taking off a horse before passing through a turnpike, or adding one after the carriage had passed through the turnpike, and so avoiding payment of the toll.

Although the Act limited the number of draught horses to be used under ordinary circumstances, the Trustees could allow waggons with broad wheels to be drawn up hill by ten horses, and waggons with narrow wheels by six horses. But the Justices of Peace at Quarter Sessions were to have the measurement of the hill brought before them, and if they did not think fit to confirm the permission it was to be considered cancelled; and when there was snow upon the ground, permission might be given to employ a greater number of horses than the number mentioned in the Act of Parliament.

Narrow wheel waggons were not permitted to be drawn by horses harnessed in pairs, and the toll they were to pay was increased to one-half more than had been hitherto demanded; but the increased toll was not payable for carts having six-inch fellies and drawn by two horses, nor by carts, &c., employed in husbandry. Drag irons also came under notice; they were to be flat, and of the full width of the fellies of the wheels.

The Act orders a direction post to be erected where several roads meet, and milestones set up: where the land was subject to floods, stones had to be placed for the guidance of travellers. The clause which made pulling down turnpike or bars a felony, punishable by death, without benefit of clergy, was also retained. But this Act repealed a large number.

The property qualification of a Trustee was not lost sight of. He was required to be possessed, in his own right or that of his wife, of a rental of 40*l.* per annum, or possessed or heir to an estate worth 800*l.*, and to confirm by oath a statement made to that effect. These qualifications, penalties, &c., are repeated in the following Act of Parliament appointing Trustees of the high road from Harlow-bush Common to Woodford, in the county of Essex.

The various Acts of Parliament which have been passed gave great powers to local Magistrates, and afforded them the support, when required, of their brother " Justices of the Peace " at Quarter Sessions. But, although they had authority, when necessary, to borrow money on the security of the tolls, in order that they might have a sufficient sum at their disposal to enable them to undertake substantial repairs; the powers conferred upon them seem not to have had the beneficial result anticipated, for in 1768 the following Act was passed through Parliament, transferring the management of the Epping Highways to Trustees.

The Act is very copious; and it appears to include all the clauses found by experience to be necessary, to enable the Trustees to divert the roads where required, and to make and maintain those within their jurisdiction.

It is printed in full, as it is the Act which created the Epping Trust, and, with the public Acts, regulated the proceeding of the Trustees in the management of all matters put under their control, until it and the preceding ones were repealed, 3 George IV, c. 44, 1822.

ACT OF PARLIAMENT CREATING THE EPPING HIGHWAY TRUST.

ANNO REGNI
GEORGII III
REGIS
MAGNÆ BRITANNIÆ, FRANCIÆ AND HIBERNIÆ,
NONO.

At the Parliament begun and holden at Westminster, the Tenth Day of May, Anno Dom. 1768, in the Eighth Year of the Reign of our Sovereign Lord George the Third, by the Grace of God, of Great Britain, France, and Ireland, King, Defender of the Faith, &c.

And from thence continued, by several Prorogations, to the Eighth Day of November, 1768; being the Second Session of the Thirteenth Parliament of Great Britain.

ANNO NONO
GEORGII III REGIS.

An Act to enlarge the term and powers of two Acts passed in the tenth year of King George the First, and the sixteenth year of His late Majesty, for repairing the road from the north part of Harlow Bush Common, in the parish of Harlow to Woodford, in the county of Essex.

Preamble.   Whereas an Act was made in the tenth year of the reign of King George the First, for repairing the highways from the north part of Harlow Bush Common, in the parish of Harlow, to Woodford, in the county of Essex, which was to continue in force for the term of twenty-one years, from the twenty-seventh day of February, one thousand seven hundred and twenty-three. And whereas the term and powers of the said Act were by an Act made in the sixteenth year of the reign of His late Majesty King George the Second, continued from the expiration thereof for the further term of twenty-one years, and to the end of the then next Session of Parliament, on the conditions therein mentioned. And whereas the money borrowed on the credit of the said Acts, for the repair of the said road, is not all repaid, and therefore and to the end the said road may be continued to be repaired and maintained, it is expedient that the term of the said Acts should be enlarged, and the provisions therein made more effectual. May it therefore please Your Majesty that it may be enacted, and be it enacted by the King's Most Excellent Majesty, by and with the advice and consent of the Lords Spiritual and Temporal, and Commons, in this present Parliament assembled, and by the authority of the same, that the

Recited Acts, &c., further continued for 21 years.   terms granted by the said Acts shall be, and the same are hereby further continued from the expiration thereof; and also of the additional term of five years, granted by an Act made in the twenty-eighth year of King George the Second, intituled, "An Act to amend an Act made in the twenty-sixth year of His present Majesty, intituled, An Act for the Amendment and Preservation of the Publick Highways and Turnpike Roads of this Kingdom, and for the more effectual Execution of the Laws relating thereto," for and during the further term of twenty one years, and to the end of the then next Session of Parliament; and that, instead of all other clauses, provisions, tolls, powers, penalties, forfeitures, payments, punishments, rules, orders, matters, and things, in the said Acts contained, the clauses, provisions, tolls, powers, penalties, forfeitures, payments, punishments, rules orders, matters, and things, in this Act contained, shall for the purposes of repairing, widening, and maintaining the road in the said Acts contained and described, take place and commence upon the first Monday in May, one thousand seven hundred and sixty-nine, and shall continue in force until the expiration of the said further term of twenty one years, and to the end of the then next Session of Parliament; which said additional term hereby granted, shall be and is hereby made subject to the payment of all money now due and owing upon the credit of the said herein recited Acts, and all interest due and to grow due thereon.

And be it further enacted by the Authority aforesaid, that His Majesty's Justices of the Peace residing and acting in the Hundreds of Harlow and Onger, and Halfhundred of Waltham, in the said county, together with Sir Anthony Thomas Abdy Baronet, Sir Charles Asgill Baronet, William Altham, William Abdy, John Archer, Mark Adston, the Reverend Stothard Abdy, Jeremiah Acres, Thomas Abrahams, Thomas Adams, Francis Allen, Thomas Appleby, the Reverend Thomas Altham, D.D., the Reverend James Altham Clerk, Samuel Altham, John Archer, Mathew Arboum, Thomas Adderley, Sir Richard Betenson Baronet, John Blake, Thomas Brand, James Barwick, Robert Boothby, Samuel Bosanquet, William Bosanquet, Jeremiah Bentham, Richard Bull, John Barrow, John Banks, John Bishop, William Broughton, George Bookuk, John Brewett, John Barrow, William Baker, Bramston Baker, Henry Barber, Henry Banks, John Ballard, Champion Branfill, Denner Bennett, senior, Richard Benyon, Thomas Bishop, Charles Bocock, Samuel Ball, Gray Burges, Samuel Butler, Richard Barnard, Robert Balliman, Peregrine Bertie, Sackvile Bate, John Boodle, William Gregg Barnston, Francis Bailey, John Brecknock, Jeremiah Bentham, Thomas Blackmore, Nathaniel Bateman, Edward Brome, John Brome, John Shute Barrington, Isaac Moodey Pingham Clerk, Daniel Binckes, John Barrow, George Bull, Adam Brown, William Bevis, Jeremiah Bentham, William Borker, Francis Bayley, James Bigg, Thomas Bridge, William Black, Samuel Bosanquet, Richard Bosanquet, Thomas Berney Branston, John Conyers, John Conyers junior, Sir Richard Chase Knight, Jemmineau Checley, George Richard Carter, Jerningham Checley, John Lomax Clay, Richard Crabb, Nathaniel Caesar Corsellis, the Reverend Thomas Chapman D.D., the Reverend John Cookson, John Crabb, Richard Collins, William Cole, William Coel, Richard Connop, Thomas Carter, James Collard, Francis Clark, Edward Cox, Edward Carver, Joseph Collins, Thomas Collier, Richard Clarke, Stanes Chamberlyne, John Cowens, William Colhoun, the

Reverend William Cheer Clerk, Nicholson Calvert, Richard Chiswell, William Clinton, Henry Cousins, Henry Cooper, Staines Chamberlayn junior, Henry Crabb, John Dickins, the Reverend William Dearling, Thomas Dew, Charles Dyson, William Dyson, Francis Dickins, Benjamin Duffield, Robert Duck, John Day, Charles Dingley, Samuel Evans, the Reverend Rice Evans, John Edmondson, John Elcock, James Eave, Joseph Ennever, Joseph Eyre, John Eyre, John Elways, John Ellis, Peter Floyer, the Reverend John Fosbrooke, the Reverend George Farran, Thomas Foster, William Ford, John Fisher, Samuel Feake, the Reverend Robert Fowler, John Fisher M.D., John Fisher junior, M.D., Paul Feilde, Ralph Freeman D.D., John Goebell, Richard Gregory, the Reverend William Gould, the Reverend Nathaniel Geering, Robert Goodwin, Robert Gough, William Green, John Gough, James Grove senior, James Grove junior, John Green, Edward Gardiner, the Reverend William Gibson Clerk, Golden Griggs, William Griffin, John Gentry, John Gawler, Bamber Gascoyne, Joseph Gascoyne, Jacob Houblon, Jacob Houblon junior, John Houblon, John Hennicher, Eliab Harvey, Edward Hillersden, Alexander Hamilton, William Hamilton, James Hannot, Thomas Hyde, Thomas Hains, the Reverend John Harris, Richard Holland, John Hantler, Philip Howlett, Joseph Hughes, Daniel Hicks, John Harvey, William Hicks, James Holland, Joseph Hoye, the Reverend Richard Hind D.D., William Hachman, John Hopkins, John Hookham, George Howland, William Holt, William Heath, Charles Harris, Thomas Heath, John Hookham, Charles Hancock, Joseph Hughes, Thomas Heslerige,   Higgons, Sir Conyers Jocelyn Baronet, William Jones, William Jaques, Arthur Jones, Thomas Jessop, William Jillett, William Jackson, George Jackson, Robert Jocelyn, Edward Johns, John Jones, the Reverend Walter Kerrick, the Reverend Charles Kippax, John Kent, John King, John King, Joseph Douglas Knight, Robert Kinscote, Sir James Long Baronet, John Luther, John Roger Lawton, Richard Lockwood, John Leachman, the Reverend William Lockwood, the Reverend John Lindsay, Mathew Law, George Lee, the Reverend Thomas Lipyeatte, the Reverend Jonathan Lipyeatte, John Lockwood, Edward Langford, the Reverend   Lawrence, John Law, William Lukin, George Lake, John Lake, Sir William Maynard Baronet, Massey Morley M.D., Carew Mildmay, Robert Moxon, William Molleson, John Mullox, Thomas Mansfield, William Marden, Thomas Martin, Abraham Millbank, Thomas Millbank, Philip Martin,   Milward of Nasing, Robert Martin, William Milles, William Masterman, Nash Mason, Anthony Merry, Francis Mitten, Thomas Milward, William Mollison, Mathew Martin, James Noel, Martin Noel, William Naylor, the Reverend   Natt Clerk, Miles Nightingale, John Nanfan, Thomas Oliver, Edward Parker, Richard Prince, John Prince, the Reverend John Pooley, James Palmer, Richard Palmer, Thomas Parker, John Plumb, Samuel Playle, Mathew Playle, Heyman Prescott, Peter Pain, Edward Parson, Edward Parson junior, William Plumer, William Poole, John Pitkin, John Pincent, George Parris, William Parris, Richard Parris, John Raymond, Charles Raymond, the Reverend Philip Rosenhagen, William Rogers, William

Rogers, John Russell, John Rigg, Mathew Raper, John Raper, William Rivitt William Robertson, John Redington, James Rayment, Sir Charles Smyth Baronet, George Scott, Thomas Scott, William Southby, Barrow Starmingford, Charles Selwyn near Harlow, Andrew Searle, the Reverend William Smyth, the Reverend Thomas Smith, James Streeter, Thomas Grubb Stacey, Thomas Stacey, John Searle, John Squirrell, Nymphas Stace, James Sedgwick Mathew Scott, Thomas Shirley, Charles Smith, the Reverend William Salisbury Clerk, the Reverend Francis Stanley, the Reverend Thomas Salt, William Smyth, the Reverend William Sclater, Nathaniel Smith, Thomas Selwin, William Sotheby, Samuel Southhouse, Robert Speed, James Scrubby, Joshua Scrubby, John Strut, Joseph Smith, Richard Stanley, the Reverend Francis Stanley the younger, Richard Salway the Right Honourable John Earl Tilney in the Kingdom of Ireland, Frederick Tensh, Anthony Todd, the Reverend Robert Tooke, the Reverend James Trebeck, Thomas Tripp, Swan Labrata, Samuel Thompson, Thomas Towers, Abraham Thorogood, James Turvin the Reverend Charles Torriano, Sir Thomas Spencer Wilson Baronet, Sir William Wake, Thomas Walton, Beacher Walton, Sir Edward Walpole Knight of th Bath, the Reverend Thomas Waste the Reverend Henry Wray, Thomas Winspear, Thomas Weaver, Richard Wright, Richard Waylett, Patrick Waters, Samuel Wingall, Michael Welch, Bartholomew Wright, George Wright, Jacob Wright, John Warner Richard Wright, Godfrey Webster, Thomas Wright, Thomas Watton, John Arnold Wallinger, Ralph Winter, the Reverend Edward Wise Clerk, the Reverend Samuel Wise, John Walker Clerk, John Wenham, Edward Wise, Isaac Whittington, James Wyatt, White, George White, Thomas Wolfe the Honourable Charles Yorke, John Young, Thomas Young and their successors, to be elected in manner herein after mentioned, are hereby appointed Trustees for repairing, widening, and keeping in repair, the said road from the north part of Harlow Bush Common, in the parish of Harlow, to Woodford, in the county of Essex, and for putting in execution all other the Powers by this Act given.

Provided nevertheless, and be it further enacted by the authority aforesaid, that no person shall be capable of acting as a Trustee in the execution of this Act, unless he shall be in his own right, or in the right of his wife, in the actual possession or receipt of the rents and profits of lands, tenements, or hereditaments, of the clear yearly value of fifty pounds, above reprizes; or possessed of a personal estate of the value of one thousand pounds; or shall be heir apparent of a person possessed of an estate in lands, tenements, or hereditaments, of the clear yearly value of one hundred pounds; and if any person, not being so qualified shall presume to act contrary to the intent and meaning hereof, every such person shall, for every such offence, forfeit and pay the sum of fifty pounds to any person or persons who shall sue for the same, to be recovered in any of His Majesty's Courts of Record, by action of debt, or on the case, or by Bill, suit, or information, wherein no essoin, protection, or wager of law, or more than one imparlance shall be allowed; and every person so prosecuted shall prove that he is qualified as aforesaid, or otherwise shall pay the said penalty, upon proof given of his having acted as a Trustee in the execution of this Act.

And be it further enacted by the authority aforesaid, that the said Trustees, or any five or more of them, shall meet together at the house of Grace Stokes, commonly called Epping Place, upon the first Tuesday in May, one thousand seven hundred and sixty-nine, and proceed to the execution of this Act ; and shall then, and from time to time afterwards, adjourn themselves to meet at such house or place, upon some part of the said road, as the said Trustees, or any five or more of them, shall think most convenient : and if at any meeting, appointed to be held by virtue of this Act, there shall not appear a sufficient number of Trustees to act, and to adjourn to another day ; or in case the Trustees, at any time so assembled, shall omit or neglect to adjourn themselves, the clerk or clerks to the said Trustees shall, from time to time, in either of such cases, by notice in writing to be affixed upon all the turnpikes which shall be erected cross the said road, or by advertisement in some weekly journal or newspaper usually circulated in the neighbourhood of the said road, at least ten days before the next meeting, appoint the Trustees to meet at the place where the last meeting was appointed to be held, on that day three weeks upon which such last meeting

was appointed ; and the said Trustees, at all their meetings, shall defray their own expences ; and that all orders and determinations of the said Trustees in the execution of this Act, shall be at a meeting to be held in pursuance of this Act, and not otherwise, except as hereinafter is excepted : and that no such order

or determination shall be made unless the majority of the Trustees present at a meeting (every Trustee composing such majority not being personally interested in the matter or matters in question) shall concur therein, and such majority not being less than the number of Trustees by this Act authorized to make

such order or determination ; nor shall any such order or determination be revoked or altered at any subsequent meeting, unless nine Trustees, neither of them being personally interested as aforesaid, shall be present, nor unless the person or persons applying to revoke or alter any such order or determination shall give notice in writing to the clerk to the said Trustees, to be by him fixed up at all the gates or turnpikes then standing cross the said road, or advertised in manner aforesaid, at least ten days previous to any meeting to be held for such

purpose ; nor shall any Trustee be capable of acting in the execution of any of the powers hereby granted, during the time he shall hold any place of profit under this Act, but all such Trustees as are Justices of the Peace may act in the execution of this Act, notwithstanding their being Trustees, except only in such cases were (*sic*) they shall be personally interested ; nor shall any meeting of Trustees by virtue of this Act be on any account begun to be held before the hour of ten in the forenoon, or after four in the afternoon ; and if any meeting shall at any time be held contrary to this direction, all business which shall be done or transacted at such meeting shall be, and the same is hereby declared to be, null and void.

Provided always, and be it further enacted by the authority aforesaid, that two Trustees shall be sufficient for the purpose of adjourning ; and if it shall at any time happen, that no Trustee shall apper (sic) at the time and place appointed for any of the meetings of Trustees to be held under this Act; then, in case the clerk or clerks to the said Trustees shall refuse or neglect to give notice, or shall by any means be prevented from giving notice as aforesaid, or in case there shall be no clerk appointed, it shall and may be lawful for any two or more of the Trustees appointed to put this Act in execution at any time or times (the space of ten days after such refusal, neglect, or prevention, of the clerk or clerks having first intervened) to appoint such Trustees to meet at some house in or near the said road on that day three weeks, mentioned in such notice, which said notice shall be in writing, and shall be affixed on all the turnpikes erected by virtue of this Act across the said road, or advertised in some weekly journal or newspaper as aforesaid, either of which methods shall be deemed and taken to be sufficient notice for any such meeting.

Provided likewise, and be it further enacted by the authority aforesaid, that if after any adjournment by virtue of this Act, or after such refusal or neglect as aforesaid, it shall at any time be thought necessary for the better execution of this Act, that an early day of meeting should be appointed, the person acting as clerk to the said Trustees, upon an order in writing, signed by five or more of the said Trustees, naming the time and place of such meeting, shall, as soon as may be, give notice thereof by advertisement in some journal or newspaper as aforesaid, and thereby appoint a meeting of Trustees to be held at such time and place as shall be by such order directed, such time not being less than fourteen days after the publication of the respective journal or newspaper, and specifying in such notice the particular business intended to be transacted at such meeting; and such business when so done and concluded upon at such meeting, shall have the same effect as it could have had in case it had been done at any meeting of Trustees herein otherwise authorized or directed to be held; but any other business done at such meeting than what shall be so specified, shall be to all intents and purposes void and of none effect. *Meetings on emergency.*

And be it further enacted by the authority aforesaid, that when and so often as any Trustee shall die, or refuse to act, it shall be lawful for the surviving or remaining Trustees, or any seven or more of them, by writing under their hands and seals, to elect one other person qualified as aforesaid to be a Trustee in the room of each Trustee so deceased or refusing to act; but notice in writing of the time and place of meeting for every such election shall be given by the clerk or clerks to the said Trustees, by affixing the same in writing upon all the turnpikes across the said road, and by advertising the same in manner aforesaid, at least fourteen days before every such meeting, and all persons who shall be so elected are hereby vested with the same powers for putting this Act in execution as the persons in whose places they shall be respectively chosen were vested with. *Or death, &c. of Trustees, other to be chosen.*

And be it further enacted by the authority aforesaid, that the said Trustees, or any five or more of them, may continue the turnpikes and tollhouses already erected upon the said road, except as is herein after excepted, and may and shall cause to be erected any turnpike or turnpikes in, upon, or cross, any part or *Trustees may erect turnpikes and tollhouses.*

parts of the said road, except also as herein after is excepted, and also upon the side or sides thereof, and cross any street, lane, or way, leading into or out of the same, and also to be erected or provided a tollhouse or tollhouses, with suitable out buildings, at or near each turnpike; and also to take in and enclose from the common or wastes near the said road a garden spot to each toll house suitable and convenient thereto, so as such garden spot does not exceed four poles square, and also to provide and maintain a lamp or lamps with proper furniture at or near each turnpike, and from time to time to take down or remove any such turnpike or turnpikes and tollhouses, or to alter the same, or any part or parts thereof respectively, as they the said Trustees, or any five or more of them, shall think meet or expedient, and that the tolls following shall be demanded and taken at every such turnpike by such person or persons as the said Trustees, or any five or more of them, shall from time to time appoint for that purpose, or to whom the same shall be lett, before any cattle or carriage shall be permitted to pass through the same, that is to say,—

And take toll thereat.

The tolls.

For every coach, chariot, chaise, or calash, drawn by one pair of horses, mares, geldings, or mules, six pence; and drawn by four horses, mares, geldings, or mules, nine pence; and drawn by six horses, mares, geldings, or mules, one shilling.

For every chaise drawn by one horse, mare, gelding, or mule, three pence.

For every cart drawn by one horse, mare, gelding, mule, or ass, three pence; and if drawn by more than one horse, mare, gelding, mule, or ass, if a-breast, eight pence; and drawn by more than one horse, mare, gelding, mule, or ass, at, length, six pence.

For every cart drawn by three or more horses, mares, geldings, mules, or asses, nine pence.

For every wagon or wain, one shilling.

For every horse, mare, gelding, mule, or ass, laden or unladen, and not drawing, one penny.

For oxen or neat cattle, ten pence per score; and so in proportion for a greater or less number.

For sheep, calves, and swine, five pence per score: and so in proportion for any greater or less number.

Tolls may be levied by distress and sale.

Which said respective sums of money shall be demanded and taken in the name of or as a toll, and if any person or persons, subject to the payment of any of the said tolls, shall, after demand thereof made, neglect or refuse to pay the same, or any part thereof; it shall be lawful for the person or persons appointed as aforesaid to collect such tolls, by himself, or taking such assistance as he shall think necessary, to seize and distrain any horse or horses, or other cattle, together with their bridles, gears, harness, or accoutrements, or their loading, or any goods, or carriage, upon which such toll is by this Act imposed, or any of the goods and chattels of such person or persons so neglecting or refusing to pay the same; and if such toll, and the reasonable

Distress may

charges of such seizure and distress shall not be paid within the space of four days after such seizure and distress made, the person or persons so seizing and distraining shall and may sell the horse or horses, cattle, carriages, goods, chattels, or things so seized and distrained, returning the overplus (if any be) upon demand, to the owner thereof, after such tolls, and the reasonable charges occasioned by such seizure, distress, and sale, shall be deducted; and that all the tolls collected or levied by virtue of this Act shall be, and are hereby vested in the said Trustees, and shall be applied, or may be assigned in such manner as is herein after-mentioned. *be sold after days.*

Tolls vested in Trustees.

And be it further enacted by the authority aforesaid, that the said Trustees, or any five or more of them, shall and they are hereby directed and required at their first meeting in pursuance of this Act, to cause the gate or turnpike now erected, and standing at or near a place called Epping Place, near the town of Epping, to be immediately taken down and removed to that side of the windmill, belonging to John Conyers, Esquire, near Epping Place, which is nearest to the town of Epping. *Epping Gate to be removed near to Mr. Conyers' windmill.*

And be it farther enacted by the authority aforesaid, that the tolls by this Act granted shall be collected in manner following; that is to say, for the space of one calendar month at the gate to be erected near to the said windmill; and at the gate called the Lower Gate, for the space of one other calendar month; and so in monthly alternate periods, during the continuance of the said former Acts, and this Act: the first of the said collections to be made at the said gate near the said windmill: anything in the said former Acts, or this Act, to the contrary notwithstanding. *Tolls to be taken at one gate only, by alternate monthly periods.*

And be it further enacted by the authority aforesaid, that no person or persons shall be subject to pay any toll more than once in any one day, to be computed from twelve of the clock in one night to twelve of the clock in the succeeding night, for passing with the same horse, cattle, or carriage, through all or any turnpike or turnpikes to be continued or erected by virtue of this Act, such person or persons producing a note or ticket, denoting that such toll has been paid on that day; which notes or tickets the collectors of the tolls are hereby required to deliver gratis, on receipt of the toll. *Tolls to be paid but once a day.*

Provided also, and be it further enacted by the authority aforesaid, that if any dispute shall happen about the quantity of the tolls due, or the charges of keeping the said distress, it shall be lawful for the said collector, or person distraining, to detain the same, or the money arising from the sale thereof as the case may happen, till the quantity of the tolls, or charges of distraining and selling the distress, as the case shall happen, shall be ascertained by some Justice of the Peace for the county of Essex, who shall examine the said collector upon oath, and assess the charges of such distress and sale, and also the collector's attendance for that purpose upon the said Justice; all which sum, or sums, so assessed, shall be paid to the said collector, before he shall be bound to return the said distress, or the overplus after sale thereof. *Justices to determine differences.*

And be it further enacted by the authority aforesaid, that it shall and may be lawful for the said Trustees, or any five or more of them, and they are hereby *Trustees may compound* with travellers.

impowered from time to time as they shall think proper, to compound or agree by the year, with all or any the inhabitants of the several parishes or places through which any part of the said road leads, for the passage of their respective cattle and carriages, not travelling for hire, through all or any of the gates or turnpikes upon the said road, for any sum and sums of money, for and in lieu of the payment of tolls, which composition money shall be paid yearly in advance.

Turnpikes, &c., vested in Trustees.

And be it further enacted by the authority aforesaid, that the right and property of all the turnpikes and tollhouses already erected, or to be by virtue of this Act erected, upon the said road, and the right and property of the materials provided for building or repairing the same, or any of the out-buildings, lamps, and other conveniences and requisites, and of all materials which shall be actually got or collected for repairing the said road, shall be, and are hereby vested in the said Trustees, and they, or any five or more of them, are hereby impowered to bring, or cause to be brought, an action, or actions, in the name or names of any two or more of them, or of their Treasurer or Treasurers, Clerk or Clerks, or to prefer, or order the preferring of indictments against any person or persons who shall injure the same, or any part or parts thereof, or disturb them in the possession thereof, or to take or retain, or hold possession thereof, after being required, by the order of any five or more of the said Trustees, to deliver up the same.

Application of the tolls.

And be it further enacted by the authority aforesaid, that out of the money already raised upon the credit of the said recited Acts, or out of the first monies to be raised by virtue of this Act, the said Trustees, or any five or more of them, shall in the first place, pay and discharge all the expences and costs relative to procuring and passing this Act; and the remainder of the money so raised shall, from time to time, be applied in putting this Act in execution, and in repaying the principal monies borrowed, and the interest due thereupon.

Exemptions from toll

Provided always, and it is hereby enacted, that no toll shall be taken by virtue of this Act for any horse, cattle, or beast, drawing or not drawing, employed only in the conveyance or carriage of any stones, gravel, or other materials, for repairing the said road, or for repairing any of the highways in any of the parishes or places in which any part of the said road is situated, or in the carriage or conveyance of any dung, soil, chalk, chalk rubbish, mould, or compost of any kind, for manuring of any garden, or other land or ground, in any of the parishes through or in which any part of the said road shall lead or lie; or employed in the plowing, sowing, tilling, cultivating, or stocking, of any land or ground in any of such parishes or places, or in the carriage or conveyance of any hay, straw, or corn in the straw, not sold or disposed of, but passing to be laid up in the houses, out-houses, or grounds, of the owner or owners thereof, in any of the said parishes: or drawing or conveying any plough, harrow, or other implement of husbandry; or for any horse, or other cattle or beast going to or from water or pasture; or for the horses of any officers or soldiers upon their march, or for the horses or other cattle or beast employed in the conveyance or carriage of their arms or baggage; or for any post horse carrying or drawing the mail; or for any horse or other cattle, drawing or not drawing, employed in the carrying or conveying any person or persons going to or returning from any election of a Knight or Knights of the Shire, to serve in Parliament for the said county of Essex, on the days of such election, or on the day before or day after any such election shall begin or be concluded; and if any person shall claim and take the benefit of any of the exemptions aforesaid, not being intitled to the same, every such person shall, for every such offence, forfeit the sum of forty shillings.

And be it further enacted, that, if any person or persons shall forcibly or wilfully go or pass with any horse, beast, or carriage, through any turnpike by virtue of this Act to be continued, erected, or set up, without paying the toll or tolls by this Act directed to be paid for the same; or shall knowingly and designedly assault, interrupt, or obstruct, any or either of the collectors or persons in the collecting or receiving any or either of the said tolls, or any otherwise in the execution of his, her, or their office or offices of collector or collectors; or shall forge, counterfeit, or alter, or shall deliver to, or receive of any other person or persons, any ticket or tickets, with intent to avoid the payment of any of the said tolls, or any part thereof; or if any person or persons shall take off, or cause to be taken off, any horse or other beast from any carriage, or having passed through any turnpike, shall afterwards add or put any horse or other beast to any such carriage, and draw therewith upon any part of the said road, so as to increase the number of horses or other beasts drawing the said carriage, after the same shall have passed through the said turnpike, with intent to evade, or having thereby evaded the payment of any of the said tolls, or any part thereof; or if any person or persons shall go or pass with any horse, beast, or carriage, through or over any land, ground, or place, being by the side of, or near to, the said road, the same not being a publick highway; or if any person or persons owning or occupying any land, ground, or place, not being a publick highway, shall knowingly and wittingly permit or suffer any other person or persons to go or pass with any horse, beast, or carriage, through or over such land, ground, or place, in order or with intent that the payment of any of the said tolls, or any part thereof, should be avoided; or if any person or persons shall do any other act, in order or with intent to avoid the payment of the said tolls, or any part thereof, such persons, and every of them, so offending, shall, for every such offence, forfeit and pay the sum of five pounds, over and besides such damages and punishments as they and every of them respectively shall be liable to by law; and shall and may be lawful for the said collectors of the said tolls, and for every of them, and all other persons by them required to assist in that respect, to seize any horse or horses, beast or beasts, or goods belonging to, or in the possession or under the care of, any person or persons so offending in the premisses; and the same to take to any Justice of the Peace of the county or place where such offence or offences shall be committed, and before him to make complaint of such offence or offences; and such Justice may, and is hereby required to examine the nature of the offence or offences so complained of, and by the confession of the party or parties complained of, or upon the oath or oaths of one or more witness or witnesses, if the said Justice shall see cause, to convict the party or parties complained of, if he, she, or they, shall or shall not appear before him, in the respective penalties aforesaid; and for non-payment thereof, and of the tolls that shall be due, though the same shall not be demanded, by warrant under his hand and seal, to cause the said horse or horses, beast or beasts, or goods, to be sold for payment of the said tolls and penalties, and the charges of seizing, keeping, and selling the same, and of such conviction; and after payment thereof, to render the overplus of the money arising by such sale (if any there shall be) to the owner or owners of the said horse or horses, beast or beasts, or goods, or to the person or persons under whose care or in whose possession they respectively was or were when so seized as aforesaid; and if no such distress as aforesaid can or shall be made, then the aforesaid penalties, forfeitures, and tolls shall be levied and recovered by such means, and in such manner, as are herein after mentioned and provided for the levying and recovering of penalties and forfeitures imposed by this Act; one moiety whereof, when raised, shall be paid to the informer, and the other moiety shall be applied in such manner as the other penalties are herein after directed to be applied.

Penalty on leaving any empty carriage or rubbish in the road.

And be it further enacted, that if any person shall leave any waggon, cart, or other carriage in, upon, or on the side of any part of the said road, without any horse or other beast of draught yoked thereto, or to draw the same; or shall knowingly or wilfully lay any sort of timber, or any stone, hay, straw, dung, manure, soil, rubbish, or other matter or thing whatsoever in any part of the said road, or on the side or sides thereof, to the prejudice or annoyance thereof; every person so offending shall, for every such offence, forfeit and pay the sum of twenty shillings.

Trustees may fence off commons.

And whereas several parts of the said road lead over downs, moors, commons, common fields, or waste grounds, and the payment of the tolls hereby granted may, by reason of the width of the said downs, moors, commons, or waste grounds be easily avoided, be it therefore enacted by the Authority aforesaid, That the said Trustees, or any five or more of them, shall and may, if they see occasion, fence and ditch off such parts of the said downs, moors, commons, common fields, or waste grounds as they shall think necessary in order to prevent the payment of the said tolls being evaded.

Trustees may lease, &c., the tolls.

And be it further enacted by the authority aforesaid, that the said Trustees, or any seven or more of them, may, and are hereby authorized and impowered, at any time or times, twenty-one days' notice in writing being affixed on all the turnpike gates which shall be then standing upon the said road, and also advertised in manner aforesaid; to lease or farm by the year all the tolls granted by this Act, or any part or parts thereof, to any person or persons whomsoever, at or for the largest yearly sum or sums that can be gotten for the same, taking sufficient security for the payment thereof; provided that such leases or agreements be in writing, and signed by the person or persons taking or farming the same, and by seven of the said Trustees, and be not made for more than three years at any one time; and that the money which shall be so agreed to be paid for the said tolls shall be made payable, and shall be paid to the said Trustees, or any five or more of them, or to such person as they or any five or more of them shall, by any writing under their hands and seals, authorize and impower to receive the same, by quarterly payments, and that the person or persons to whom the same shall be lett, shall always pay down one quarter's rent in advance: and in case any agreement shall be made for letting or farming the said tolls, or any part thereof, contrary to the true intent and meaning of this Act; or if any default shall be made in paying the full money agreed to be paid for the said tolls, or any part or parts thereof, contrary to the true intent and meaning of this Act; that then, and in either of the cases aforesaid, every such agreement shall be void, and the person or persons to whom the said tolls shall have been letten or farmed as aforesaid shall be liable to account for the same to the said Trustees, or any five or more of them; and the same shall be levied and recovered upon and from him and them by the same ways and means, and in such manner, as the tolls granted by this Act are herein directed to be levied and recovered from the collectors thereof.

And be it further enacted by the authority aforesaid, that it shall and may be lawful for the said Trustees, or any seven of them, at their first, or any subsequent meeting to be held in pursuance of this Act, upon the credit of the tolls, to borrow and take up at interest such sum or sums of money as they, or any seven or more of them, shall think fit; and may and are hereby impowered to assign over and mortgage the said tolls, or any part or parts thereof, the costs and charges of such assignments or mortgages to be paid out of such tolls, as a security to any person or persons, or their Trustees, who shall advance the same, by the following words of assignment under their hands or by any other words for that purpose:

By virtue of an Act made in the   year of the reign of His Majesty King George the Third, intituled an Act

We,   of the Trustees, do assign unto A. B, his executors, administrators, or assigns, in consideration of the sum of
from this   day of   , in the year of our Lord
until the said sum of   with interest at the rate of   per centum per annum shall be repaid, such proportion of the tolls arising by virtue of this Act, as the said sum of   shall bear to the whole sum advanced on the credit on the same.

And copies of all such mortgages or assignments shall be entered in a book or books to be kept for that purpose by the clerk or treasurer to the said Trustees; but no money shall be borrowed upon the credit of the said tolls, after such first meeting, unless notice be for that purpose fixed in writing upon all the turnpikes in or upon the said road, and advertised in manner aforesaid, at least twenty-one days before the borrowing thereof; and all and every person or persons

Assignments may be transferred.

to whom any such assignment or assignments shall be made as aforesaid, or who shall be intitled to the money thereby secured, may from time to time assign or transfer his, her, or their right, title, interest, or benefit, to the principal and interest thereby secured to any person or persons whatsoever, indorsing on the back of such security, before one credible witness, the following words, or words to the like effect :—

Form of transfer.

I do transfer this assignment, with all my right and title to the principal hereby secured, and to all the interest now due, unto
his executors administrators, or assigns, dated this   day of

             G. H.

Witness, J. K.

Which said transfer or assignment shall be produced and notified to the said clerk or clerks, treasurer or treasurers, who shall cause an entry or memorial to be made thereof, containing the numbers, dates, names of the parties, and sums of money therein transferred, in the said book or books to be kept for the entering the said original assignments : for which the said clerk or clerks,

Clerk's fee.

treasurer or treasurers, shall be paid such sum as the said Trustees, or any five or more of them, shall appoint, not exceeding the sum of two shillings and six pence ; and after such entry made, but not till then, every such assignment shall intitle such assignee, his, her, and their executors, administrators, and assigns, to the benefit thereof and payment thereon, and every such assignee may in like manner assign again, and so *toties quoties ;* but in case any sum or sums so assigned shall not exceed the sum of one hundred pounds, it shall and may be lawful to and for the respective person or persons intitled to such assignment respectively, by an indorsement of his, her, or their proper name, without witness, to transfer his, her, or their property in such assignment or assignments, to any other person or persons, without an entry to be made thereof in the said book or books to be kept for entering the original mortgages or assignments ; and all such transfers and assignments shall intitle such assignee, his, her, or their executors, administrators, and assigns, to the benefit thereof and payment thereon, and such assignee may in like manner assign or transfer the same again, and so *toties quoties ;* and it shall not be in the power of such person or persons who shall have made such assignments respectively, to make void, release, or discharge the same, or any monies thereby due, or any part

All creditors deemed equal in degree.

thereof ; and all and every person and persons to whom any such mortgage or assignment shall be made as aforesaid, shall be, in proportion to the sum or sums therein mentioned, creditors on such tolls, on the credit whereof such sum or sums are advanced, in equal degree one with another, and shall have no preference in respect of the priority of any such monies.

Trustees may appoint officers.

And be it further enacted by the authority aforesaid, that the said Trustees, or any five or more of them, may from time to time, by writing under their hands, continue or appoint one or more collector or collectors of the tolls, and one or more clerk or clerks, treasurer or treasurers, and surveyor or surveyors of the said road, and such other officers as the said Trustees, or any five or more of them, shall think necessary; and from time to time to remove any or either of such officers and other persons, and appoint others in the room of such of them as shall be so removed, or shall die; and out of the monies to arise by virtue of this Act make such allowances to the said officers and persons, as to them the said Trustees, or any five or more of them, shall seem reasonable; and all such officers and persons shall under their hands, at such time and times, and in such manner as the said Trustees, or any five or more of them, shall direct, deliver to such Trustees, or such person or persons as they, or any five or more of them, shall appoint, true and perfect accounts in writing of all the monies which shall have been by such officer or officers and person or persons respectively, received by virtue of this Act, and how much thereof hath been paid and disbursed, and for what purposes, together with the proper vouchers for such payments, and shall pay all such monies as remain in their respective hands to the said Trustees, or any five or more of them, or to such person or persons as they shall appoint; and all the said officers and persons, so accounting as aforesaid, shall, upon oath, if thereunto required by the said Trustees, or any five or more of them (which oath the said Trustees, or any two or more of them, are hereby impowered to administer), verify their said accounts; and if any such officer or person shall not make and render, or refuse to verify upon oath, any such account, or to produce or deliver up the vouchers relating to the same, or to make payment as aforesaid, or shall not deliver to the said Trustees, or any five or more of them, within fourteen days after being thereunto required by any five or more of such Trustees, all the books, papers, and writings, in his custody or power, relating to the execution of this Act, or shall refuse or neglect to pay such money as upon the balance of any account or accounts, shall appear to be in their respective hands, to the said Trustees, or any five or more of them, or as they shall direct or appoint; then, and in either of the cases aforesaid, such Trustees, or any five or more of them, may and are hereby authorized and impowered to bring or cause to brought (sic) any action or actions in the name of such Trustees, or in the name or names of any two or more of them, against the officer or officers, person or persons, so neglecting or refusing as aforesaid, in order for the recovery of the monies that shall be in the hands of such officer or officers, person or persons, respectively; or if complaint shall be made of any such refusal or neglect as aforesaid, to any one or more of the Justices of the Peace for the county or place wherein such officer or officers, person or persons, so neglecting or refusing, shall be and reside, such Justice or Justices may, and is and are hereby authorized and required, by a warrant or warrants under his or their hand and seal, or hands and seals, to cause the officer or officers, person or persons, so refusing or neglecting, to be brought before him or them, and upon his and their appearing, or not being to be found, to hear and determine the matter in a summary way, and to settle the said account or accounts, if produced, in such manner as the said Trustees, or any five or more of them, by virtue of this Act might have done : and if, upon the confession of the party or parties, or by the testimony of any credible witness or witnesses upon oath (which oath such Justice or Justices is and are hereby impowered and required to administer without any fee or reward) it shall appear to such Justice or Justices, that any of the monies that shall have been collected or raised, by virtue of this Act, shall be in the hands of such officer or officers, person or persons, such Justice or Justices may, and is and are hereby authorized and required, upon non-payment thereof, by a warrant or warrants under his or their hand and seal, or hands and seals, to cause such money to be levied by distress and sale of the goods and chattles of such officer or officers, person or persons respectively ; and if no goods or chattles of such officer or officers, person or persons, can be found sufficient to answer and satisfy the said money, and the charges of distraining for the same, then, and in any of the cases aforesaid, such Justice or Justices shall commit every such offender to the common gaol for the county or place where such offender shall reside, or be apprehended, until he shall give and make a true and perfect account and payment, as aforesaid, or until he shall compound with the said Trustees, or any five or more of them, and shall have paid such composition in such manner as they shall appoint (which composition the said Trustees, or any five or more of them, are hereby impowered to make) or until he shall deliver up such books papers, and writings as aforesaid, or give satisfaction in respect thereof to the said Trustees, or any five or more of them.

And be it further enacted by the authority aforesaid, that the said Trustees, or any five or more of them, shall, and they are hereby required to take such security from their treasurer, as to them, or any five or more of them. shall seem requisite.

And be it further enacted by the authority aforesaid, that no victualler or retailer of ale, beer, cyder. or spirituous liquors shall be capable of holding any place of profit under this Act.

And be it further enacted, that when and as often as any collector of the tolls directed by this Act to be taken shall die, or be incapable of performing his or her duty, or shall be negligent, or misbehave himself or herself therein, it shall and may be lawful for any five or more of the said Trustees, though not assembled at a meeting in pursuance of this Act, by any writing under their hands, to appoint any other person to collect such tolls ; and the person so appointed shall have the same authority for recovery thereof as the person he or she shall succeed was vested with, until the said Trustees, or any five or more of them, shall, at a meeting to be held by virtue of this Act, appoint a collector of such tolls.

And be it further enacted, that if any toll-gatherer, or person appointed by the said Trustees, or any five or more of them, in manner directed by this Act, to collect and receive any of the tolls hereby granted, shall, at any time or times, neglect or refuse to quit his or her employment, conformable to the orders of the said Trustees, or any five or more of them, and to deliver up the posses-

Marginal notes:

Balance by distress and sale.

For want of distress, person to be committed,

until payment or composition made.

Treasurer, &c., to give security.

Victuallers not to hold any place of profit, &c.

Trustees may appoint a collector in case of death, &c.,

and oblige gate-keepers to deliver up possession of gates when required.

sion of the turnpike or toll-gate, and toll-house, to the said Trustees, or to such person or persons as they, or any five or more of them, shall appoint, and shall be convicted of such neglect or refusal before one or more Justice or Justices of the Peace of the county of Essex, either upon confession of the party, or by the oath of one or more witness or witnesses; then it shall and may be lawful to and for such Justice or Justices, and he and they is and are hereby required to issue his or their warrant or warrants to the constable, tything-man, or other officer or officers of the peace of the county or place, to turn such toll gatherer or collector out of the possession of the said turnpike or toll-gate, and toll-house, and to deliver the possession thereof to such person or persons as the said Trustees, or any five or more of them, shall have directed or appointed, in manner aforesaid; and also to bring the toll-gatherer or toll-gatherers, or collectors, before such Justice or Justices, who is and are hereby impowered and required to commit him or them to the House of Correction, there to be kept to hard labour for any time not exceeding the space of two months.

And be it further enacted by the authority aforesaid, that the surveyor or surveyors for the said road, or any of them, and such other person and persons as shall be employed by such surveyor or surveyors, or by the said Trustees, or any five or more of them, is and are hereby impowered to cut, dig, gather, take, and carry away any furze, heath, gravel, sand, or other materials, proper for the repairing of the said road, out of and from any waste ground or common, river or brook, in any parish, town, or place, in which any part of the said road lies, or in any neighbouring parish, town, or place, without paying anything for the same; such surveyors, or other persons, filling up the pits or quarries, levelling the ground, or sloping down the banks, where such materials shall be taken, or railing or fencing off such pits or quarries, so that the same may not be dangerous to passengers or cattle: and if such quantities of furze, heath, stones, or other materials, proper and sufficient for that purpose, cannot be had or found in or upon such waste ground or commons, rivers or brooks, contiguous to that part of the said road intended therewith to be repaired; then, and in such case, the said surveyor or surveyors, or other person as aforesaid, may, by order of the said Trustees, or any five or more of them, dig, gather, take, and carry away, any such materials as aforesaid, in, upon, or out of, from, and over the lands of any person or persons, not being a yard, garden, park, paddock, planted walk, or avenue, to any house, or any inclosed ground, planted and set apart as a nursery for trees,) paying or tendering payment for the same, and for the damages done to such private lands, over which any materials, gotten in any waste ground, common, river, or brook, or private ground, shall be conveyed, as the said Trustees, or any five or more of them, shall adjudge reasonable: and in case of any difference between the said Trustees, surveyor or surveyors, or other person or persons appointed and employed as aforesaid, and the said owners or occupiers, or any or either of them, concerning such payments and damages as aforesaid, the Justices of the Peace, at their next

Surveyors may dig gravel, &c.

without paying for the same.

Levelling the pits.

Materials may be taken from private grounds

making satisfaction to the owners.

Justices to determine differences.

General Quarter Sessions, to be holden in and for the said county, on six days notice thereof being given in writing, by the said surveyor or surveyors to the said owner or occupier, owners or occupiers, or by the said owner or occupier, owners or occupiers, to the said surveyor or surveyors, or to be left at their respective places of abode, with some or one of their respective families, shall hear, settle, and determine, the matter of such payments and damages, and the judgement or order of the said Justices therein shall be final and conclusive to all parties.

Penalty on taking away materials, &c. got by order of the surveyor, and on surveyors not taking away stones which are picked and heaped.

And be it enacted by the authority aforesaid, that if the owner or occupier of any ground or soil, or any person whatsoever, shall take away any materials which shall have been digged or gathered in any lands, fields, wastes or grounds, river or brook, for the purpose of repairing the said road, or shall get or take away any materials out of any pit or quarry, which shall have been made for the purpose of getting such materials for repairing the said road, before the said surveyors or their workmen shall have discontinued working therein for the space of six weeks (except the owner or occupier of any private ground, and persons authorized by such owner or occupier to get materials therein for his own private use only, and not for sale), or if the said surveyors shall neglect or refuse, after fourteen days' notice to them given for that purpose by the owner or occupier of any lands or grounds, to remove and carry away any such stones as shall by their orders be picked up and laid in heaps upon any lands or grounds; every person so offending in either of the said cases shall forfeit for every such offence the sum of five pounds.

Surveyors may remove annoyances, &c.

and cleanse ditches, &c.

Owners neglecting to remove the same, after notice;

and cut down trees, &c.

And be it further enacted by the authority aforesaid, that it shall and may be lawful for the said Trustees, or any five or more of them, or the said surveyor or surveyors, and such person or persons as he or they shall appoint, from time to time to remove and prevent all annoyances on any part of the said road, by filth, dung, ashes, rubbish, straw, or otherwise, and convert the same to his or their own use or uses, and to turn any watercourses, sinks, or drains, running along, into, or out of the said road, to the prejudice thereof, and to open, scour, cleanse, widen, or make deeper, any watercourses or ditches adjoining thereto, and make the same as deep and large as he or they shall think necessary, in case the owners or occupiers of the premises shall neglect to open, scour, cleanse, widen, or deepen such watercourses or ditches, or remove such other annoyances, in such manner as the said Trustees, or any five or more of them, or the surveyor or surveyors shall require, for the space of ten days next after notice in writing given for that purpose under the hand or hands of such surveyor or surveyors; and that it shall be lawful for such surveyor or surveyors, from time to time, to lop or top any trees (timber trees excepted) and cut down any shrubs or bushes growing in the said road, or in the hedges or banks adjacent thereto; and to cut down or reduce all such hedges to the heighth (*sic*) of three feet, and take, carry away, and sell the wood so cut, and apply the money, arising thereby, in repair of the road whereon or near whereunto the same stood, in case the owners or occupiers shall neglect to lop or top, cut down, and remove such trees, shrubs, or bushes, or reduce such hedges, in such manner as the said Trustees, or any five or more of them shall require, for the space of thirty days next after notice in writing given for that purpose, to be left at the capital or mansion house belonging to the land on which the same shall stand, or where the occupier or tenant shall reside, under the hands of five or more of the said Trustees; the charges whereof to be settled by the said Trustees, or any five or more of them, shall be reimbursed by such owners or occupiers, and be recovered and applied in such manner as the penalties and forfeitures are herein after directed to be recovered and applied: and if, after removal of any of the said annoyances, any person shall again offend in the like kind, every such person shall, for every such offence, forfeit the sum of two pounds.

Charges to be reimbursed to the surveyors.

Penalty on a second offence.

And be it further enacted by the authority aforesaid, that it shall be lawful for the said surveyor or surveyors of the said road, or such person or persons as he or they shall appoint (such surveyor or surveyors having an order for that purpose from the said Trustees, or any five or more of them) to make, or cause to be made causeways, and also ditches or drains in and upon the said road, and also through any ground lying contiguous thereto: and also to make a road through the grounds adjoining or lying near to any hollow way, narrow or ruinous part of the said road (such ground respectively not being the ground whereon any house stands, nor a yard, garden, orchard, park, paddock, planted walk, or avenue to any house, or any inclosed ground, planted and set apart as a nursery for trees) to be made use of as a publick highway, whilst the old road is repairing and widening: and also by order of any five or more of the said Trustees, to build, erect, repair, and keep in repair, any bridge or bridges, arch or arches, upon any part or parts of the said road, and cross any river, stream, brook, water, ditch, or drain therein, or contiguous thereto, making such recompence to the owners and occupiers of the private grounds respectively for the damages they shall or may thereby sustain, as shall be judged reasonable by the said Trustees, or any five or more of them, but that no satisfaction shall be made for doing or performing any of the works aforesaid upon or through any moor, common, or waste ground.

Surveyors may make causeways, &c.

and make a temporary road;

erect bridges, &c.

making satisfaction to the owners.

And be it further enacted by the authority aforesaid, that if any person or persons shall assault, interrupt, or hinder, or cause to be assaulted, interrupted, or hindered, any or either of the said turnpike surveyors, or any other person or persons by them, or either of them, or by the said Trustees, or any five or more of them, employed in the cutting, digging, taking, or carrying, of any furze, heath, sand, gravel, stones, or other materials for the altering, widening, or repairing, the road by this Act intended to be repaired, or in topping, lopping, cutting down, or carrying of any tree, lop, top, or overhangings, or digging, cleansing, or scouring, any new or other ditch, drain, or watercourse as aforesaid, or doing any other act in or for the repairing, widening, or altering, varying, turning, shortening, or amending, the said road, by virtue of the powers by this Act given, or any of them, every such person shall, for every such offence, forfeit the sum of five pounds.

Penalty on obstructing surveyors, &c. in their duty.

Persons liable to repair bridges, &c. to continue so.

And be it further enacted, that where any particular part of the said road, or any bridge, drain, or sewer, being in and upon the said road hereby intended to be repaired, which hath been accustomed or ought to be repaired and maintained by any particular person or persons, body politic or corporate, by reason of the tenure of any lands, tenements, or hereditaments, or by the said county or any township therein, every such part of the said road, bridge, drain, or sewer, so lying in and upon the said road, shall, from time to time, be maintained and kept in repair by such person or persons, body politic or corporate, township or townships, parishes, tythings and places, and in such manner as the same were respectively maintained and kept in repair before the passing of this Act ; and it shall and may be lawful for the Justices of the Peace for the county wherein such particular part of the road, bridge, drain, or sewer, shall lie, and they are hereby required and impowered, at their Petty or Special Sessions, upon application to them made by the said Trustees, or any five or more of them, or their clerk or clerks for the time being, to adjudge and determine where, how, and in what manner, the same, from time to time, shall be maintained and kept in repair.

Trustees may compound for statute-work.

And be it further enacted, that it shall and may be lawful to and for the said Trustees, or any five or more of them, from time to time, during the continuance of this Act, to compound and agree with all or any of the said person or persons, bodies politic or corporate, township or townships, tythings or places, who is, are, or shall be liable or chargeable for or towards repairing of any such particular part of the said road, bridges, drain, or sewer (except the bridges liable to be repaired by the county, which shall continue to be respectively repaired as aforesaid) for a certain sum of money, by the year or otherwise, as the said Trustees, or any five or more of them, shall think fit, in lieu of such particular works or repairs to be done by such particular person or persons, body politic or corporate, township or townships, tythings, or places as aforesaid.

Owners, &c. of lands, &c. liable to the repair of the road, to continue so.

And be it further enacted, that if any rents, profits, or sum or sums of money, issuing as aforesaid, shall remain liable and chargeable, and the possessors and occupiers of such lands, tenements, and hereditaments, are hereby directed and required to pay such rents and profits to such person or persons as the said Trustees, or any five or more of them, shall appoint to receive the same ; and upon default of payment thereof, it shall and may be lawful to and for any one or more Justice or Justices of the Peace of the county wherein such lands, tenements, or hereditaments, shall be, by warrant under his or their hand and seal, or hands and seals, to levy the same by distress and sale of the goods of such person or persons as shall neglect or refuse to make such payment as aforesaid, together with the costs and charges of such distress and sale ; and such rents, profits, sum or sums of money, when recovered, shall be applied, from time to time, for and towards the amending the part of the said road to the repairs of which such rents, profits, sum or sums of money, are or shall be so chargeable and to no other use or purpose whatsoever.

Inhabitants to do statute-work.

And be it further enacted, that all and every person and persons who by law are and shall be chargeable with statute-work within the parishes and places where any parts of the said road hereby directed to be repaired do lie, shall yearly, and every year (if thereunto required by the said Trustees, or any five or more of them) do and perform such portion of statute work, and on such part or parts of the said road within their respective townships, parishes, tythings, places, and divisions, and in such manner, as the said Trustees, or any five or more of them, or the surveyor or surveyors of the said road by them appointed, shall appoint and require; and that every person who shall rent, hold, or occupy any lands, tenements, or hereditaments, of the yearly value of fifty pounds, within any of the said townships, parishes, places, and divisions respectively, shall be deemed and taken to keep a team therein, and for every fifty pounds a-year which he shall so rent, hold, or occupy, shall do statute-work with one team upon the said road for so many days as shall be required by the said Trustees, or any five or more of them, or their surveyor or surveyors aforesaid

Persons renting £50 per ann. deemed teamholders.

And to the end that the said Trustees may know the inhabitants of, and occupiers of, lands, tenements, and hereditaments, in all the parishes, tythings, hamlets, and places, wherein any part of the said road lies, who are liable to do statute-work, and what sort of duty they ought respectively to do, be it further enacted, that the surveyor or surveyors of the highways, of and for every of the said parishes, tythings, hamlets, and places, where, or in or for which any surveyor or surveyors usually have been, or ought to be, chosen, shall, and they are hereby required, within ten days after notice in writing, signed by the clerk, treasurer, or surveyor, to the said Trustees, shall be given to him or them, or left at his or their house or houses, or last place of habitation, for that purpose, to return and deliver in to the said Trustees, at any meeting to be by them held agreeable to such notice, true and perfect lists in writing, upon oath, if thereunto required by the said Trustees, or any five or more of them, of the names of all the inhabitants of, and occupiers of, lands, tenements, and hereditaments, in such parishes, tythings, hamlets, and places respectively, that are liable to do their statute-work or duty (which oath the said Trustees, or any five or more of them are hereby impowered to administer) and shall, in such lists, and every of them, distinguish and set forth which of such inhabitants and occupiers keep a team or teams, or are deemed by this Act to keep a team or teams, and which of them are labourers, or liable to do their statute duties as labourers only; and if the surveyor or surveyors of the several parishes, tythings, hamlets, or places, wherein any part of the said road shall lie, shall not deliver in such lists, as aforesaid, respectively, at or before such times, and in such manner, as by this Act are required and directed to be delivered, or shall refuse to verify the same, upon oath, if thereunto required; or if the name or names of any person or persons, who ought to have been inserted in such list or lists, are, by design, omitted; or if such surveyor or surveyors shall refuse or decline to give publick summons or notices to such person or persons who ought, by law, to do and perform such statute labour or duty as aforesaid, according to the directions of the said surveyor or surveyors appointed by the said Trustees, such parish surveyor or surveyors, and every of

Surveyors of the highways to deliver in lists of persons liable to do statute-work.

Penalty on surveyors, &c. neglecting to deliver in such lists

them, shall forfeit and pay, for every such default, the sum of ten pounds. And

if any or either of the inhabitants of, or occupiers of, lands, tenements, or hereditaments, in the said several parishes, tythings, hamlets, or places, being obliged by law to do statute duty in and upon the highways, shall not do so much statute-work in and upon the said road, at such times and places, and in such manner, as they shall, by the said surveyor or surveyors appointed by the said Trustees, be directed or appointed to do, such inhabitants and occupiers, and every of them, shall, for every such neglect or default, forfeit and pay the several sums hereafter mentioned ; that is to say, every such inhabitant or person who shall keep, or, by virtue of this Act, shall be deemed to keep, a team or teams, for every day's default, the sum of ten shillings ; and every other inhabitant or person liable to work on the said road as a labourer only, for every day's default, the sum of one shilling and sixpence ; and if any person or persons who shall come as a labourer or labourers, or be sent with any team or draught, to work on the said road, shall not attend at the time and place

appointed, or shall be found idle or negligent by the said turnpike surveyor or surveyors, such surveyor and surveyors is and are hereby impowered to remove and turn off such person and persons ; and in that case the respective forfeitures and payments before mentioned shall be incurred and made payable, as if such person or persons had refused or neglected to come, or such team or draught had not been sent out.

Provided always, and be it further enacted, that if the surveyor or surveyors of the highways for the time being of any of the parishes, tythings, hamlets, or places, wherein the said road, directed by this Act to be repaired, lies, shall think the said Trustees, or their surveyor or surveyors, have directed or appointed too large a proportion of the statute-work in any parish, tything, hamlet, or place, to be done on the said road, it shall and may be lawful for such surveyor or surveyors of the highways to appeal to two or more Justices of the Peace of the county or place, who are hereby authorized to convene the parties concerned before them, and to hear and determine the matter in dispute.

Provided always, that in case the parties, or either of them, shall be dissatisfied with such determination, it shall be lawful for them, or any of them, to appeal to the Quarter Sessions, in such and the same manner, as is herein after authorized and directed in other cases where persons shall think themselves aggrieved.

And be it further enacted, that it shall and may be lawful to and for the said Trustees, or any five or more of them, from time to time, to compound and agree with the inhabitants of all or any of the said townships, parishes, places, and divisions, from, to, or through which the said road leads (their consent being first signified at a vestry, or other publick meeting of such inhabitants, summoned to assemble for that purpose) or with any of the said inhabitants respectively, for a certain sum of money by the year, or otherwise, as the said Trustees, or any five or more of them, shall think reasonable, in lieu of the statute or other work to be by them, or any of them, done on the said road.

And be it further enacted, that in case any composition-money agreed to be paid in lieu of any statute or days work to be done by the inhabitants of any township, parish, place, or division, as aforesaid, or by any of them respectively, or in respect of any lands, tenements, or hereditaments, liable or chargeable by tenure or otherwise, as aforesaid, shall not be paid within three calendar months next after the same shall become payable according to such composition or agreement, that then it shall and may be lawful to and for any one or more Justice or Justices of the Peace of the county wherein such township, parish, place, or division, or such lands, tenements, or hereditaments, shall be, by warrant under his or their hand and seal, or hands and seals, to impower such person or persons as shall be authorized by the said Trustees, or any five or more of them, to receive such composition-money (oath being first made that the same has been demanded and remains unpaid, which oath the said Justice or Justices is and are hereby impowered to administer) to levy the same by distress and sale of the goods and chattles of the person or persons so having compounded as aforesaid, or of the surveyor or surveyors of the highways for the time being of such township, parish, tything, place, or division, in respect of whose statute or days work such composition shall be made, returning the overplus of any be upon demand, after the charges of such distress and sale shall be thereout first deducted.

Composition-money, how to be recovered.

And be it further enacted, that if any surveyor or surveyors of the highways for the time being of any township, parish, place, or division, for or in lieu of whose statute or days work such composition shall be made as aforesaid, shall pay the composition-money; or if such composition-money shall be recovered and levied of his and their goods and chattles in manner herein before directed, then, and in either of the said cases, such surveyor or surveyors shall be repaid or reimbursed the composition-money which shall be so paid or recovered of him or them as aforesaid, together with the costs and charges of such distress and sale in such manner as, by the laws now in being, surveyors of the highways of this kingdom are to be repaid or reimbursed the monies by them expended in buying materials for amending the highways.

Surveyors paying the composition-money, how to be reimbursed.

And be it further enacted by the authority aforesaid, that nothing in this Act contained shall extend to compel or oblige the inhabitants of any parish or place to do or perform more than one day's statute-work in any one year upon the said road, or any part or parts thereof; anything in this Act to the contrary notwithstanding.

No person to do more than one day's statute-work.

And be it further enacted by the authority aforesaid, that the said Trustees, or any five or more of them, shall be and are hereby fully impowered from time to time to widen the said road, or to divert, turn, shorten, vary, or alter, the course or path of any part or parts thereof, through any moor or waste ground, without making any satisfaction for the same; and also through any private grounds or hereditaments, first making satisfaction to the owners thereof and

Road may be turned, diverted, &c.

persons interested therein for the damage they may thereby sustain; and for that purpose it shall be lawful for the said Trustees, or any five or more of them, from time to time, to contract and agree with the owners of and persons interested in any lands or hereditaments for the purchase or exchange thereof, or for the loss or damage such owners or persons may sustain by such widening, diverting, turning, shortening, varying, or altering, the course or path of any part or parts of such road through such lands or hereditaments: and it shall be lawful for all bodies politick, corporate or collegiate, corporations aggregate or sole, husbands, guardians, trustees, and feoffees in trust, committees, executors, administrators, and all other trustees whatsoever, not only for and on behalf of themselves, their heirs and successors, but also for and on behalf of their cestuique trusts, whether femes covert, infants, or issue unborn, lunaticks, ideots, or other person or persons whatsoever, and to and for all femes covert, who are or shall be seised or interested in their own right, and to and for all and every person and persons whomsoever who are or shall be possessed of or interested in any such lands or hereditaments, to contract with the said Trustees, or any five or more of them, for the satisfaction to be made for such damages as aforesaid, or to exchange with, sell, and convey unto them, or any five or more of them, all or any of such lands or hereditaments, or any part thereof, for the purpose aforesaid; and all contracts, exchanges, sales, and conveyances, which shall be so made, shall be valid to all intents and purposes; any law, statute, usage, or other matter whatsoever, to the contrary notwithstanding; and all such bodies politick, corporate or collegiate, corporations aggregate or sole, husbands, guardians, trustees, feoffees, committees, executors, administrators, and all other persons, shall be and are hereby indemnified for what they shall do by virtue of this Act: and if any such body politick, corporate or collegiate, corporations aggregate or sole, husbands, guardians, trustees, feoffees, committees, executors, administrators, or any other person or persons, interested in any such lands or hereditaments, upon notice to him, her, or them, given or left in writing at the dwelling-house or houses, or other place or places of abode of such person or persons, or of the principal officer or officers of any such body politick, corporate or collegiate, corporations aggregate or sole, or at the house of the tenant in possession of the lands or hereditaments through which any part of such road is intended to be diverted, turned, or altered, for the space of twenty-one days next after such notice given or left, neglect or refuse to treat, or shall not agree in the premisses, or by reason of absence shall be prevented from treating; then, and in every such case, the said Trustees, or any five or more of them, shall cause such damage and recompence to be enquired into and ascertained by a jury of twelve indifferent men of the said county of Essex; and in order thereto the said Trustees, or any five or more of them, are hereby impowered and required, from time to time, as occasion shall be, to summon and call before such jury, and examine upon oath, all and every such person and persons whomsoever who shall be thought necessary or proper to be examined concerning the premisses (which oath any one or more of the said Trustees is and are hereby impowered to administer) and such Trustees, or any five or more of them, shall, by ordering a view, or otherwise, use all ways and means as well for their own as for the said jury's information of the premisses; and after the said jury shall have inquired of and assessed such damage and recompence, they the said Trustees, or any five or more of them, shall thereupon order, adjudge, and determine, the sum or sums of money so assessed by the said jury, to be paid to the said owners and other persons interested in the said lands or hereditaments, according to the verdict or inquisition of such jury, which said verdict or inquisition, and judgement, order or determination thereupon, shall be final, binding, and conclusive, to all intents and purposes, against all parties and persons whomsoever claiming or to claim in possession, reversion or otherwise, their heirs and successors, as well absent as present, infants, femes covert, lunaticks, ideots, and persons under any disability whatsoever, bodies politick, corporate and collegiate, corporations aggregate or sole, as well as all other persons whomsoever; and for summoning and returning such juries, the said Trustees, or any five or more of them, are hereby impowered to issue their warrant or warrants to the sheriff of the county of Essex, requiring him to impannel, summon, and return, an indifferent jury of twenty four persons qualified to serve upon juries, to appear before such Trustees, or any five or more of them, at such time and place as in such warrant or warrants shall be appointed; and such sheriff, or his deputy or deputies, is and are hereby required to impannel, summon, and return, such number of persons accordingly; and out of the persons so summoned, impannelled, and returned, or out of such of them as shall appear upon such summons, the said Trustees, or any five or more of them, shall and they are hereby required to swear, or cause to be sworn, twelve men, who shall be the jury for the purposes aforesaid, and in default of a sufficient number of jurymen, the said sheriff, or his deputy or deputies, or any five or more of the said Trustees, shall return other honest and indifferent men of the standers by, or that can speedily be procured to attend that service, to the number of twelve, and all persons concerned shall have their lawful challenges against any of the said jurymen when they come to be sworn: and the said Trustees, or any five or more of them, acting in the premisses, shall have power from time to time to impose any reasonable fine or fines upon such sheriff, his deputy or deputies, bailiffs or agents, making default in the premisses, and on any of the persons that shall be summoned and returned on such jury, and who shall not appear, or appearing, shall refuse to be sworn on the said jury, or being so sworn, shall refuse to give, or not giving their verdict, or in any other manner wilfully neglect their duty therein, contrary to the true intent and meaning of this Act: and on any of the persons who, being required to give evidence before the said jury, shall refuse or neglect to appear, or appearing shall refuse to be examined or to give evidence; and which fine or fines shall be levied, recovered, and applied in such manner as the penalties and forfeitures are herein after directed to be levied, recovered, and applied, so that no such fine be more than ten pounds, nor less than two pounds, on any one person for any one offence.

And be it further enacted by the authority aforesaid, that every sum of money or recompence to be agreed for or assessed as aforesaid, shall be paid out of the tolls aforesaid, or out of the monies to be borrowed upon the credit of such tolls, to the parties or persons respectively intitled to such monies, or to their agents; and upon payment, or in case of refusal to accept the same, upon leaving the same in the hands of the treasurer or treasurers to the said Trustees, for the use of such parties or persons, it shall be lawful for any person or persons authorized by writing under the hands of the said Trustees, or any five or more of them, to widen, divert, or turn such

road through such lands or hereditaments, and to do all and every act, matter, and thing, with relation to such lands or hereditaments, as the said Trustees, or any five or more of them, shall think fit; and the said Trustees, or any five or more of them, shall cause such parts of the said road as shall be widened, diverted, or turned, through any private grounds, to be ditched and fenced from the adjoining lands; and all lands and hereditaments which shall be made a part or parts of the said road, by virtue of this Act, shall be for ever thereafter to all intents and purposes a common highway, and shall be repaired and kept in repair, in such manner as the road hereby appointed to be repaired is by this Act to be amended; and from thenceforth all parties and persons

whatsoever shall be divested of all right and title to such lands and hereditaments; and after any such new road shall be compleated, the lands constituting the former road, unless leading over some moor or waste ground, or to some village, town, or place, to which such new road doth not lead, shall be vested in, and shall and may be exchanged or sold, and conveyed by the said Trustees, or any five or more of them, for the best price that can be gotten for the same,

and the money arising by such sale shall be applied to the repair of that part of the said road so diverted and turned: but this Act shall not extend to the taking down any dwelling-house or other building, or to take in any land that is a garden, orchard, yard, park, paddock, planted walk, or avenue to a house, or any part thereof without the consent of the owner or proprietor thereof.

Provided always, that no person shall act as a Trustee in any case relating to the contracting for, exchanging, or purchasing of any lands or hereditaments, wherein he shall be particularly concerned or interested.

Provided also, that in case the owner or owners of any lands adjoining to the lands constituting the former road shall signify in writing to any five or more of the said Trustees, before the new road shall be compleated, his, her, or their desire to purchase so much of the said former road as shall adjoin to his, her, or their lands; such owner or owners shall be allowed to purchase the same in preference to any other person.

And be it further enacted, that in case any jury shall give in and deliver a verdict or assessment for more monies, as a recompence for the right, interest, or property of any person or persons in any lands or hereditaments, or for any such loss or damage, than what shall have been agreed to and offered by the said Trustees, or any five or more of them, before the summoning or returning the jury, as a recompence or satisfaction for any such right, interest, or property, or loss or damage as aforesaid; that then, and in such case, the costs and expenses of summoning and maintaining the jury and witnesses, shall be borne and paid by the said Trustees, or any five or more of them, out of the tolls hereby granted, or out of any money to be borrowed upon the credit thereof; but if any such jury shall give and deliver a verdict or assessment for no more or for less money than shall have been agreed (sic) to and offered by the said Trustees, or any five or more of them, before the summoning and returning the said jury, as a recompence or satisfaction for any such right, interest, or property in, or loss or damage as aforesaid; that then the costs and expences of summoning and maintaining the said jury and witnesses, shall be borne and paid by the person or persons with whom the said Trustees shall have such controversy or dispute.

And be it further enacted by the authority aforesaid, that the said Trustees, or any five or more of them, may, and they are hereby impowered and required to cause the said road to be measured, and stones or posts to be set up, in, upon, or near the sides thereof, at the distance of one mile from each other, with inscriptions thereon, denoting the distance of every such stone or post, from any town or place, as they shall think fit; and also within the same time, to erect guide or direction posts, with such inscriptions thereon, as the said Trustees, or any five or more of them, shall think proper. And if any person or persons shall wilfully pull down, break, or damage any such stone or post, or obliterate any inscription that shall have been made thereon, or shall cause or procure the same to be done, and be thereof convicted upon oath by one or more credible witnesses or witnesses, or by his or her own confession, before any Justice of the Peace for the county or place wherein such offences shall be committed (which oath, such Justice is hereby impowered and required to administer without fee or reward) every such person, so offending, shall forfeit the sum of two pounds for every such stone or post so pulled down, broke, or damaged, or inscription so obliterated; whereof one moiety shall be paid to the informer, and the other moiety shall be applied in such manner as the penalties and forfeitures are hereinafter directed to be applied; and in case such penalties shall not be forthwith paid, such Justice of the Peace shall commit such person or persons to the House of Correction, for any space not exceeding two months, nor less than ten days, unless such forfeitures and all reasonable charges shall be sooner paid; and every such offender, in either of the said cases, shall and may, by the authority of this Act, and without any other warrant, be apprehended by any person or persons who shall see any such offence committed, and shall be immediately delivered to a constable, or other peace officer, who shall convey such offender to be dealt with according to the directions of this Act.

And be it further enacted by the authority aforesaid, that if any person or persons shall hale or draw, or cause to be haled or drawn, upon any part of the said road, any tree or piece of timber, or any stone, otherwise than upon wheel upon wheel carriages.

carriages, or shall suffer any part of any tree or piece of timber which shall be conveyed upon any wheel carriage, to drag or trail upon any part of the said road, to the prejudice thereof; every such person shall, for every such offence, forfeit and pay the sum of forty shillings.

Penalties and forfeitures, how to be recovered and applied.

And be it further enacted by the authority aforesaid, that all the penalties, forfeitures, and fines, hereby inflicted or authorized to be imposed (if the manner of levying and recovery thereof is not otherwise directed) shall upon proof of the offence respectively before any one Justice of the Peace for the county or place wherein the offence shall be committed, or any one Justice of the Peace for the county or place wherein the offender shall be and reside, either by the confession of the party or parties offending, or by the oath of one or more witness or witnesses (which oath such Justice is hereby impowered and required to administer without fee or reward) be levied by distress and sale of the goods and chattles of the party or parties offending, by warrant under the hand and seal of such Justice (which warrant such Justice is hereby impowered and required to grant for those purposes); and the overplus, after such penalties, forfeitures, and fines, and the charges of such distress and sale are recovered and deducted, shall be returned upon demand unto the owner or owners of such goods and chattels; and the penalties, forfeitures, and fines, when paid or levied, shall be (if not otherwise directed to be applied by this Act) from time to time paid to any five or more of the said Trustees, or to their treasurer or treasurers, and applied in the repair of the said road; and in case sufficient distress shall not be found, or such penalties and forfeitures shall not be forthwith paid, it shall be lawful for any one Justice of the Peace, as aforesaid, and he is hereby authorized and required, by warrant or warrants under his hand and seal, to cause such offender or offenders to be committed to the common gaol or House of Correction of the county or place, there to remain without bail or mainprize for any time not exceeding two calendar months, unless such penalties, forfeitures, and fines, and all reasonable charges, shall be sooner paid and satisfied.

Constables, &c. to execute orders of the Trustees.

And it is hereby further enacted by the authority aforesaid, that if any high constable, petty constable, headborough, tythingman, or other person whatsoever duly authorized for that purpose, shall willingly, knowingly, or contemptuously, neglect or refuse to obey and execute any summons or other precept in writing under the hands and seals of any five or more of the said Trustees for putting this Act into execution, every such high constable, petty constable, headborough, tythingman, or other person so authorized, offending in the premises, shall, for each and every such offence, forfeit and pay any sum not exceeding two pounds, one moiety to the informer, and the other moiety thereof to the said Trustees, or to their treasurer or treasurers, to be applied for and towards the amending and repairing the road in this Act mentioned, to be levied on such person or persons in the same manner as the other penalties and forfeitures are in and by this Act directed to be levied; and the said Trustees,

Trustees may

or any five or more of them, may, and are hereby impowered to direct the

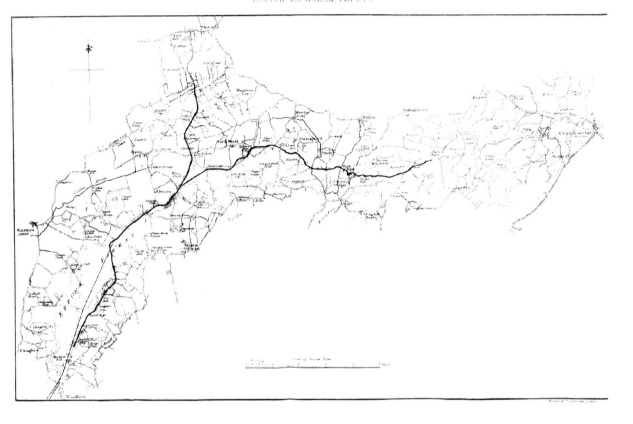

treasurer for the time being to reimburse such constable, or other officer or reward such constables. officers, for his or their loss of time, trouble, or other necessary expences in the due execution of his or their duty in pursuance of this Act, such sum or sums of money as such Trustees shall think fit, and out of such tolls as shall be collected by virtue of this Act.

And for the more easy and speedy conviction of offenders against this Act, be it further enacted by the authority aforesaid, that all and every the Justice or Justices of the Peace, before whom any person or persons shall be convicted of any offence against this Act, shall and may cause the conviction to be drawn up in the following form of words, as the case shall happen, or in any form of words to the same effect.

Be it remembered that on the   in the   Form of conviction. year of His Majesty's Reign, A. B. is convicted before   of His Majesty's Justices of the Peace for the said county of   (specifying the offence, and time, and place, when and where the same was committed as the case shall be).

Given under our hands and seals the day and year aforesaid.

Provided always, and be it further enacted by the authority aforesaid, that Persons aggrieved may appeal to the Quarter Sessions. if any person shall think himself or herself aggrieved by anything done in pursuance of this Act, and for which no particular method of relief hath been already appointed, such person may appeal to the Justices of the Peace at any General Quarter Sessions of the Peace to be held for the county or place wherein the cause of complaint shall arise, and within three months after the cause of such complaint shall have arisen; such appellant first giving, or causing to be given, six days notice at the least in writing, of his or her intention to bring such appeal, and of the matter thereof, to the clerk or treasurer to the said Trustees, and within two days after such notice, entering into recognizance before some Justice of the Peace for such county or place, with two sufficient sureties, conditioned to try such appeal at, and abide the order of, and to pay such costs as shall be awarded by the Justices at such Quarter Sessions, and the said Justices at such sessions, upon due proof of such notice being given as aforesaid, and of Notice of appeal to be given. the entering into such recognizance, shall hear and signally determine the causes and matters of such appeal in a summary way, and award such costs to the parties appealing or appealed against, as they, the said Justices, shall think proper, and the determination of such Quarter Sessions shall be final, binding, and conclusive, to all intents and purposes.

And be it further enacted, that no order made touching or concerning any Proceedings not to be quashed for want of form, of the matters aforesaid, or any other proceedings to be had touching the conviction or convictions of any offender or offenders against this Act, shall be removed or removeable by certiorari or any other writ or process whatsoever, into any of His Majesty's Courts of Record at Westminster; and that where any nor removeable by Certiorari. distress shall be made for any sum or sums of money to be levied by virtue of this Act, the distress itself shall not be deemed to be unlawful, nor the party or Distress not unlawful for want of form, parties making the same be deemed a trespasser or trespassers, on account of any defect or want of form in the summons, conviction, warrant of distress, or other proceedings relating thereunto ; nor shall the party or parties distraining be deemed a trespasser or trespassers ab initio on account of any irregularity which shall be afterwards done by the party or parties distraining ; but the person or persons aggrieved by such irregularity shall and may recover full satisfaction for the special damage in an action upon the case ; but no plaintiff or plaintiffs shall recover in any action for such irregularity as aforesaid, if tender of amends hath been made by or on behalf of the party distraining before such action brought.

And be it further enacted, that no nomination, appointment, information, order, judgement, conviction, warrant, mortgage, or assignment, transfer or other security, for the borrowing of money, or other writing whatsoever, under the hand and seal, or hands and seals of, or only signed by, any Trustee or Trustees, for putting this Act in execution, or by any Justice or Justices of the Peace, or exhibited before them, or any of them, touching, concerning, or in execution of any of the powers or authorities hereby vested in such Trustee or Trustees, Justice or Justices of the Peace, or any of them, or transfer or assignment of any of the securities aforesaid, made by any person or persons, shall be charged or chargeable with any stamp duty whatsoever.

And be it further enacted, that all orders and proceedings of the said Trustees at their several meetings to be held by adjournment, or upon notice to be given by the clerk, or, in case of his neglect or default, by two Trustees as aforesaid, shall be entered in a book or books to be kept for that purpose, and such orders and proceedings, when entered, shall be signed by the said Trustees or any five or more of them, and the said orders and proceedings, so signed, shall be deemed and taken to be original proceedings, and shall and may be produced and read in evidence in all cases of appeals, suits, actions, and other proceedings, touching anything done by the authority of this Act.

Provided always, and be it further enacted by the authority aforesaid, that no action or suit shall be commenced against any person or persons for anything done in pursuance of this Act, until twenty-one days notice shall be thereof given to the clerk or clerks to the said Trustees ; or after sufficient satisfaction or tender thereof hath been made to the party or parties aggrieved, or after six calendar months next after the fact committed, and every such action or suit shall be laid or brought in the county where the matter shall arise, and not elsewhere, and the defendant and defendants in every such action or suit, shall and may, at his or their election, plead specially, or the general issue, not guilty, and give this Act and the special matter in evidence, at any trial to be had thereupon, and that the same was done in pursuance and by the authority of this Act ; and if the same shall appear to be so done, or that such action or suit shall be brought before twenty-one days notice shall be thereof given as aforesaid, or after the time limited for bringing the same as aforesaid, or shall be brought in any other county, then the jury shall find for the defendant or defendants ; and upon such verdict, or if the plaintiff or plaintiffs shall be non-suited, or discontinue his, her, or their action or suit, after the defendant or defendants shall have appeared, or if upon demurrer judgement shall be given against the plaintiff or plaintiffs, then the defendant or defendants shall recover treble costs, and have such remedy for the same, as any defendant or defendants hath or have in other cases by law. *Treble c*

And be it enacted by the authority aforesaid, that this Act shall be deemed, adjudged, and taken to be a Publick Act, and be judicially taken notice of as such by all such judges, justices, and other persons whatsoever, without specially pleading the same. *Publick*

FINIS.

CHAPTER III.

The Roads through Epping prior to the Establishment of the Epping Highway Trust.

THE earliest mention made of a road in the neighbourhood of Epping relates to the portion of the high road between Thornwood Common, through the forest* to the town. In the tenth year of Henry VIII John Baker left a sum of money, out of the rental of Stonards (or Stonehurst Farm, in the parish of Theydon Garnon), to keep up the stump road from the corner of Thornwood Common to the town of Epping, in which he carried on the business of a mercer.

For more than two hundred years the bequest relieved the inhabitants of the Parish of Epping of some of the expense of keeping up the roads. The portion of the rental of Stonards' Farm devoted to the keeping up of the stump road, supplied during ten years (from 1705 to 1714 inclusive) 2,303 loads of gravel, at the expenditure of £174 11s. 3d. Although the will mentions only the stump road from Thornwood Common (the boundary mentioned is Wintry Brook) to the town of Epping, the benefit of the trust had been extended as far as Buckhurst Hill, and included the repair of bridges. One near the chapel was repaired in 1721, and there are entries for the repairs of bridges at Golden's Hill and Fairmead Bottom.

The last entry in the account book of payment for gravel is in 1750—61 loads of screened stones, £6 2s.

As Acts of Parliament had given power to Justices of the Peace to erect turnpikes and collect tolls for making and repairing the road, some of the Trustees of Stonards' Charity

---

* In the Ordnance Map it is marked Wintry Wood, but Wintry Wood and Wintry Park were on the other side. See Map.

evidently believed that the object for which the bequest was made had ceased to exist : for in 1758 there is an entry of a sum of money paid for counsel's fees and witnesses' expenses to Chelmsford Quarter Sessions "concerning a dispute arising out of the trust."

The difference of opinion is not, however, mentioned in the account book ; neither is there any record of the decision of the magistrates. But, as there is no further entry of an outlay for gravel, and there is for the first time an entry (1763) of there having been given to the poor of Epping £10 8s. 8d., and the donation continuing, it may be concluded that the opinion of the magistrates was adverse to there being any further expenditure on the road ; and, that so it happened the Trustees had the money in hand which they distributed amongst the poor. The matter was, however, definitely settled by the Lord Chancellor, April 3rd, 1780. He gave it as his opinion that "The charitable uses for which the rents for Stonards' Farm are given to the Trustees are such as do require the direction of the Court of Chancery for explanation. The amendment of the highway between London and Harlow, which was the main object of the Charity, is no longer necessary, as it has become a turnpike road."

John Baker's object, it is stated, was to induce the traffic to leave the road to London, by Coopersale, Stewart's Green, &c., and to pass through the town, about a mile distant from the road where at present it crosses the Ongar Road, making it the highway to London : in which it is said he succeeded.

There was not at that time, nor until the following century, a road from Loughton, by Golden's Hill and the Wake Arms, to Epping. The forest land extended as a green, or common, to the chapel of St. John the Baptist. Some of it still remains as "the green," and also portions between the road and the houses on the right hand side of the road, on entering the town from

---

* Extracted from the Account Book of Stonards' Charity, in the possession of Mr. Windus, Clerk to the Trustees.

London.   The portion on the left hand has been enclosed and is now built upon; but the hedge-rows at the back of the houses still show its ancient boundary.   The houses on the right hand are built, it is said, on the causeway, which may have been a portion of the Purlieu Bank, still to be seen on Bell Common, and more distinctly in the lower forest, near to the late Thornwood Gate.   It separates the parish of Epping from Theydon Garnon and part of Theydon Bois.   All Epping parish and part of Theydon Bois is within the forest boundary, but all Theydon Garnon is outside its limits.

The boundary of the forest, as follows, is copied from the "Gentleman's History of Essex."   The places mentioned are marked in the Trustees' map, and the boundary can therefore be easily made out.   After giving the boundaries by Hainault Forest, &c., &c., to the River Roden, it continues :—

"And from thence by the river aforesaid to Aybridge, and passing over the bridge aforesaid by the king's highway leading straight to the parish church of Theydon Bois, and so going on by the king's highway aforesaid to the mansion house of the rector of Theydon Bois to the gate called Theydon Green Gate, and thence by the hedge called Hedge Purlieu, to a corner of a certain hedge called Priors-horne Corner; and so by the hedge aforesaid called Purlieu Hedge to the end of a certain lane called Hawcock Lane; and to the bank near the end of the town of Epping called Purlieu Bank; and going by the bank aforesaid to a place called Bennet's Corner according to the bounds, limits, and divisions of the parishes of Epping and Theydon Gernon, including within the forest aforesaid all the parish of Epping lying within the bank aforesaid, and excluding out of the forest, all the parish of Theydon Gernon; and going by the bank aforesaid to the end of the lane called Duck Lane, and to the corner of the great waste called 'Thornwood Common' and so going by the bank aforesaid, called Purlieu Bank, lying near the hedge on the south part of the common aforesaid to a current of water, which runs down from a ditch lying near the hedge aforesaid, and the aforesaid bank called Purlieu Bank near a certain elm, which is the sole limit and boundary between the parish of Epping aforesaid and North Weald Basset, and also between the half-hundreds of Harlow and Waltham; and further going by the current of water aforesaid, to the ditch, before and near the mansion house of one William Spranger, situate upon the side of the waste and common of Thornwood aforesaid; and from thence returning by the ditch aforesaid, to the mansion house of one David Hudson, likewise situate on the side of the common aforesaid; and by the metes and divisions dividing the aforesaid two half-hundreds of Harlow and Waltham, to a certain free hay, called Lincely Gate, including within the forest aforesaid parcel of the waste or common called Thornwood Common, as it lies within the current of water aforesaid."

Morant, who mentions John Baker's bequest and its object, does not say what direction the travellers took after leaving Epping town, and the question as to the route they pursued is therefore open to consideration, and suggestion.

Roads, however much they may have been altered, run in their original direction, and often small portions of the primitive ones remain.

To those who know Epping, and also on reference to a map,* the road which runs by Kendal Lodge and by the Bower can be followed across Hawcock Lane (Ivy Chimneys) up the opposite hill, to a house which, by the remains of a moat and the general appearance of the ground on which it is situated, seems to occupy the site of a nobler building. The road is continued by a footpath through some fields in the direction of Theydon Garnon Church, near to which it enters the old London road, through Aybridge.

It is difficult to understand why Baker's bequest should have had the effect of turning the traffic through the town, or what benefit a traveller would have derived by passing through it, if the road he had to traverse joined the old London road, through Aybridge to London. But it is not unlikely that the road turned out of Epping, when it reached the Green, in front

---

* See the Trustees' Map.

of the Chapel, into Hemnal or Back Street, and skirting the Common (Bell Common) on the Theydon side of the Purlieu Bank, was continued into Theydon Bois.

Theydon Bois was a village soon after the Conquest. It was in the possession of "De Bosco," who gave the church in the twelfth century to the Priory of Bartholomew the Great, in Smithfield; there can be no doubt but what during the several hundred years intervening, between that date and the making the road through the forest, there were means of communication between it and the town of Epping, in one direction, and with Loughton in the other.

The intercourse between Loughton and Epping, the market town of the district, would have been carried on through Theydon Bois, that being the shortest route before the road from Loughton was made through the forest. It therefore seems as if John Baker's idea was, that if he could maintain the stump road from Thornwood Common to the town, travellers would pass through it, and so into London by Theydon Bois and Loughton, a route which would considerably lessen the distance between London and Epping.

The traffic having set this way for many years, skirting the royal forest into Epping, must have made it evident that a direct road through it from Loughton would be of great advantage to travellers.

But Epping Forest was a royal forest, well known to Henry VIII, and his two daughters, Queens of England. Henry VIII hunted in it; Queen Mary lived for some time at Copt Hall, Epping, which, as well as Queen Elizabeth's Lodge, well known to visitors to Chingford, was within the forest boundaries.

That the forest was closely watched, and the deer carefully guarded is generally admitted; and the following abstract of a deed in the British Museum, shows the means adopted for their preservation to have been of a very oppressive character :—

*　　　*　　　*　　　*　　　*

Item that the lieu tenaunt Rydyng foster and Ranger of the same forest Certyffy at th............ perticulerly in a byll the certente of the deer kyllyd and seruyd by euery of them w^t the .... to them directyd and gyvyn.

Item the Clerke of the Swanymote euery yere wⁱⁿ xij days next after the fest of Saynt Michell or wⁱⁿ couenyent tyme after to make relaĉon to the kynges hyghnes of the Certente of the deer kyllyd in the same forest in the sayd yere and before hym presentyd as ys aforsayd.

Item yf any deer be kyllyd by chaunce and recouered so that the fflesche be of any goodnes then the keper in whose walke any suche deer be recouered dilyuer and brynge the same to the lieu tenaunt in his absens to the Rydyng foster or Ranger to thentent that yf the sayd deer be mete for the kynges hyghnesse then that yt be sent to his hyghnes and yf couenyent tyme serue not then that yt be distrybutyd by the discreĉon of the lieu tenaunt or in his absens by the sayd Rydyng forster or Ranger best for the savegarde of the kynges game.

Item the sayd lieu tenaunt Rydyng foster or Ranger to Certyfy at the next Swanymote to the Clerke how and 'too' what persons the same deer so kyllyd by chaunce and recouered ys distributyd.

Item that noo keper hurt or suffer any person to hunt wⁱⁿ his walke for any 'fee deer warrant or ĉomaundement' but suche as 'shalbe appoyntyd by the said lieu tenaunt and in hys absens of the seid other officeres or suche other person as' byfore this tyme hath vsed to hunt for ther disport and plesure for the kyllynge of ther fee deer.

Item euery keper yf he lyst to call his neyhures or borderers to assyst hym to hunt and serue his warrant or ĉomaundement to thentent they may take sport and therby to increase frend-chyppe and amyte.

Item the freholderes to hunt and take disports for the kyllynge of ther feer deer by the ouer syght of the lieu tenaunt and in his absens of the Rydyng foster or Ranger.

Item that noo keper his seruauntes or deputeez vse or kepe in ther howses or walke any Crosebow except yt be the lieu tenaunt.

Item that noo keper suffer noo crosebow to be kept or vsyd in his walke as nere as he can except the person that so hathe or vse yt may Justyfy the kepyng therof' by the kynges lawez and yf he fynde or seyse any suche crosebow lett yt be delyuered to the Clerke of the Sanymote* to thentent that dew punysche ment may be poursuyd accordynge to the kynges lawez and cherapon informaĉon to be gyvyn in theschequer.

Item† yf any keper suspect any person in his walke to kepe any Crosebow in hys howse then lett hym take w^t hym a verderer or constable of the parishe

---

* *(Sic.)*

† Contra legem, *marginal note.*

where the party so suspect dwellyth and serche the howsez yf any be founde lett yt be delyuered as ys aforsayd.

Item that euery noble man may hunt and take his disport and plesure in the same forest accordyng at ther perylle accordyng as the kynges lawez wylle suffer them and the keper to gyve them the lokynge ouer and to make them suche sport as yt aperteyneth to a noble man and the sayd keper to Certyffye the same at the next Swanymote.

Item that the Warrantes comaundementes and other fee deer be taken equally wher yt may be moste conuenyently sparyd by the ouersyght and discrecon of the sayd lieu tenaunt Rydyng foster and Ranger or one of them in absens of the resydew.

Item noo keper or foster lieu tenaunt Rydyng foster Ranger or ther seruantes hunt and any wyse by nyght onles yt be for the recouere of sum hurt or chasyd deer.

Item that noo person taken by the keperes or any other offyceres be comyttyd to warde or lettyn to baylle onles he be examyned by the lieu tenaunt Rydyng foster Ranger and Steward 'or too of them.'

Item that the obligacons for the baylle remayn wt the Steward of recorde.

Item that every keper obserue thez articlez apon peyn of the forfeture of his offyce and that apon dew examynacon and dew proue hadde byfor the lieu teuaunt Rydyng foster Ranger and Steward of the Swanymote the sayd offender to be dischargyd of the exersyng of his sayd office tyll the kynges plesure be further knowyng.

Item theez ffee deer to be alowed as hereafter folowyth.

ffyrst the Justices of the forest.

Item the lieu tenaunt.

Item the Steward.

Item the Rydyng foster.

Item the Ranger.

Item euery keper.

Item my lorde of Waltam.

Item my lady of Barkyng.

Item the ffreholderes.

(British Museum : Royal Roll, 14 B. xxxvi.)

The year 1603 brought in another dynasty; the Stuarts from Scotland. James I could not have had, from association, the same interest in the forest as that which influenced his predecessors, causing them, or their representatives, to be unwilling that it should be cut up by a high road; and the deer and game disturbed by the traffic passing over it. He is said, on his accession to the English throne, to have been anxious

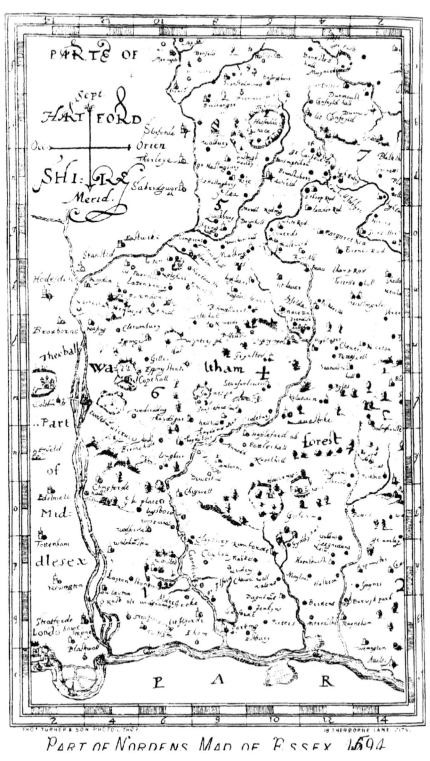

PART OF NORDENS MAP OF ESSEX 1594

to meet the wishes of his new subjects, for any adequate consideration.

Dr. Lingard writes, " He exhorted them to make known their grievances, and promised that the liberality of the sovereign to his people should be commensurate with their liberality towards him." And, as in 1611 a portion of the Crown lands were offered for sale, it is most probable that the " grievance " consisting of the obstruction caused by the royal forest, to a direct route from London into Norfolk and Suffolk, or the Eastern Counties, was brought under the notice of the King ; and that he, for an adequate consideration, allowed sufficient forest land to be purchased to make the road from Loughton by Golden's Hill to Epping.

In 1622 a new aisle was added to the Chapel of St. John. In the County histories it is said the addition was rendered necessary on account of the great increase in the number of the inhabitants. There was no cause, as Epping is a purely agricultural, and not a manufacturing town, for the great increase in the number of its inhabitants, except a large addition to the traffic through the town ; which would necessarily arise by opening up the road from Loughton through the forest. It may therefore be supposed that between 1611 and 1622 the road over Golden's Hill through the town of Epping by Wintry Wood to Thornwood Common became an important road into the Eastern Counties.

It is shown in the portion of Nordon's Map, 1594, in which is marked the road by Theydon Garnon and Abridge to London, that there was no road at that date through the forest. By the drawing of Winchelsea House, taken by Walter Metcalfe, Esquire, from an old deed relating to the property, the present road from Loughton, in front of it, was in existence in 1632. Winchelsea House stood on the triangular ground on which is now Epping Place, and the land detached by the road from the forest had been in the possession of Lady Winchelsea, sufficiently long for her to enclose, and build a mansion on.

There is no information respecting the condition of the

high road from Harlow Bush Common to Woodford, when the Act of Parliament made over its management to Trustees, or Commissioners.

As, in the minute book of the Trustees' proceedings, no mention is made of ruts, or other inconveniences arising from the use of narrow wheels, or from waggons being overloaded, it may be inferred that, by the assistance of the money bequeathed by Thomas Baker, the road had been kept gravelled, and sufficiently hard to bear the traffic passing over it, during the greater part of the year ; but it is more than probable, frost and snow, and bad drainage, reduced it in winter to a condition similar to that of the Chelmsford Road, described in the "People's History of Essex," where it is stated that in 1795 "seven loaded waggons remained stuck fast, sunk up to their axle-trees, in the Great Trunk Road, between Ingatestone and Chelmsford," a distance of six miles.

CHAPTER IV.

The Proceedings of the Trustees of the Epping Highways.

The Trustees of the Epping Highway assembled at Epping Place in May, 1769, as directed.

The minute book commences with the following entry :—

"EPPING TURNPIKE ROAD.—At the first meeting of the Trustees, held at Epping Place on Tuesday evening, 2nd day of May, 1769, for putting in execution an Act of this present Session of Parliament for enlarging the term and powers of two Acts passed in the 10th year of King George I, and 16th of His late Majesty, for repairing the road from the north part of Harlow Bush Common, in the parish of Harlow, to Woodford, in the county of Essex. The order and determination of the Trustees was as follows :—

Present—

Sir Anth. Thos. Abdy (Bart.).	Richard Collins.
W. Altham, Esq.	William Cole.
Mr. Thos. Addorly.	John Cozens.
James Barwick.	Henry Cozens.
Jeremiah Boultham.	John Dickens.
John Bishop.	Thomas Dew.
John Browitt.	Joseph Eyre.
Robert Bulman.	John Eyre.
Daniel Binches.	Rev. Robert Fowler.
John Conyers, Esq.	Thomas Forster.
John Crabb.	Thomas Ford.

William Green.
Jacob Houblon, Esq. (junior).
Edward Hillersden.
Richard Holland.
John Hantler.
Joseph Hughes.
William Jackson.
William Jaques.
John Kent.
John Rogers Lawton.
Rev. John Lindsay.
Rev. Thomas Lipyeatt.
Rev. Anthony Natt.
Edward Parker, Esq.

James Palmer.
Richard Palmer.
Edward Pearson, Esq. (junior).
Thomas Parker.
Rev. William Smyth.
John Searle.
Rev. Thomas Salt.
Rev. Francis Hawley.
Swan Tabrum.
Richard Wright.
Frederick Warters.
Michael Welsh.
— Speed.

John Conyers, Esq., was appointed Treasurer.
William Dare and Thomas Smith, joint clerks.
William Hatchman (senior), surveyor.

The meeting being the first, was very well attended, the number of Trustees being much larger than were gathered together at any subsequent ones; and there was business of importance to be transacted.

The first order was "that a board should be forthwith painted and hung at each of the gates, mentioning the particular tolls to be demanded, and taken according to the Act just passed, which is to take place at 12 o'clock this night."

The next was that the tolls should be taken at the present gate near Epping Place for this month, and that the lower gate (*i.e.*, Thornwood Common Gate) be thrown open during that time, and during the following month tolls were to be taken at the lower gate, and the one by Epping left open. But the most important business was the position of a new turnpike.

By a clause in the Act appointing the Trustees, one of the duties imposed upon them, was the removal of the turnpike at the west end of the town.

"And be it further enacted that the said Trustees, or any five or more of them, shall, and they are hereby directed and required at their first meeting in pursuance of this Act, to cause the gate or turnpike now erected at or near a place called Epping Place, near to the town of Epping, to be immediately taken down and removed to that side of the windmill belonging to John Conyers, Esq., near Epping Place, which is nearest to the town of Epping."

The precise situation of the turnpike not being mentioned, leaves its position a matter for consideration. The corner of the Bury Lane would coincide with the statement that it was situated at or near to Epping Place, for the land belonging to it abuts upon the lane. The supposition that the turnpike stood at the corner of the Bury Lane is strengthened by tradition; and for many years at that spot there was in existence the remains of a large post, which had been sawn off near to the ground. An old inhabitant says that he had always understood it to be the remains of the turnpike post.

There is not any reason given for removal of the turnpike; it was some distance from the town. A long piece of grass land, known as the Walk, extended from the Bury Lane to the green in front of the late Chapel, now the new Church—St. John the Baptist: the cottages by the Bury Lane are built at one end of it, and the garden wall of "Crows" encloses the other. It existed as "the Walk" for about ten years after the removal of the turnpike. Amongst the title deeds of "Ockeridge" (occupying a large portion of "the Walk") is one by which the lord of the manor effected an exchange of a portion of it with Mr. Parker, of Bury Farm, for a cottage and land near to the windmill. It is mentioned in the deed that Mr. Conyers (the lord of the manor) enclosed the waste somewhere about the year 1779. The turnpike, however, had to be removed, and two propositions were brought before the meeting as follows :—

"It being proposed that the new gate and rails should be

fixed across the road and common from the house in the possession of John Bishop, to the house in the possession of Peter White, as being the shortest and least expensive (and which is nearest to the town)." This proposition was objected to, and it was proposed "That the same should be from the hedge near the corner of Hornfield, in the possession of John Tanner, to the large elm tree near the house now in the occupation of William Roberts (nearest the windmill)," upon which two propositions the Trustees divided.

For the first proposition (nearest the town).	For the second proposition (nearest the mill).
Mr. Altham.	Mr. Barwick.
Mr. Boutham.	John Bishop.
Mr. Conyers.	Mr. Bulman.
John Cozens.	Mr. Brewitt.
Henry Cozens.	Mr. Binches.
Jos. Eyre.	John Crabb.
John Eyre.	Richard Collins.
Rev. Mr. Fowler.	William Cole.
William Green.	Mr. Dickens.
Mr. Houblon.	Mr. Dew.
Mr. Hillesdon.	Mr. Thos. Forster.
Jos. Hughes.	Mr. Ford.
William Jackson.	Mr. Holland.
Rev. Mr. Lindsay.	Mr. Hantler.
Rev. Mr. Lipyeatt.	Mr. Jaques.
Rev. Mr. Natt.	Mr. Kent.
Edward Parker, Esq.	Mr. Lawton.
Mr. Parsons.	Mr. James Palmer.
Rev. Mr. Smyth.	Mr. Richard Palmer.
Rev. Mr. Salt.	Mr. Thomas Parker.
Rev. Mr. Hawley.	Mr. Richard Wright.
Mr. Tabrum.	Mr. Patrick Warters.
	Mr. Welsh.
	Mr. Speed.

Whereupon it was ordered that the gates and rails at Epping Place be removed as soon as convenient, and fixed as proposed by the amendment which has been carried, and also that John Palmer should furnish an estimate of the cost of a gate hung like that at Lea Bridge.*

It was also ordered that the present toll gatherers be continued alternately, until otherwise ordered, at their respective gates.

It would be interesting to know what were the circumstances which guided the decision of those who voted for the motion, and those who voted for the amendment.

A turnpike at the corner of the Bury Lane would, unless there were side bars, have permitted the carts and carriages from Epping Uplands, Nazing, Parndon, &c., to have passed over the high road without paying toll at Epping turnpike gate, as they could have gone on the west side of Epping Place, and so have avoided the gate. They could have gone to Loughton, Woodford, or Waltham Abbey, without contributing by the payment of a toll towards the repairing and maintaining the high road. The removal of the turnpike must have had for its object either doing away with the expense of a side bar, if one existed, or for the purpose of taking tolls from the inhabitants of the places named whose carts and waggons had not previously contributed towards the expense of keeping the road in repair. The position of the turnpike proposed by those who voted for the motion was nearer to the town than that proposed by the amendment. But the amendment seems to have proposed a more advantageous position, as it does not divide Bell Common. The fence ran along a road which joined the high road, used apparently by those who lived by Hawcock Lane, Theydon Bois, and Theydon Garnon, etc.

* Note 1757, 13 George II.—An Act was passed for Building a Bridge over the River Lea at a place called Jeremy's Ferry, and for making, repairing, and widening the road from thence into the great road at Snaresbrook, in the County of Essex, and Clapton, in the County of Middlesex.

At the next meeting, May 10th, 1769, it was ordered that there should only be one gatekeeper for the two gates at the weekly salary of sixteen shillings, finding fire and candles for himself, and that the surveyor shall, when necessary, remove his goods from one house to the other. At each house there was to be a fixed bedstead.

It was decided that the clerks' salary should be one guinea a day for their attendance at the meetings of this trust, and ten shillings a day for expenses.

Surveyor's salary was to be fixed at twenty-five pounds a year, the sand to be sold for one shilling a load, and be accounted for by the surveyor.

It was also ordered that one load in twenty of the gravel carted from the property of William Haltham, in Latton, shall be laid on that part of the road in the parish of Latton over which it shall be carted.

John Palmer having furnished the required estimate, it was agreed that the turnpike house be erected on the right-hand side of the road going to London, in brick work, with a lean-to (but no cellar), according to the plan delivered, and to be surveyed and valued.

A high railing was also to be made twenty yards from the gate, and then a double ditch with posts and two rails on the bank. The work was to be completed in six weeks; John Conyers and John Dickens, and any other of the Trustees who desired to attend, were to look over the building and railing whilst in progress. The cost of the whole was £234 14s. 3d. The bill was delivered August following, and ordered by the Trustees to be paid.

As the ditch and railing between the turnpike and the elm tree, near Roberts' house, closed the access from Theydon Bois to Epping, which had for so many years, perhaps hundreds, been maintained as a road running over Bell Common on the Theydon Bois side of the Purlieu Bank, the surveyor was ordered to have the road from the elm tree, running by the side of the ditch and rail recently erected, to the London road, by the turnpike, put in a good state of repair as a means of com-

munication between Theydon Bois and the high road, and so
through the turnpike to Epping.

It was also ordered that a gate should be put in the fence
which closed the old road across Bell Common, and that it be
left unlocked for the use of passengers from Theydon Bois into
the town of Epping during the months when the tolls were
taken at Thornwood Common.

Although the double ditch and railing along the side of
Bell Common which separated it from the other portion
of the common terminating in the Forest, appeared to be
sufficient to prevent any horses, carriages, or cattle evading the
payment of tolls at the Epping Gate, the drovers who attended
the fairs at Epping and Harlow Bush Common found means of
pursuing their journeys without passing through the turnpike.
They made their way by the back of the windmill along
Gaylins Lane, entering the town at the further end, and
so evaded the toll. This practice had existed during many
years, for it was not until 1783 that the Trustees took any
action in the matter, when the following minute is made :—
" Ordered that a turnpike be erected and set up across the
lane called Gaylins Lane, at a place called Ivy Chimnies, which
leads into Epping town, and that a person be appointed during
the time the fairs are held at Harlow Bush Common and
Epping, to receive toll there, to prevent drovers and others
evading the toll at those times as they have heretofore done."

The gate at Gaylins Lane was only to be closed and tolls
collected during the fairs at Harlow Bush, including a few days
for their dispersion   But it was subsequently found that the
evasion of the tolls by entering the town by Gaylins Lane was
not confined to the drovers, and such people, at fair-time ; but
appeared to have been a common practice with many, for
17 February, 1785, a minute is entered as follows : —" It being
made apparent to the Trustees that many people evade the toll
by going down Gaylins Lane, and then coming into the town of
Epping by the private road leading by Mr. Dickens' house, and
that it is necessary some step should be taken to prevent such
practice, it is therefore ordered that it be referred to the

Rev. Mr. Abdy and Dr. Gould, John Doubleday, and others of the Trustees, to survey the road at the end of Gaylins Lane and such other places as may be necessary, to see how the inconvenience could be remedied, and to make their report at the next meeting.

"The Trustees, also thinking a check ought to be sometimes set at the turnpikes, do therefore order that Joseph Powers do, on the first of March next, take the tolls of the upper gate for that month, and that he shall do the same at the lower gate for the month of April."

The report connected with Gaylins Lane, ordered to be made by the Committee appointed at the last meeting, was duly handed in on the 2nd of April. It stated that the only way to prevent the toll being evaded was to make a fence at the end of Mill field to the gate of the field called Bowlands, in the occupation of Harry White, and on the other side of the Mill field to the turnpike gate. The estimate made by Mr. Palmer for erecting the fence in the place proposed was £107 3s. 8d., and as he was present at the meeting he had instructions to carry out the plan.

At the same meeting it appears that the Trustees were not satisfied with the amount of tolls taken, and ordered that the services of Joseph Powers be continued during the ensuing four months from the first of May next, as at this time of the year there was less traffic on the road.

At the meeting, 25th September, 1789, a letter having been received from a Mr. Reade, objecting to the obstruction on the road to Theydon Bois into Epping over Bell Common, caused by the gate and fence erected across it from the turnpike, Mr. Jessops (the clerk) was "directed to inform him that the Trustees are of an opinion that they are justified in keeping the gate in question, on the road leading to Theydon Bois, shut or open at such times as they think proper." It was ordered that a Minute of the above be entered on the turnpike book, and a copy sent to Mr. Reade.

The clerk was further ordered to advertise in the

Chelmsford paper that if any person should at any time break any of the fences on the turnpike road, they would be prosecuted as the law directs.

Mr. Reade was evidently not satisfied, for at the first meeting in January, 1790, a letter from him was taken into consideration; when the clerk was ordered to write in reply that the Trustees cannot comply with his request, but if he conceives himself aggrieved, he can apply to the Quarter Sessions under the "General Turnpike Act."

It was decided further that the advertisement ordered at the previous meeting should be again inserted, "stating the clause that makes it felony to break in turnpike gates and fences, and offering a reward, as before, for such person as will give information as to who last broke the fence; and also adding the clause that subjects persons to a penalty for avoiding the tolls, as at Norton Heath "—it appears that they had been much evaded.

(January 30th.) The advertisement resulted in information being given by Whitbread that the fence at the end of Gaylins Lane had been, on Tuesday, 26th inst., broken in by John Bishop, of Theydon Bois, labourer. "The Trustees ordered that Bishop should be prosecuted for the offence, and appointed a committee for that purpose, also giving them power to prosecute any person whatsoever who shall have broken open, or shall hereafter break open, any fence or fences belonging to the turnpike."

It appears that Mr. Reade had written another letter to the clerk of the Trustees, which somewhat roused their indignation. The letter, dated the 9th January, declared his belief "that the advertisements which appeared in the 'Chelmsford and County Chronicle' were inserted by the sole authority of the Rev. Mr. Abdy and the Treasurer, without the approbation of the Trustees."

The Trustees, in answer, moved a resolution as follows:— "We do not only, highly approve of the insertion of the paragraph, but also of the steps taken by the said Mr. Abdy in that behalf."

They evidently, however, did not feel quite satisfied with their treatment of Mr. Reade's objection to the road from the "Ivy Chimnies" over Bell Common into the town, being closed.

The clauses in the Act of Parliament creating the Epping Highway Trust, when giving the Trustees power to erect turnpike gates and toll-bars across roads or lanes, stated that the roads and lanes are such as lead into turnpike roads. As the road across Bell Common did not at either end run into a turnpike road, it is to be supposed that some of the Trustees, very reasonably, were afraid they might have exceeded their powers, and therefore wished counsel to be consulted as to the limits of the clause which had regulated their action. The case was submitted to the consideration of F. Gould, Esq., who set the question at rest by giving his opinion that the clause justified their erecting the fence objected to.

But, nevertheless, with the desire of lessening as much as possible the inconvenience arising from their closing the road, they permitted inhabitants living near it to compound for the tolls, and to have keys of the gate in the fence.

The clause in the Act of Parliament permitting Trustees to put toll-bars or turnpikes across lands or roads running into highways gave rise to much dissatisfaction, as it compelled those using them to pay tolls, from which no benefit was derived. For, although the Act brought the side roads to a certain extent within the Trust, they derived no benefit from the money collected. Duck Lane is a road joining the highway at Thornwood Common, across it a toll-bar had been erected. It is evident that many persons objected to the interference with the free right of way which they had enjoyed from the earliest times, and resisted the payment of toll. For the collector was ordered by the Trustees to immediately give notice to the clerk, if he was threatened with an action-at-law for not permitting anyone to pass through the gate without paying toll. The inhabitants of North Weald Bassett made application for relief from the payment of tolls at the new turnpike when, although they passed through the gate they did

not continue their journey on the turnpike road. Their request
was taken into consideration, June 29, 1793, by the Trustees,
and the relief they asked for granted; and it was moreover
ordered that the tolls they had paid should be returned to
them. It was also decided that the inhabitants of Thornwood hamlet should not be asked for tolls when going to
church, and the amount of the tolls they had paid be returned
to them.

As the parishes through which highways passed had to
do ' statute" labour on the roads, the provision in the Act
10 George I, 1714, permitting the inhabitants to compound by
a small annual payment for the tolls, in order to diminish as far
as possible the additional burden which the turnpike tolls
imposed upon them, was continued in the subsequent Highway
Acts.

The following list contains the names of those persons who
"compounded" with the Trustees in 1769 for liberty to pass
through the turnpike on the " Epping Trust" without paying
tolls. Compounding for a year at different dates was, however, found to be inconvenient, so that an order was issued
the following year (November 10th, 1770) and entered on the
Minute Books, that the names of those wishing to compound for
these tolls must be submitted at a meeting of the Trustees,
especially called, for taking the applications into consideration;
and that the composition must be made for one year, commencing 29th September in each year, so that until the
following year, therefore, no application for "compounding"
could be received and accepted.

Compounded for Tolls, 1769.

John Conyers, at the first meeting, for his horses, carriages,
family, and servants, for one guinea a year (21s.), paid in
advance.

The Rev. Mr. Salt, the resident minister of Epping (i.e.,
of the Chapel) compounded for 2s.

					£	s.	d.
Richard Palmer	-	-	-	-	1	11	6
Mr. Jacques	-	-	-	-	0	10	6
William Cole	-	-	-	-	1	1	0
Joseph Doubleday	-	-	-	-	0	10	6
John Tanner	-	-	-	-	1	1	0
Francis Surridge	-	-	-	-	0	5	3
Philip Hould	-	-	-	-	0	10	6
William —	-	-	-	-	1	1	0
Richard Lee	-	-	-	-	0	10	6
John Crab, North Weald Basset		-			0	10	6
Michael Welsh, Epping	-		-		0	10	6
Richard Newman, Epping		-			0	10	6
Thomas Lincoln, Epping		-			0	10	6
William Altham, Esq., Latton		-			2	2	0
William Cole, Epping	-		-		1	1	0
Richard Dore	-	-	-		0	2	6
Daniel Bink, North Weald		-		-	0	10	6

The Trustees found many little matters, unnoticed by their predecessors in the management of the Epping Highway, required their attention; for October 10th, 1769, they gave instructions that posts and rails were to be put to the bridge at Loughton ponds, and that the bridge and road be widened, and posts and rails be put to the same against the road turning to Loughton Church; also that a brick arch be made near the "Crown" at Loughton, in place of the wooden one (drain pipe).

In the following year, May 18th, 1770, posts and rails were put up, by order of the Trustees, on the sides of the turnpike road at or near the bridge between the "Horseshoes" and "Rundles."

The condition of the gatehouse at Thornwood Common is not mentioned, but it must have been a wooden structure of no great value; for June 8th, 1770, the Messrs. Palmer were instructed to erect a new turnpike in brick near Thornwood Common, on the right-hand side of the road. It could not have been built on the site of the old one, for it was ordered to be removed to a convenient spot, at Duck Lane gate; and that the surveyor should find a proper person to live there free of rent, and collect the tolls, at any salary not exceeding six-pence per week (so in the Minute Book). The order for the removal of the turnpike was either not carried out, or the Trustees found the removal did not fulfil their wishes: for it was ordered to be sold July 6th, 1771, and to be removed within three days. It sold for £6 19s. 0d., and the auctioneer was paid ten shillings and sixpence for the trouble of selling it.

Nov. 20th, 1773.—The Trustees put in force their power of altering the tolls payable, and directed a notice to be put up at the Epping turnpike gate, or either of the turnpikes, that waggons, wains, or carts having the fellies of the wheels of less breadth than six inches, and the horses, &c., drawing them, should pay one-half more toll than they had previously paid; and that waggons, wains, carts, &c., "moving upon rollers of the breadth of sixteen inches on each side thereof, with flat surface, should be permitted to pass toll free till Michaelmas day next, and after that day to pay only half the toll payable by other waggons, wains, &c."

During several years the attention of the Trustees was given to the work carried on at Golden's and Buckhurst Hills; and the road about Epping is scarcely mentioned in the minutes until 1778. The road at the east or Harlow end of the town was very narrow, and the hill very steep. At the meeting of the Trustees, January 2nd, in that year, it was ordered, that the road leading out of Epping from the collar-maker's to Butler's Weir be widened. August, 1773.—The road opposite the pond was "ordered to be widened at least four feet, that part of the road being com-plained of as being too narrow;" and at the following meeting the road was ordered to be raised. The work done on the roads can now be seen; but "Butler's Weir," a large pond, has disappeared. It may, therefore, be as well to mention that about the middle of the present century the fencing of the Grove Estate was carried so far forward as to enclose the pond (Butler's Weir) and some cottages which the then owner had purchased, and also some of the "green" or waste land. Butler's Weir must at one time have been of a considerable size, as weir means a sheet of water;* and it was of sufficient importance to give a name to the hill leading on to the plain. In the title deeds of "Spriggs' Oak" it is described as being situate on Butler's Weir Hill.

Mr. John Conyers and Mr. Dakins had been appointed to superintend the work whilst in progress for widening the road, and carrying it across the hollow at the bottom of the hill, as a causeway or raised road. But, as they were not present at the meeting in June when the accounts were sent in, and should have been paid, fifty pounds were ordered to be paid to the contractor on account, and the balance seems to have been paid in December, as there is the entry: "Mr. Finlason was paid his bill for the work done." It has, unfortunately, happened that time has obliterated the figures showing the amount; it, however, seems to have been in excess of the sum expected, for it is stated, "The Trustees being much concerned to find that such frequent impositions are attempted by the workmen employed on the turnpike road when no estimate is brought in, it is therefore ordered that no work or job shall be directed to be done on the said turnpike road which shall amount to above five pounds, without an estimate having been first produced and agreed, and inserted in the proceedings of the day." Mr. Champness was ordered to place posts and rails opposite Butler's Weir on the newly made road, to prevent carriages being overturned by going too far.

In the minutes of the fifty-second meeting of the Trustees on August 29th, 1774, there is an entry to the effect that John Hatchman, the surveyor, had considered himself, by right of his office, exempt from the payment of tolls when passing and

---

* *See* Halliwell's "Dictionary of Archaic Words."

repassing through the turnpike gates. It is stated, however, as follows:—" By this office he is not exempt from paying thereof, for his waggons, carts, and carriages travelling on the said road. And whereas it appears that the amount of the tolls so omitted to be paid is, on the whole, seven pounds and four shillings; and the expense of obtaining the information is one pound." In December, 1775, the sum was deducted from money due to him.

CHAPTER V.

GOLDEN'S HILL.

THE hills, Golden's and Buckhurst Hills, forming the valley in which Loughton is situated, were serious difficulties in the way of the traffic into the eastern counties through Epping. In whichever direction a waggon, or cart, or any other vehicle was travelling, it had to descend and ascend very steep hills: if its destination was London, it had to make its way up Buckhurst Hill, and if travelling eastward up Golden's Hill, the greater portion of which is still remaining. But, although the impediment to the development of the traffic must have been very evident, the road had existed for 150 years and no steps, apparently, taken to lessen the gradients of the hills, until the Local Highway Act put them under management of Trustees, who, at their ninth meeting, June, 1770, directed their clerk, Mr. Hatcham, to write to Mr. W. Kentish at St. Albans, instructing him to make a survey of Golden's Hill, and to send in an estimate of the cost of making the ascent more easy.

His plans and report are not in existence. But they were evidently not satisfactory; for the Trustees ordered, July 3rd, 1770, that he be paid, for his journey from St. Albans and four days surveying, four guineas; and that Mr. James Barwick, one of the Trustees, be directed to employ Mr. Finlason to survey the hill, and to furnish plans for the consideration of the Trustees at a future meeting. At the same time the difficulty of the ascent of this hill, and also Buckhurst Hill, had evidently their serious attention; for there is the entry in the Minute Book: "Mr. Swan Tabrum and William Hatchman, junior, were ordered to view Golden's and Buckhurst Hills, and report the length of each, and how far it may

be proper to allow a greater number of horses to draw waggons
and other carriages up the said hills." Having examined the
hills as instructed they stated the measurement of Golden's
Hill to be four hundred and forty-eight yards, and Buckhurst
Hill [spelt Buckott's] four hundred and eight yards. Whereupon it was ordered " that an order of allowances be signed,
permitting carriages with nine-inch wheels [at the fellies] to be
drawn by ten horses, and carriages with less breadth wheels
than nine inches to be drawn with six horses, up the said hills,"
which order was to be presented at the next Quarter Session
to be confirmed, and for that purpose the measurements of the
hills were, no doubt, made, as required by the Act of Parliament.

Nov. 1770.—Mr. Finlason produced his plan for lowering
Golden's Hill before the meeting; when a committee was
appointed to examine it, of which Mr. Richard Lomax Clay,
and William Hamilton, Esqre., both residing at or near
Golden s Hill, were the appointed members. But any other of
the Trustees might attend their meetings.

At the meeting of the Trustees in January of the year
following, 1771, the committee brought in their report, and
stated that Messrs. Glyn and William Finlason estimated the
cost of lowering the hill, according to the plan supplied by
William Finlason, at £360. This offer was accepted by the
Trustees, and they gave instructions to the committee to
confer with the owners of such land as would be required
for the widening of the hill, respecting the compensation they
would ask for the land proposed to be taken. The work could
not be undertaken at once on account of the frosts; and the
delay afforded Messrs. Glyn and Finlason time to reconsider
their estimate; for at the next meeting, 16 February, 1771, they
stated they could not do all the work necessary, mentioning
carpenters' and bricklayers' work, and find materials, for the sum
mentioned, £360, so they brought in a supplementary estimate,
for additional work and materials, amounting to £70, making the
total £430. The Trustees, however, would not sanction the
increase on the estimate, and instructed their clerk to draw a contract deed, and submit it to Sir Anthony Thomas Abdy, for his

perusal and approbation.   Soon after this the work on Golden's
Hill must have been commenced; for at the meeting in April of
the same year it was ordered, that as Messrs. Glyn and Finlason
had begun "the lowering of the hill called Golden's Hill, the
clerk be instructed to acquaint John Conyers, the treasurer,
thereof; and that he is desired to pay them, as agreed by the
Article for that purpose, and formerly ordered; and that one
of the clerks do likewise inform the same treasurer, that he is
desired to contract for the land necessary to be purchased for
the new intended road, according to the Articles."

As it was not likely the treasurer, "the Lord of the Manor
of Epping," would be at home at all times when money was
wanted, the surveyor, Mr. Hutchinson, was empowered to pay
the contractors forty pounds forthwith, on account of the
work done, and to continue to pay them, in the absence of the
treasurer.

The work was commenced on the Epping side of the hill,
for the land on the Loughton side had not, at the time of the
meeting in May, 1771, been purchased.   Mr. Richard Dore, one
of the clerks, having made inquiry, by the direction of Mr. John
Conyers, about the purchase of the land necessary for widening
and lowering Golden's Hill, reported that "the executors of
Mr. John Lawton, of Loughton, late deceased, to whom the
ground belongs, have fixed the value of the land, containing
twenty-two perches, at £8 5s., the same being garden ground;"
the fence which would be required was to be made at the
expense of the Road Trustees.

The road over the hill became dangerous to passengers,
owing to the cutting which was being made, so Messrs.
Champness and Palmer were ordered to immediately run a
small slight temporary rail along the side of the "new intended
road," so far "as the same shall appear to be dangerous to
travellers, and at a proper distance to keep travellers off that
part of the road where the same is sunk."

At the twenty-first meeting of the Trustees, in June, 1771,
although there is no mention made in the minutes of any
disagreement between the contractors and the Trustees, it

seems as if some difficulty had arisen, for there is the following minute :—

"That the former contract, as agreed with Messrs. Glyn and Finlason for making a new road over Golden's Hill, and lowering the same, as executed, be confirmed, and carried on without any alteration of the plan or expense for doing the same; except only, that the said contractors for the said work having at this meeting agreed to leave at least fourteen feet wide of the gravel of the old road, from the top of the said hill to the bottom thereof, and to take down the road opposite the house of Richard Lomax Clay, Esquire, according to an estimate delivered in and signed by them, amounting in the whole to £62 7s. 4d."

At the meeting in October a complaint was brought that a postchaise had been overturned by the gravel being improperly laid. Other inconveniences having also arisen, railings were ordered to be placed at the spot to prevent similar accidents happening.

During the winter months the work on the hill had evidently been suspended, and not re-commenced when the Trustees met in March, 1772; for it was ordered " that Messrs. Glyn and Finlason do as soon as possible and immediately set about the performance of their agreement of making the new intended road and lowering the hill."

At the twenty-eighth meeting, in August, 1772, by desire of Mr. Glyn, one of the contractors for lowering the hill, the Trustees assembled at Golden's Hill in order to survey the work done, as the hill was cut through. They reported "that the undertaking to reduce the said hill appears not to have been pursued according to the meaning of the contract for the same." Mr. John Glyn being present, he was ordered to proceed to the reducing of the said hill as fast as possible, and in every respect according to the written contract entered into and signed by him, and the clerk was to send him "an attested copy of the said contract and plan of the road, for him to attend to in the performance of his duty."

The Contractors could not have made satisfactory progress

with the work they had in hand ; for in the following September it was ordered that no further time be lost, "and for the better enabling them to proceed with the work the treasurer was ordered, 8 September, 1772, to pay them £35 on account of work done. The clerk, Richard Dore, was also instructed, 9th October, to wait on Mr. William Black, one of the Trustees, and to request him to take a survey of Golden's Hill, and to report the condition of the same at the next meeting. Mr. Black, however, was away from home.

Four meetings were summoned, but there had not been a sufficient number of Trustees present to form a quorum until May 15th, 1773. In the six winter months country gentlemen found more agreeable occupation in field sports than in attending committee meetings, etc., so the condition of Golden's Hill seems to have received no attention from the Trustees until they again assembled, when Mr. Black brought in his report in accordance with the instructions issued at the last meeting.

His report is not mentioned, but it was evidently unsatisfactory, for it was ordered "that the original contract entered into and agreed upon with the said Trustees, and Messrs. Glyn and Finlason for making a new road on Golden's Hill and reducing the same, be confirmed and strictly attended to, by carrying on the same without any alterations, of the said contract, or additional expense for doing thereof, save and except as hereinafter mentioned."

"The said John Glynn being here personally present at this meeting, doth hereby promise and agree to obey the above order and forthwith to proceed to finishing and completing the said work and undertaking agreeable thereto and to the said contract. [That is to say] That he will sink the said hill sixteen feet perpendicular in that part thereof that is opposite to the corner of the wall of Richard Lomax Clay, Esq., at Golden's Hill aforesaid next to the 'Red Lion,' and that he will raise the same at least sixteen feet at the bottom of the said hill opposite to the 'Plume of Feathers.' And, make the same road with the most easy declivity that may be, from opposite the 'Shoe Maker' at the beginning thereof, to the corner

of the hedge below the wheeler's shop, at the bottom of the said dell, after such sinking and raising as aforesaid; and to finish the said work and undertaking, in like manner, by the 30th day of October now next ensuing the date hereof."

"And it is further ordered by the said Trustees and agreed unto by the said John Glyn that as soon as the said road shall be completed and finished as in manner above particularly mentioned, the treasurer, John Conyers, Esq., do, upon the part of the said Trustees pay or cause to be paid unto him, the said John Glyn, so much of the sum of £360 [being the full consideration money mentioned in the contract] therein agreed to be paid to Messrs. Glyn and Finlason for lowering and reducing the said hill, as shall then be remaining unpaid."

A surveyor was to be appointed on the part of the Trustees, and another by Mr. Glyn to certify that the work had been satisfactorily done and that Mr. Glyn was entitled to be paid the full amount due to him on his contract. Messrs. Glyn and Finlason, having undertaken to complete the work in October 1773, there was a meeting of the Trustees, at which John Conyers and John Archer, Esq., reported to the gentlemen present, that they yesterday took a survey of that part of the road called Golden's Hill, and finding "that John Glyn, who undertook on the 15th May last, to finish the said road agreeable to his contract, by this day, hath neglected to do so, and that the said road now remains unfinished, and in a ruinous and miry condition; and it also appearing that the said John Glyn has had due notice to attend the Trustees at this meeting; but has refused so to do, and by his letter now produced and read, it further appearing that the said John Glyn doth not intend to proceed to finish the said road agreeable to his contract, but persists in trifling with the said Trustees, and doth not mean to do anything more to the said road till next summer. It is therefore the opinion of the gentlemen present, and we do order and direct that our clerks, or one of them do forthwith wait upon William Black, Esq., and request him to appoint a surveyor to estimate and value the work done at the said road by Messrs. Glyn and

Finlason and make a report to the Trustees on the twenty-sixth day of November next." And public notice was to be given that proposals would then be received from any person willing to complete and finish the work, making it a good road according to the specification, which appears to have been drawn by Mr. William Finlason, as he was awarded a sum of five guineas for the plan and estimate. At the same meeting, November 26th, 1773, the clerks were directed to lay a proper case before counsel for his opinion, as to whether the Trustees could by law recover the money which had been paid to Mr. Glyn, in excess of the value of the work done. And with that view Mr. Black was to obtain a valuation and lay it before the Trustees. Owing to illness, however, of the person employed by Mr. Black, the report was not made until April, 1774, for which he did not send in his account until 1795, when the amount, £6 16s. 6d., was ordered to be paid.* It was stated that the cost of the work done on Golden's Hill should not have exceeded £212 16s., and as the treasurer had paid Mr. Glyn £300 it follows that the contractors had received £87 4s. in excess of the valuation. Whereupon it was ordered that the case, mentioned at a previous meeting, should be completed and submitted to Mr. Dunning, the counsel selected, for his opinion.

Mr. William Finlason, of Cheshunt, having undertaken to complete the work at Golden's Hill; his offer was accepted by the Trustees, subject to the following conditions :—" That under their directions he would carry on the work in such manner that the hill might be sunk sixteen feet in the highest and steepest, and raise the bottom at least sixteen feet computed from the height the same was before it was begun

---

* It seems incredible that an account should be so long outstanding; but the minute made January 2nd, 1795 leaves no doubt as to the date of the survey for which the sum was paid. "William Black, Esq., having sent in a bill of £6 16s. 6d., for work done by him in the year 1774, at Golden's Hill, in surveying the road there, it is ordered the Treasurer do pay the same."

upon by Mr. Glyn." He was to be paid at the rate of one and a-half guineas for his trouble* in superintending the completion of the road. He was repaid weekly the sum of money he paid away, and he had to confirm the accounts rendered to the Trustees, by oath. In January of the following year, 1774, arrangements were made for digging and carting gravel. The surveyor was ordered to get together, near to Golden's Hill, as much gravel and stones as he could obtain, in order to complete and finish the road. And, at the meeting in July, he was directed to put the gravel on the road; so that it may be concluded the work on the hill was finished.

But there were other matters connected with the hill to occupy the attention of the Trustees.

The road being much raised above the level of the land on either side, the best means of guarding against accidents to travellers was discussed at a subsequent meeting (April, 1774). In consideration of the many inconveniences arising from the sides of the new intended road at Golden's Hill, from the side railing thereon: We order and determine, that instead thereof, on both sides the road from the cottage opposite to the late Lawton's house at Golden's Hill to the bottom thereof, there shall be made and set up mud or earth work banks, to be erected, with the soil arising from the said road, at least four feet high, and not less than three feet wide, for the safety of the passengers and travellers on the said road. These banks can now be seen on the sides of the hill.

As it seemed to the members who were present, William Altham, Robert Boothby, Esqs., Francis Mitten and John Archer, gentlemen, that the alteration of the road would obstruct the approach to the house of Mr. Lomax Clay, a clerk was instructed to inform him that the Trustees will order to be removed, at the expense of the Trust, all the earth out of the road, in as easy an ascent as possible from the road up into his door, and will also order the present brick walls before and

---

* The payment was no doubt per week, but the minute does not say so.

by the side of his house, to be rebuilt in a manner satisfactory
to him.

In May there was another meeting of the Trustees, at
which W. Altham and J. Barwick, Esqs., having surveyed the
hill, brought in a report of its condition, and also a statement of
what alterations they thought should be made to complete the
work connected with the alteration to the hill. In accordance
with the report of these gentlemen it was ordered that the
bridge at the bottom of the hill on "this side [the Epping
side] Mr. Clay's house be widened by William Finlason, and
that part of the field belonging to Mrs. Rogers at the bottom
of Golden's Hill be taken into the road; and proper steps be
immediately taken to compel her to give up the same to the
Trustees, in case she refuses." The land taken was to be valued
at thirty years' purchase, and the surveyor was instructed to
pay her £10. An agreement was also to be made with the
trustees of the late Mr. Lawton, as to the value of a portion
of a garden and field adjoining Golden's Hill, which the
Trustees desired to purchase, to enable them to complete the
work they had in hand. Mr. Lomax Clay, not having given
any attention to the message sent to him, the clerk was obliged
to call again upon him.

The new road having stopped up the old road to
Airwaker's house he was paid £2 1s. towards the expense
of making another, and a proper road, from the turnpike road
to his farm, was to be made at the expense of the Trustees.

12th May, 1775.—It appearing that thirty-three poles of
Mr. Airwaker's land had been taken by the Trustees, Mr. Lally
was to be paid £16 10s. for the use of Mrs. Rogers. She had
already been paid £10, so that £26 10s. was the estimated
value of thirty-three poles. In addition to the money paid
for Mrs. Rogers' use, the Trustees were to make another
pond in the place of the one they had filled up, and a ditch
and bank next the road, planted with a thick-set hedge,
protected by fencing until it should be fully grown. With
the exception of making a new road to Mr. Bouler's house
at Loughton, with hand-rails on one side, and repairing some

cottages which were reported to be dangerous, because the foundation had been rendered unsafe, through cutting away the ground, to lower the hill, these works appear to have been thought finished at the meeting in December, 1775; and Mr. Hatcham was paid the balance due to him, £343 7s. 3d. 1777.—There is the entry "William Finlason was paid a further gratuity of £20 for his finishing Golden's Hill so much to the satisfaction of the Trustees."

At the meeting, April, 1774, the Trustees had sent a clerk to Mr. Lomax Clay promising to remedy any inconvenience to him, or injury done to his premises, through the alterations to the road and lowering Golden's Hill; but it is not until 1781 that the condition of his premises is again brought under the notice of the Trustees, when it is stated, "The surveyor having brought in an estimate of what is necessary to be done at the old Golden's Hill, and it appearing that Richard Lomax Clay, Esquire, expects to have the wall rebuilt in case that plan and estimate is carried into execution, and that the same will cost the sum of £84 8s. 3d., beside £68 for reducing the road from his house, and bringing the same into the new road, it is ordered that nothing further therein be done except securing the present road."

The want of funds no doubt influenced the decision of the Trustees, for it is assigned as a reason for stopping work at Buckhurst Hill.

But on the 29th December, 1783, it was ordered "that the cross road leading from Debden Green by Mr. Clay's house at Loughton be sloped down to the turnpike road at Golden's Hill, and that the materials of the old road be made useful." So up to that date the road to Debden Green must have turned into the old road at Golden's Hill, and not been brought across it to join the present road.

In May, 1784, it is entered in the minutes that nothing has at present been done at the cross road at Mr. Clay's house since the order was given for sloping the same on 29th December last, on account of some objection made by Mr. Clay as to the manner to be pursued in sloping down

K

the same. It is therefore ordered that it be referred to a committee of five, who at a meeting on the 15th May, 1784, reported "that having viewed and surveyed the cross road, they consider it may be sloped in a direct line to the turnpike road, by beginning the same at the blue fence opposite the south front of Mr. Clay's house, carrying the reduction thereof in an easy manner into the turnpike road; thereby discontinuing the narrow road that is now railed in: also this reduction may be done without prejudice to Mr. Clay's house and wall, and would be the most proper way of carrying the order of May last into execution." In September Mr. Perkins, who had been employed to certify the completion of Mr. Palmer's work at Buckhurst Hill in a satisfactory manner, was instructed to examine the plans of the work proposed to be done at Mr. Clay's house, and to inform the Trustees whether they were suitable. But he could not attend the meeting in February, 1785, on account of having a bad cold, and so his instructions were cancelled. It was not until June in the following year that steps were taken to carry out the necessary alterations. It was then ordered that the clerk should wait upon Mr. Lomax Clay, and inform him that the Trustees were ready to make a good road to his house, agreeable to the directions in the report of the committee who viewed the same May 15th, 1784, in case he chose to let the workmen see about it; and if he had any objection thereto, to desire him to attend the next meeting and state the same. At the said meeting, the clerk reported that he had seen Mr. Clay, who had requested to be shown a plan of the manner in which the Trustees intended to make good the road to his house. Mr. Moore, the surveyor, was directed to attend on the 7th of August to view the place, and to give his opinion as to the advisability of carrying out the plans of the 15th May, 1784, or whether any other plans would be preferable. Mr. Moore stated that the alterations could not be made in a direct line without breaking into Mr. Clay's courtyard, in the front of his house, and Mr. Clay very naturally raising objections to the plan, it was finally settled (23rd September, 1786) that he should undertake the work himself on receipt from the Trustees of £200, paid to him in full for all demands for injury done to his gardens, &c.

Golden's Hill was not again brought under the notice of the Trustees, except for occasional repairs to the railings by the side of the road, until October, 1825, when the necessity for a drain at the bottom of the hill to carry off the water from the road was taken into consideration, resulting in the order that a brick drain, eighteen inches diameter, should be made. At the meeting of the Trustees, held April, 1826, it was mentioned that the Rev. Mr. Hamilton acquiesced in a proposal for turning the road at the bottom of the hill through his field, according to a plan suggested by Mr. South, the surveyor, who was ordered to attend, with the plan and estimate of the costs, at the next meeting. In May his plan and estimate were produced, and, being approved of by the Trustees, it was ordered to be carried out.

It was also proposed to alter the course of a road near the 14th milestone, but the minute does not say whether it was in the Loughton or Ongar Road. It is merely stated that the alteration of the road marked out near the 14th milestone appearing to be less calculated to benefit the public than the adoption of the old horsepath to the eastward, the surveyor, Mr. South, was ordered to prepare estimates for making such alterations on each line, and produce them at the next meeting.

On the Loughton Road the 14th milestone was by the "Wake Arms," but the road had been used for many years, and it does not appear that there was any horsepath, or that any alteration on the road was necessary.

At the top of Golden's Hill, leading from the ridge of hills, there was a horsepath through the forest passing by Ambresbury Bank to Epping; it is known as "The Mill Ride," and is supposed to have been a pack-horse road, but it evidently crossed the high road near to the then 13th milestone.

CHAPTER VI.

BUCKHURST HILL.

THE attention of the Trustees had been given to the steep gradient of Buckhurst Hill in 1770, when they ordered it to be measured, with the view of obtaining the consent of the magistrates in Quarter Sessions, to their permitting a greater number of horses to be used in drawing waggons, wains, carts, &c., up the hill than was allowed under ordinary circumstances.* But it is not again mentioned until at the meeting of the Trustees in December, 1774, their attention was directed to the state of Buckhurst Hill, when Mr. Hatcham, the surveyor, was directed to fill up several holes thereon.

No other notice of the hill appears in the Minute Book until 27th March, 1777, and then James Barwick, Esq., was "desired to survey Buckotts Hill with a surveyor and report at the next meeting what sum it may be reduced for." He brought in his report at the next meeting as instructed, but, for some cause unexplained, its consideration was deferred until the meeting in December, at which Mr. Finlason, the surveyor, attended with the report. There were not, however, a sufficient number of Trustees present, and its consideration was again postponed. Something, however, had been done, for in January, 1778, Mr. Finlason brought in his account for widening the road at Buckotts Hill, and other jobs—£95 4s.

It was over two years—viz., 19th May, 1780—before the state of Buckhurst Hill again had the attention of the Trustees.

---

* *See* Golden's Hill, in foregoing chapter.

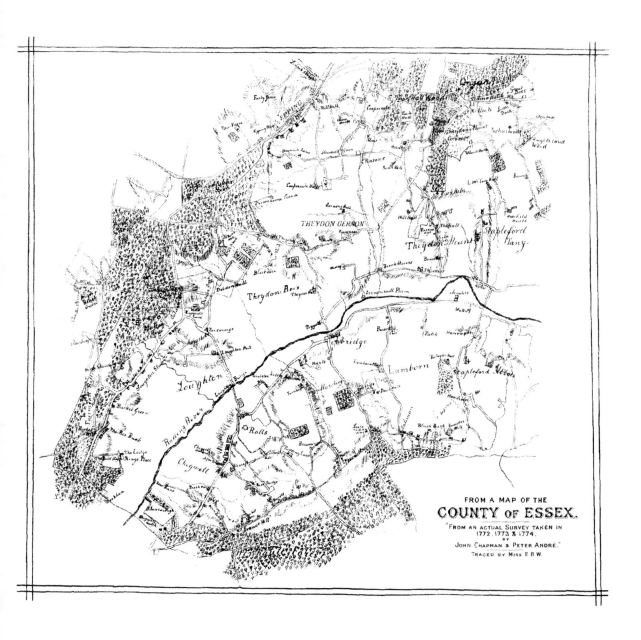

FROM A MAP OF THE
COUNTY OF ESSEX.
"FROM AN ACTUAL SURVEY TAKEN IN
1772, 1773 & 1774.
BY
JOHN CHAPMAN & PETER ANDRÉ."
TRACED BY MISS E.B.W.

At the meeting on that date, the report prepared in 1777, relating to the reduction of the gradient of the hill, having been brought before the Trustees, it was ordered that the surveyor should "at once stake out" the boundaries of Buckotts Hill for reducing the same, and cause an advertisement to be put in the county paper, also the "Daily Advertiser," "that such persons as are willing to contract for reducing the hill according to the plan left for their inspection with Joseph Doubleday, or any other plan such persons inclining to contract shall judge less expensive, and more commodious; do bring in an estimate at the next meeting." Mr. William Finlason attended with his estimate (£970 7s. 9d.) of the cost of the work to be done according to the plan produced. No other plan having been submitted, it was thought advisable that the further consideration of the matter should be deferred, and that there should be a meeting of the Trustees at the "Roebuck," Buckhurst Hill, in August, to view the proposed alterations. Accordingly, on the 7th of August, the Trustees met at the "Roebuck" to make the survey mentioned, when they came to the conclusion that before entering on such expensive works the surveyor of the Bishop Stortford roads, Mr. Mott, should be consulted. It was therefore ordered, that he should be requested to obtain the consent of the Trustees of the Bishop Stortford roads to his compliance with their wishes.

Mr. Mott was paid two guineas for his attendance, the result of his inspection being that he approved of the plan submitted, and the estimate of the cost. At the meeting of the Trustees in the following month, it was arranged that an agreement should be entered into with Mr. Finlason for reducing the road over Buckotts (alias Buckhurst) Hill according to the plans brought forward by him, and the estimate he had produced, viz., £976 7s. 9d.; it being, moreover, the opinion of the Board that if Mr. Finlason could give security for the completion of the job, it would be for their interest to let him do it.

But after this arrangement had been made it seems that some of the Trustees were doubtful as to their legal right to

charge the tolls with the cost of reducing Buckhurst Hill; and
fearing that each Trustee would be personally liable for the
money expended by them in carrying out the plans submitted,
it was proposed at the meeting held 19th September, 1780,
that the contract they had agreed to make with Mr. Finlason
should be revoked, and that the hill be reduced, in the
manner mentioned, under the direction and inspection of the
Trustees.

By way of commencement, their surveyor, Mr. Finlason,
was instructed to begin the work as soon as convenient, and to
report at their several meetings the progress made and expenses
incurred. The minutes of the meetings up to the present time
lead to the idea that no other surveyor than Mr. Finlason was
employed; but an entry made at this date as follows :—" It
was ordered that three pounds fifteen shillings and eleven pence
be paid to the surveyor, James Turnbull, who was recommended by Mr. Wright, for his plan, and expenses attending
the meeting, and for his estimate mentioned in the former
order,"—points to the conclusion that the Trustees had consented to additional information being obtained, or that the
plan produced by Mr. Finlason, and approved by Mr. Mott,
was prepared by Mr. Turnbull.

There not being, however, during the winter months, a
sufficient number of the Trustees present at any meeting to
transact the business on hand, it was not until May, 1781, that
the minutes of the meeting in September of the previous year
were confirmed. But it appears that Mr. Finlason had, nevertheless, been carrying on the work at Buckhurst Hill, for at the
May meeting, 1781, he reported that he had begun the work.
An order was then made that he should be paid the money
expended for labourers' work, team labour, and other incidental
expenses, according to the bill he had laid before the meeting.
At the same time it was arranged with the treasurer that
Mr. Finlason should always have from £40 to £50 in hand.
He was also ordered to hire as many teams as he could employ,
and make all possible expedition in reducing the hill. He
evidently had some difficulty in obtaining labourers, as there

is, July, 1781, the following entry in the Minute Book :—"The Trustees having that day viewed the hill, and being of opinion it will be for the advantage of the publick to have the road over the said hill finished before summer is over, and finding that they cannot get hands to work on the said hill during the harvest without increasing men's wages, it is ordered that twelve shillings a week be paid the labourers during those times from" (the word has disappeared through the ink having perished) "till 7 o'clock in the evening, and as many engaged as can work thereon." The meeting adjourned to the following Friday, "to settle the surveyor's account, and proceed in the execution of the trust reposed in us." The surveyor's account, duly audited, was presented, amounting to £218 14s. 5d., for work done at Buckhurst Hill between the 11th of May and the 30th of June, and it was "ordered to be entered in the treasurer's book." (Mr. Finlason had received the money as directed at the meeting in May.) The balance in the treasurer's hands was £220. Up to October following, the work at Buckhurst Hill had gone on without interruption, when it was reported that the balance in the treasurer's hand, after paying the surveyor's bill, was £91 10s. 0d.; whereupon orders were given "that no more work be done at Buckhurst Hill till further orders." The Trustees gave no attention to the "execution of the trust reposed in us" until the 25th of March, with the exception of a meeting in January, 1782, when it was stated that there was not sufficient money in hand to satisfy a bill presented for payment, but that it was to be paid out of the first money collected. On the above date in March, they borrowed money on the security of the tolls, as allowed by the Act of Parliament (£200), when the accounts due were paid, and attention was again given to the alterations which had been suspended.

Having made a survey of the work already done, the Trustees gave it as their opinion, "that it would be to the advantage of the public to make a short road from the old highway by Mr. Laybank's house, into the new road now making at the said hill, before the upper part of the hill is

completed." They ordered that the same be done forthwith.
and the lower portion of the hill be completed. £50 was to be
paid on account of the said work.

In July of the same year the Trustees again visited Buckhurst Hill, and at the following meeting the work there was
stopped, and a meeting summoned for October in order to
consider what was to be done. No cause is mentioned for
stopping the work, but at the meeting in October an explanation is afforded by the entry that "as part of the ground has
fallen in upon the old road, we order that so much thereof be
removed as encroaches upon the same." It was ordered that
in addition, a rail be put across the new road leading from
Laybank's house, also a bank thrown up at each end of the
hill, and a slight railing put by the side of the old road at the
bottom of Buckotts Hill, where it is dangerous. At the same
time they gave it as their opinion "that nothing further could
be done at present."

The plans for the alteration and improvement of Buckhurst Hill, which had been laid before the Trustees and
approved by them, having disappeared (like the plan for improving Golden's Hill), it cannot be stated with certainty what
they were. The map of the roads comprised within the Epping
Trust, and the entries in the Minute Book, seem to be the only
sources of information.

A short road was made at the bottom of the hill opposite
Mr. Laybank's house to the new road. The map shows that
the high road through Loughton takes at the bottom of the hill
a sudden turn to the right. This turn seems to be the short
road mentioned in the minutes.

Nearly at the top of the hill there is a road turning to
the left ; it runs close to the "Roebuck Inn," and bending
to the right, joins the road on the level ground at the top of
the hill.*

A road running in a direct line from Loughton to the
"Roebuck" would be so very steep that even the ten horses

---

* *See* Map by Chapman and André.

permitted at the meeting in 1770 to be used for drawing a waggon up Golden's and Buckhurst Hills, would scarcely be able to do so. It may therefore be concluded that the old road wound up the hill; the middle portion of the hill now existing being part of it; also, that the road seen at the present time in front of the "Roebuck," continuing into the road to Woodford, is the upper portion.

The plan, then, probably consisted in making a cutting through the top of the hill, and with the excavated soil filling up the valley at the bottom. The carts carrying the earth so obtained would make use of the middle portion of the old road. There was apparently no stoppage of the traffic between Woodford and Loughton, for on the occasion of the landslip, measures were taken to prevent passengers inadvertently going on the road in course of construction.

The order that the lower portion of the road should be completed before work was commenced in the upper, indicates that the "new intended road" consisted of two distinct portions, an upper and a lower. When the lower portion was completed, so as to be in a suitable condition for the public use, the contractor was to proceed with the upper—that is, the portion from the spot where the road turns off to the "Roebuck" to where it now joins the road to Woodford.

At a meeting of the Trustees in February, 1783, as there was in the hands of the treasurer £67 13s. 11d., they decided that the work at Buckhurst Hill should be carried on for one week, and then Mr. Finlason, their road surveyor, who had the work in hand, was ordered to take his instructions from the committee who had been appointed to superintend the work. But satisfactory progress could not have been made, for in May following, the Rev. Mr. Abdy, one of the committee appointed, stated that he had attended at the hill as directed, and found the alteration could not be completed without the expenditure of a considerable sum of money.

The information evidently surprised those Trustees who were at the meeting, and it probably caused them much disappointment to learn that the plan they had adopted of carrying on the work themselves, by their surveyor and a committee of inspection, had so completely failed. The work was ordered to be stopped, and the clerk was instructed to advertise in the Chelmsford paper for tenders from those persons willing to contract for the completion of Buckhurst Hill. At the same time Mr. John Palmer was desired to survey the hill, and give his opinion as to the amount of money required to finish the alterations according to the plans. His estimate was brought before the June meeting, when Mr. Finlason, not agreeing with Mr. Palmer as to certain suggestions he made, a contract was entered into with Mr. John Palmer to complete the work from Mr. Laybank's house to the bottom of the hill for £340. The work now went on rapidly. In the following September an estimate was submitted by Mr. Palmer, and accepted by the Trustees, to complete the upper portion of the hill from Mr. Laybank's house to the "top thereof next to the turnpike road near the 'Baldfaced Stag.'"

Mr. Finlason must have had much trouble and anxiety whilst employed in altering, &c., Buckhurst Hill; but his trials were at an end, for having taken an inn in Epping, he was not by the Act of Parliament allowed to continue his position of road surveyor. He was dismissed by his employers at the meeting, 29th December, with a gratuity of £20, for which he pleaded very hard, on the grounds that much extra work had been put upon him.

Although the making of the present Buckhurst Hill was commenced in 1781, it was not completed until 1784. In March of that year Mr. Palmer was instructed to carry out the lowering of the upper portion of the hill according to the plan furnished by Mr. Turnbull; and in the June following, Mr. William Perkins, of Holloway Down, was instructed to see if the lowering of the hill had been done in accordance with Mr. Turnbull's plan. The report he handed in was, no doubt, satisfactory, for in October an assignment was made of the tolls to the amount of £200 to Mr. Palmer as security for the amount due to him. The Trustees then advertised for a further loan, on the security of the tolls; and on the loan being effected a

short time after, the debt was paid. The year following, a
footpath by the side of the road up the hill was constructed with
the materials taken off the road in Loughton, in consequence of
complaints which had been made.

There was more work to be done; the landslip had not
been properly dealt with. On March 13th, 1786, £20 was
voted for "clearing the ground which had fallen in, and flinging
back that which is fallen in." In June, 1787, there was another
slip. Mr. Bowers, the surveyor who was at the time employed
on the road to Writtle, was ordered to rail off the most
dangerous parts of the hill until he could conveniently cart
sufficient earth from the top to support the bank, and slope the
road in the same manner as had been done in other parts of
the hill.

At a meeting, held at the "Red Lion," Ongar, March, 1789,
the state of Buckhurst Hill was brought before the notice of
the Trustees, and it was decided at the next meeting that they
should meet in July, at the "Roebuck," Buckhurst Hill, when
they surveyed the new road. It seemed necessary, for security,
that the road should either have banks on each side, or else
posts and rails, to prevent accidents happening to passengers.
The surveyor was therefore ordered to put up banks on each
side such as he thinks will answer the purpose, as specimens,
for the inspection of the Trustees, and that in the meantime a
temporary railing be erected. The cost was not to exceed
£20. No more notice is taken of the state of Buckhurst Hill
until a meeting on the 23rd of September, 1791, when the
following is entered in the Minute Book:—

"Ordered that the surveyor shall at the next meeting
bring in a plan for sloping down the road in such manner as will
make it safe for passengers."

At the January meeting, 1792, there was a proposal to
make the roadway, which was in some places only twenty feet,
forty feet wide. But the further consideration was adjourned,
till June, when it was ordered to be made a uniform width
of thirty feet; and two years after, posts and rails were put

on each side of the road to make it safe for foot passengers. The cost was £62 13s.

The cutting through Buckhurst Hill opened up a spring of water or, perhaps better stated, cut through a vein of surface gravel, out of which water filtered. Some of the inhabitants of Loughton, where there is but little water, wished to utilise the spring by carrying the little stream by the side of the road, and applied to the Trustees for permission to do so. At the meeting, September 17th, 1796, the Trustees, having taken the application into consideration, decided that the request might be granted, and the work carried on under the supervision of William Turner. The bed of gravel was, no doubt, soon drained, and the flow of water stopped except in very wet weather. Some years since there was a dipping well on the " Roebuck " side of the cutting, and the bank on the other side, thirty-five years ago, was well stocked with rabbits.

As there is no further mention made in the Minute Book of the road on Buckhurst Hill, it may be concluded it was maintained in a satisfactory condition; but, July 3rd, 1837, the attention of the Trustees was drawn to the injury done to the footpaths by the drivers of carts and waggons running the wheels, when going down hill, against their sides or edges in order to lessen the strain upon their horses, by impeding the progress of the vehicles they were drawing. With the intention of putting a stop to the objectionable proceeding of the drivers, and to protect the footpaths, an order was made that posts should be put along the edge of the footpath on the off side of Buckhurst and Golden's Hill.*

The posts still exist on Buckhurst Hill, driven into the ground to a level with the bank or edge of the road on the near side.

At the bottom of Buckhurst Hill there is a pond of considerable size. At the annual meeting in February, 1863, its condition was brought under the notice of the Trustees. It is

---

* On the near sides of vehicles descending the hill there are no footpaths.

stated it was necessary to protect the public on passing and repassing it. A committee was appointed to examine the pond and report at the next meeting; the report was as follows.— "In reference to the nuisance at Buckhurst Hill pond—that the parties complaining refuse now to contribute towards the expenses (which the Trust surveyor estimated upwards of £50)," whereupon it was resolved "that the surveyor be instructed to cause no further outlay than should be absolutely necessary to protect the public from injury and the Trustees from responsibility."

CHAPTER VII.

THE ROAD FROM EPPING, THROUGH WRITTLE, TO CHELMSFORD.

JUNE 19, 1786.—Business of great importance was brought before the meeting of Trustees of the Epping Turnpike Roads, held on that day ; the nature of which is explained by the following entry in the Minute Book :—

"A petition being this day presented from the inhabitants of the parish of North Weald Bassett, praying the Trustees to extend the powers of the said Act* and carry the Epping turnpike road through their parish, and so towards Chelmsford, it was ordered that a special meeting be held at this place ('Epping Place Inn') on the 8th day of July next, 'to take the prayer of the said petition into consideration ; and that the Clerk do meantime put an advertisement in the newspapers circulating in this county, of such a meeting being then to be held for the purpose aforesaid.'"

It was resolved unanimously by the Trustees who attended the meeting so advertised, that "the opening a communication for coaches and carriages between Epping and Chelmsford would be highly beneficial to this part of the county." They thought, however, such a road would be very burdensome to the parishes through which it would pass ; and so carried a resolution that application should be made to Parliament "for renewing the present Epping Turnpike Act, and extending its power by making a new road from Epping through the several parishes of North Weald Bassett, High Ongar, Bob-

---

* The Epping Turnpike Act of 1769.

bingworth, Chipping Ongar, and Shelley to the Four-wants-way, in that parish, upon proper terms and conditions;" which would enable them, by erecting turnpikes and taking tolls from all who used the road, to relieve the parishes from any other burden than the "statute labour," which previous Acts of Parliament had imposed upon them.

It was evidently not the intention of the Trustees, when they approved of the above-mentioned resolution, to undertake the twenty miles of road between Epping and Chelmsford. For they instructed their clerk to take a copy of the resolution to the Trustees of the Essex Roads, at their next meeting, and request them to take the same into consideration; and determine how far it will be eligible for them to carry their turnpike road to the Four-wants-way at Shelley to join the above-mentioned new road.

At the next meeting the clerk reported that he had carried out his instructions.

The Trustees of the Essex roads desired him to acquaint the Trustees of the Epping roads, that, as they had already so great a length of road under their care, they did not choose to make a new road; but they had no objection to the Epping Trustees making a turnpike road from Epping to Chelmsford if they chose to do so. Whereupon the clerk was directed, in the next and following months, to advertise in the county papers the Trustees' intention to apply to Parliament for an Act to extend their powers, &c., &c.

23rd September, 1786.—At this meeting the clerk reported he had, in accordance with his instructions, advertised in the Essex newspaper—"That it is the intention of the Trustees to apply to Parliament at the next (this) meeting for a renewal of the Epping Turnpike Act, and to extend the powers of the said Act, and also for to enable them to carry the same from that part of the road that lies near to the seventeenth milestone*

---

* This is now the 16th, as the new road from the "Wake Arms" to Woodford shortened the distance from London by one mile.

in Epping, through the several parishes of North Weald Bassett, Bobbingworth, Ongar, Chipping Ongar, and Shelley to the Four-wants-way, in the same parish of Shelley, and so from thence through the parish of Norton Mandeville, and through Writtle to the parish of Chelmsford, in the same county."

Conyers, Esq., moved that application should be made to Parliament for the proposed Act; and the Trustees, after having fully discussed the subject, were unanimous in their opinion, that such a road would be highly beneficial to the county. They accordingly directed their clerk to take the necessary steps for applying for the said Act. They were, however, careful to order a clause to be put in the draft of the Act (which was to be left ten days at Epping for the inspection of persons interested), giving them the power to raise the tolls should the amount collected not be sufficient to pay the interest on the money borrowed. A further sum of £700 was to be obtained on the security of the tolls.

As, by the advertisement inserted in the Essex papers, those persons who had complaint to make against the formation of the contemplated new road to Chelmsford, were invited to be present at a meeting of the Trustees in November, and to bring forward their objections; several of the inhabitants of Writtle attended, and pointed out the hardship it would be to their parish to erect any turnpike that would subject them to pay tolls in going to and from Chelmsford. In consequence an order was made, and entered in the minutes, that no toll-gate should be erected in the parish of Writtle so long as the inhabitants of that parish kept up a good and sufficient road, for coach and other carriages, through the whole of the said parish, to the satisfaction of the Trustees, at their sole expense.

Mr. Moore, the surveyor, having been instructed at a previous meeting to prepare plans for, and estimate the cost of making, the new road, including bridges, drains, &c., brought in his report. It is stated, it was fully considered and examined at the meeting, and the road ordered to be made in accordance with the plan. His charge for the service rendered, seems, however, to have been in excess of the sum the Trustees thought sufficient; for, at the meeting in January, 1787, there was made an entry in the minutes, "That Mr. Moore be paid only Ten guineas, in full for his bill delivered, in case he chose to accept thereof."

At the same meeting (Jan. 1787), in consequence of Mr. Tyndall, acting for the inhabitants of Chelmsford and Writtle, objecting to the intended Act, as being likely to prejudice the market at Chelmsford; an agreement was made for the introduction of a clause in the Act, providing that no toll-house or turnpike gate should be erected between the town of Chelmsford and the town of Writtle, and that the words, " to the satisfaction of the Trustees" in the clause which relates to Writtle, be crossed out; also that the clerk do wait on Mr. Rozier in the House of Commons, and inquire if the " style of the Act can now be altered without any delay in passing the Bill, and if it can, that the same be so altered as to extend the road no further than Writtle." Mr. Rozier having explained the rules of the House of Commons, which permitted a Bill to be narrowed but not extended, it was agreed that the Act should be so far altered as to leave out the parish of Writtle. The clerk had also to wait on the county members to ask them to support the Bill by giving their assistance and interest in carrying it through the House.

The Bill readily passed the House of Commons; for, two months after Mr. Tyndall brought the objections to the Bill under the notice of the Trustees, the following entry appears in the Minute Book :—

"EPPING TURNPIKE ROAD.—At the first meeting of the Trustees appointed for putting in execution an Act of the present Session of Parliament for continuing and enlarging the term and powers of the several Acts for repairing the road from the north part of Harlow Bush Common, in the parish of Harlow, to Woodford, in the county of Essex, and for repairing and widening the road from Epping through

L.

the parish of North Weald Bassett, Bobbingworth, High Ongar, Chipping Ongar, and Shelley to the Four-wants-way, in the said parish of Shelley, and thence through the parish of High Ongar and Norton Mandeville to the parish of Writtle, in the said county, held at Epping Place in Epping, on Monday, 26th day of March, 1787, in pursuance of the last adjournment, the several Trustees whose names are underwritten took and subscribed the oath or affirmation in the said Act mentioned. And the following orders and resolutions were then made by them.

" There were present :

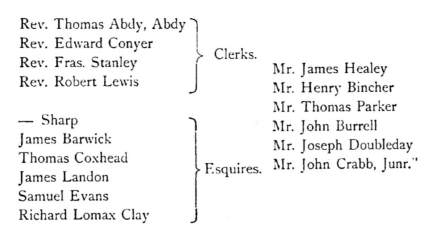

Rev. Thomas Abdy, Abdy
Rev. Edward Conyer
Rev. Fras. Stanley
Rev. Robert Lewis

⎱ Clerks.

— Sharp
James Barwick
Thomas Coxhead
James Landon
Samuel Evans
Richard Lomax Clay

⎱ Esquires.

Mr. James Healey
Mr. Henry Bincher
Mr. Thomas Parker
Mr. John Burrell
Mr. Joseph Doubleday
Mr. John Crabb, Junr."

A little later on (April 23rd) the Right Hon. George, Earl Waldegrave, and the Right Hon. John, Lord Howard, were chosen Trustees, in place of those who had resigned.

As there was only one tender for making the roads, in reply to an advertisement which had appeared in the Chelmsford paper, the Trustees, who were apparently satisfied with the mode of carrying on the work at Golden's and Buckhurst Hills, decided not to do the work by contract, but to employ their own labourers and workmen, under the superintendence of a committee appointed for that purpose, assisted by any other Trustees who might like to join.

The instructions to the committee were to select suitable places for the erection of turnpike gates and toll-houses, and to view and direct the making and repairing of the new intended road.

The clerk having brought in the bill for obtaining a new Act of Parliament: it amounted to the sum of three hundred and nine pounds seven shillings and sixpence. The Trustees, having borrowed five hundred pounds, ordered that it should be entered in the treasurer's account and paid. In the previous month the treasurer was ordered to pay two hundred pounds towards discharging the fees of the "House" when called upon. But as there is no entry of that sum having been paid, a doubt arises as to the total cost of the Act of Parliament.

There was evidently a want of promptness in fulfilling their engagements on the part of those, on whom the committee were dependent to some extent, for the means of carrying out the instructions of the Trustees: for it was ordered that the surveyors of Epping, North Bassett, High Ongar, Bobbingworth, Shelley, and Chipping Ongar, and the owner of Ongar Park Farm do make good their subscriptions, and do the work, and furnish the stones they agreed to provide for the said new road.

The next month (April 23rd) the committee appointed to superintend the new road and to decide where the toll gates should be put, brought in their report. It had the approval of the Trustees, who forthwith ordered, "That a bye gate be erected at Duck Lane opposite the cottage occupied by Thomas Godfrey, and the bye lane stopped that leads from Weald Hall Coppy to Park Corner and hedges the tenants of the farm belonging to Mr. Goff and Mr. Danberry. Also that a toll-gate be set up at Root Street, and a toll-house built upon the plan of the present toll-gates and toll-houses. Also another gate near the 'Red Lyon' at Ongar, and a bye gate contiguous thereto to prevent the tolls being evaded by going down the lane by the 'Red Lyon.'"

It is much to be regretted that the preservation of parish maps has been thought to be of little importance; parish maps are very scarce. A map of Bobbingworth, or the plan.

for which Mr. Moore was paid £10 would now be of great interest, and assist in following out the alteration proposed, when the resolution was passed "that the clerk do apply to N. Francis, of ......sterton* Lodge, near Lutterworth, Leicestershire, for his consent to carry the road through his field by Bobbingworth Mill, and to know for what sum he would sell to the Trust so much of the said field as might be wanted for that purpose." It was also ordered that application be made by the clerk to Mr. Hornsby, to know if he would sell so much of his field as would enable the Trustees to carry the turnpike road in a straight line from Shelley into the Ongar Road, and to avoid the narrow way that now leads between Evan's house and Mr. London's.

The answer received from Mr. Francis was very prompt, and must have been satisfactory; for in June the Trustees directed the surveyor to proceed at once "in making good the new turnpike road to Mr. Frank's field in the parish of Bobbingworth with all possible despatch, and that the road be carried across Mr. Frank's field in a direct line with the pollard tree pointed out by Mr. Bowers, he having given his consent thereto, and offered to make the Trustees a present of the ground; he contributed in addition 800 loads of gravel (11th August, 1787).

Mr. Hornsby also fell in with the wishes of the Trustees, and agreed that the new road should be carried through his field of arable land at Chipping Ongar in a straight line from the bottom of the "shaw,"† coming out of the corner of and through the pasture field in the occupation of Mr. London, so as to make the new and present road thirty feet wide. For this concession the Trust was to pay Mr. Hornsby fifteen years' purchase at the rate of 25s. per annum for the land wanted for the new road; and to be paid by Mr. Hornsby

---

* The first part of the name has perished.

† "Shaw," a thicket, or small wood.—Halliwell's "Dictionary of Archaic and Provincial Words."

for the old road, at the rate of twelve and a-half years' purchase, at 25s. per acre.

The Trustees were to make the fences, ditches, &c., which were required, and to be allowed to take away the gravel from the old road for use on the new, but the way was to be preserved to Mr. Evan's field gate.

It was "also ordered that the turnpike roads be 'caused' [*sic*] at a distance from the hedge, in a line with the present turnpike road, at the place where the same is unfinished, to the gullett, as a quicksand will thereby be avoided, and no drain be necessary."

In answer to an advertisement which had been put in the Chelmsford paper, several tenders for erecting turnpike gates and toll-houses had been read at the last meeting.

The following were accepted: William Patmore, for the work at High Ongar; William Champness, for the erection of new toll-gates at Park Corner, Road Street, for the sum of £133 10s.; John Surridge, gates and fencing at Duck Lane, £16 15s.

The extent of road under the management of Mr. Bowers, the surveyor, being very considerable, he was allowed to hire a horse at the expense of the Trust, in order to enable him the better to look after work. There appears to have been dissatisfaction at the manner in which it had been carried on, for in the minute allowing the horse is the following entry: "And that he, Mr. Bowers, be ordered to discharge such teams as shall be detected in bringing short measure or bad gravel, and also the labourers who shall see the same shot and not give notice thereof; and to make an agreement with them accordingly, and, that they shall forfeit all pay due to them when detected."

September, 1787.—In accordance with the practice of the Epping Trust, as allowed by the Act of Parliament, persons compounded for their tolls as follows: —

"For saddle horse

,,   ,,   ,,   and one cart or carriage

,, coaches

, chaises

, waggons

,, hay-carts, but not carts or waggons having wheels of less breadth than six inches between fellies."

} The amounts to be paid have been made, by time, to disappear.

Tickets were to be printed marked Epping and Writtle; but Mr. Joseph Doubleday having already had tickets printed, it was agreed that they should be used and the order cancelled.

The clerk was directed to advertise for tenders for erecting wooden mile posts for the new road. They were to be either square or triangular, of the best oak wood, not less than five feet long and eleven inches wide.

11th October, 1787.—The list of those who had compounded for their tolls was handed in; the lowest composition was 5s. 3d., and the highest £1 1s.

No estimates having been brought in for mile posts, and Mr. Black being out of the country, the further consideration was postponed.

On 17th of December the matter was again brought forward, when it was decided that the mile stone should be angular, and the letters on each side with figures stating the distance from Epping and Chelmsford. As the clerk informed the Trustees that the General Turnpike Act, Stat. 18 Geo. III, c. 28, ordered the tolls to be doubled on narrow-wheel wagons, they gave instructions to have the alteration made on the old table of tolls. (But they were reduced again 10th March, 1788.)

At Bobbingworth there was a lane which is called in the minutes Watery Lane. As it was considered to be objectionable, application was to be made to Sir Harboro' Death, Bart., through his agent, Mr. Hamilton, and to Mr. Poole, for their consent to carry the road through their fields. The Trustees were willing to purchase the land they wished to occupy.

June, 1788.—Sir Harboro' Death's consent having been obtained—there is an entry in the Minute Book—an agreement was to be made with landlord and tenant and Mr. Poole for the purchase of the land and for the damage done to the crops. A short time after the negotiations for the purchase of the land had been commenced, the estate from which it was taken changed hands, when an application was made on behalf of the new owner for payment. The Trustees were, however, ignorant of the above minute, so the consideration of the demand was postponed until it could be referred to the committee who superintended the construction of the road and the transactions connected with it. At the meeting held January, 1793, the Trustees were informed that no agreement had been made with Sir Harboro' Death. But it was not understood from Mr. Hamilton, who acted for Sir Harboro', that any claim would be made. Further information being required, the clerk was directed to apply to Mr. Hamilton to ascertain what was the understanding between him and the committee.

The result of the interview is not mentioned. The committee, however, had evidently been mistaken in supposing no payment was to be made for the land taken to form the new road, for the surveyor was instructed to measure the piece. It was twenty-four rods; and the price was settled to be thirty-five years' purchase on a rental of 25s. per acre and the tenant agreeing to accept one guinea compensation for the injury done to his crops.

As no residence had been built for the toll collector when the Ongar turnpike gates were erected, he lived in a neighbouring cottage. In 1807 there had been some idea of building a toll-house on the waste land adjoining the churchyard. Plans had been prepared, and land enough for the house and garden marked out; but, the Trustees having made arrangement with the owner of the cottage to rent it for some time longer, nothing further was done at that time. In 1817, however, the landlord of the cottage gave the Trustees notice to quit on the expiration of the agreement. They had, therefore, to find

another residence for the toll-collector.   The plan of 1807
was still in existence; and, with some modification, it was
adopted.   The toll-house was ordered to be built, on the
waste ground marked out in 1807, according to the plan
produced by Mr. Cure, the treasurer, and under his supervision.

It was found on being inhabited that the chimnies smoked,
and the trees in the churchyard were believed to be the cause.
So the Trustees ordered them to be lopped, the various Acts of
Parliament having conferred upon them the power to remove
any obstacle, the existence of which was injurious to the highways, toll-house, or gates, &c.

At Duck Lane there was also a cottage rented for the
toll-collector, in 1818.   An offer was made by the owner to sell
the property for £100, or to let it for £5 per annum.   But
at the next meeting of the Trustees an estimate or tender was
brought in for building a toll-house for the sum of £93 12s.
The tender was accepted, and orders given that it should be
built, but the cost was not to exceed £100.

Complaints were made by the inhabitants of North Weald
Bassett of the injustice to which they were subjected through
the existence of Duck Lane Gate; and in December, 1822, an
order was made by the Trustees that 18s., which had been
wrongfully taken from one of the complainants, should be
returned to him; and also that no tolls should for the future be
taken from any person passing through the gate, who did not
travel on the Ongar road.   At the same meeting instructions
were given for building a toll-house and gate at the Forest
end of Duck Lane.   At the September meeting there had
been made a proposal to remove the Duck Lane Gate; but
the further consideration of the matter was postponed until the
next meeting.   It seems as if the removal of the Duck Lane
Gate to the Forest end of the Lane was the change contemplated, but no mention was made at the time of the
proposed site.   The plan of erecting a new toll-house met
with the approval of the Trustees, and also the proposal to
remove the gates at Binck's Lane, and erect a new toll-

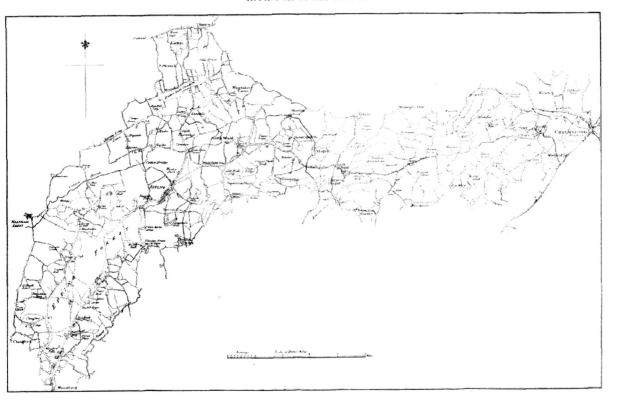

house and gates at Tyler's Green, on the same plan as the house at Nornton Heath.

A committee was appointed to select the most suitable place, &c. And, at the same time, notice was ordered to be given, agreeable to directions contained in the Turnpike Act, (3rd George IV, cap. 186), of the Trustees' intention to erect a toll-house and turnpike gate across the road at, or near, Tyler's Green, with a side gate, if necessary; and also a turnpike house and gate at the Forest end of Duck Lane, instead of the present gates in Binck's Lane, Thornwood Common side bar, and Duck Lane.

The committee which had been appointed to select a site for the new toll-house and gates, and to consider the effects of the proposed alteration, stated, at the meeting of the Trustees held February 24th, 1823, "That it would be necessary to have a plan made of the roads under the care of the Trust, with all the cross roads and lanes leading to and connected with the same."

The further consideration of building a toll-house and gate were consequently abandoned for the present, and instruction given to Mr. Powell to prepare the plans or map in accordance with the wishes of the committee. He attended the meeting May 12th, 1823, with the map, and said he had had 250 copies printed, for which, according to the bill produced, the charge was £11 16s. 6d.

The map, it is stated, was carefully examined by the Trustees present, who thereupon gave it as their opinion that it was unnecessary to erect a toll-house at Tyler's Green. A map, of which a copy is given, headed "Epping and Ongar Trust," is amongst the Trust papers, and is no doubt the one referred to as having been published for the use of the committee.

At the same meeting an order was issued that the Duck Lane and Thornwood Common side bars should be considered bye gates to the Epping turnpike road, and Epping and Ongar roads; also, that all persons passing through them should pay tolls.

Later on, however, notice having been given, as required by 3rd George IV, that at a meeting in October (1823) there would be taken into consideration the advisability of converting the Duck Lane Gate into a toll-gate and side gate, and taking such tolls as the Trustees should think proper; the subject was fully debated, when it was decided that the Duck Lane Gate should be converted into a toll-gate and side gate; and, that the same tolls should be taken there as at Thornwood and Epping Gates, but that they should not clear the Ongar Gates; that is to say, the tickets should not pass travellers through the Ongar Gates free of toll.

1824.—The Trustees ordered ground to be staked out, and converted into a garden for the toll-collector at Thornwood Gate.

One of the contractors for keeping in repair the Ongar Road, having informed the Trustees that the agent of the lord of the manor of Epping had given him notice not to remove the soil from the side of the road, a committee had been appointed to take the question into consideration, and to report to the meeting, to be held July, 1829, their opinion as to the contractor's right to do so. When, in consequence of the committee's report, the Trustees refused to admit the claim of the lord of the manor.

In spite of the care taken to prevent any pecuniary loss through carts, carriages, &c., being driven along bye-lanes, to avoid the turnpike gates and the payment of tolls, the means used appear not to have been efficient; for, October 5th, 1829, a post, rail, and a gate were ordered to be put up at the end of a green lane leading into Duck Lane.

Although no mention had been made in the Minutes of previous meetings of any question having arisen respecting the legal right of the Trustees to erect a toll-gate or bar at Duck Lane; from the two following Minutes it may be assumed that some member or members of the Trust or Highway Board had expressed an opinion that they were exceeding the powers conferred upon them either by the Local or General Turnpike Acts. At the meeting 14th April, 1834, the clerk was ordered to prepare a case to be "submitted to counsel, Mr. Thesenger, for an opinion, in order to determine the legality of fixing a side gate across a road leading to a turnpike road distant 500 yards from such road." At the same meeting the Trustees determined to take the management of the first three miles of the Ongar Road into their own hands, for the purpose of getting the road into sound and good order.

Mr. Thesenger's opinion is not recorded, but the following Minute made in June leaves no doubt of its having been in favour of the Trustees' legal power :—"A motion was moved by Mr. McNab and seconded by Charles Sotheby, Esq., that the Duck Lane gate be continued as heretofore, on the authority of the 22nd section of the local Turnpike Act."

The New Road from Woodford to the "Wake Arms," having shortened the distance between Ongar and London by about one mile, necessitated an alteration in the milestones, and gave rise to the following order in July, 1837 : That "the milestones on the Epping Road be painted and lettered and figured correctly, and that the milestones on the Ongar Road be so placed as to correspond with, and be a continuation of those on the Epping Road, so as to describe the correct distance or number of miles from London, and that they be lettered and figured accordingly."

3rd of January, 1831.—The clerk was ordered to give notice that the Trustees would at their next meeting be ready to receive tenders for repairing the Ongar Road, from the 1st of May following. And on April 11 it is entered: "Mr. Jonathan Lewis' tender for keeping in repair the last seven miles and three quarters of the Ongar Road from May 1st next for the term of seven years, provided the said road so long continues a turnpike road, at the sum of two hundred and twenty pounds per annum, on the same condition as his former contract ; and William Paine's tender for keeping in repair the first three miles of the Ongar Road with the brick arches thereon at fifty pounds per annum, were accepted."

Mr. McAdam, the surveyor, was instructed to procure

estimates for putting the drain and bridges, &c., in thorough repair, "after which they were to be kept in repair by Mr. Paine."

There is no further mention made of the Ongar Road until 1834.

February 10th.—Mr. Paine's contract would expire in May following, and the clerk was ordered, at the meeting of the Trustees on the date above-mentioned, to advertise for tenders to be produced at the next meeting, from persons willing to contract for the repair of the first three miles of the Ongar Road. But at the next meeting, April, 1834, there is no mention made of tenders having been received. And there is the following entry: "Resolved, that it is not expedient to relet the first three miles of the Ongar Road, but that the Trustees will keep the same in their own hands for the purpose of getting the same into sound and good condition." August, 1838, there is the following entry in the Minute Book: "Ordered that two hundred and fifty pounds be offered to Mr. Lewis for repairing the whole line of the Ongar Road for one year, and that the contract be entered into with him if he think fit to accept this offer."

At the next meeting the clerk reported that Mr. Lewis had accepted the contract offered, for the sum of £250, to keep the whole of the Ongar Road in repair. The contract made with him 1831 had expired, and this was a new contract for one year. But it must have been renewed each year, although no mention is made in the Minute Book of such renewal until the 15th November, 1841, when the entry is made: "It was resolved that the contract with Mr. Lewis to maintain the Ongar Road at £250 a year be continued until Michaelmas next, and that a fresh agreement be entered into accordingly." At the meeting in December, 1842, the contract was renewed for one year for £225. In February, 1843, Mr. Lewis, the contractor, was requested "not to cut down the sides of the road as complained of to the meeting, which is considered injurious to the road." January, 1844.—His contract for repairing the road was renewed for one year, and was evidently continued during the following three years. In December, 1847, there is the Minute: " Mr. Jonathan Lewis's contract for repairing the Ongar Road having expired, Sir James MacAdam was requested to repair the same road in the most convenient manner for the present, and until fresh arrangements can be made." In the following February (1848) notice was given that tenders would be received at the meeting 10th of March for keeping in repair the Ongar Road. The tender sent in was £100. This was much below the sum previously paid, and the Trustees were evidently doubtful of the contractor being able to carry out the contract to their satisfaction; for they reserved to themselves the right to terminate the contract at the end of six or nine months from the commencement. The contractor was not to be compelled to employ the number of men mentioned in the contract for one month of the hay-time and harvest.

He, however, evidently carried on the contract to the satisfaction of the Trustees; for four years after it is mentioned as having been renewed; and it was continued, by renewal, until March, 1854, when, it is stated, the Trustees proceeded to receive tenders for repairing the Ongar Road, and " Mr. Fairchild, the present contractor, having again tendered to repair the Ongar Road, from the commencement at Epping to the termination in Writtle, for the period of one year, from 25th March next, for one hundred and forty pounds, upon the terms contained in his present contract;" and the Trustees having received no lower tender, his was accepted. It was renewed in 1855, as there was no lower tender, and was by yearly renewals continued until 1863, without any complaint appearing on the Minutes. But at the meeting February, 1863, a memorial was received respecting the state of the Ongar Road. The Minute is as follows:—

" A memorial, very numerously signed by the most influential inhabitants resident in the Ongar division of the Trust, complaining of the nearly impassable, and in some places dangerous, state of the roads, and praying that the Trustees would take the matter into their serious consideration, with the view of remedying the evils complained of, was this day presented to the meeting."

The clerk had been instructed to call upon the surveyor to make a report; and as it confirmed the statement of the memorialists, it was decided that, after the expiration of the contract then running, it should not be renewed, but that the management of the division should be placed in the hands of the Trust surveyor, with power to widen where necessary, repair, and generally improve the roads.

February, 1864.—The committee, which had been appointed to superintend the improvements on the Ongar division of the Trust, submitted to the meeting a plan setting out certain alterations which the members deemed necessary, and which they were enabled to carry out through the liberality of Mr. Cure, who had presented the Trustees with the land necessary for the purpose, on the condition of their making good the fences, &c. The recommendation of the committee was adopted, and the surveyor was directed to forthwith carry out the proposed work. It was also proposed and carried that the surveyor should have his salary raised to one hundred pounds, as much more work had to be done by him.

At their meeting, July 7th, 1865, very important business came before the Trustees; the meeting had been summoned by advertisements, for the purpose of "determining whether all, or any, and which, of the several toll gates and side bars now placed on or by the sides of the said turnpike roads, should be removed and placed elsewhere, or discontinued, and whether any toll gate and side bars should be erected on or by the side of the said road, and in what situations the same shall be placed. The question was fully discussed, when it was moved, "that in consequence of the difficulties arising in the collection of the tolls at the Duck Lane side gates, situated in the parish of North Weald Bassett, it is expedient that such gates be abolished at the expiration of the present agreement, the gates and bars removed, and the materials of the toll house sold or otherwise disposed of;" this motion, on being seconded and put to the meeting by the Chairman, was unanimously carried. It was then moved and seconded, and carried unanimously, "that the materials forming the toll house and premises (exclusive of the gates, bars, and posts) be offered to the lord of the manor and owner of the soil for £25, that being the computed value of such material, if severed." But at the meeting, September, 1865, it is stated that the question disposing of the site of the Duck Lane toll-house was discussed, when it was resolved that the toll-house should be pulled down at the expiration of the existing lease, and the material sold, and that the site of the building be offered to the owner of the adjoining land, at the price at which it may be valued by a competent surveyor.

It may here be pointed out that the Duck Lane gate was placed in a very unsuitable position. The road was at times rendered impassable by the overflowing of the watercourse which runs parallel with that portion leading from Thornwood Common. A bed of withies at present shows that there is occasionally a supply of water sufficient to flood the piece of land between it and the watercourse, and form an osier bed.

The liability to floods gave rise to the following Minute: 29th September, 1851. — "A letter was received from the surveyor of North Weald Bassett, dated 20th inst., stating that it was the desire of the parishioners of that parish to construct an arched brick drain over the road, in front of the toll-house situate at Duck Lane, by which means the incessant flooding of the road in the front of the toll house would be prevented and the road rendered passable during the winter season. And further stating, that as such alteration would be a mutual benefit and improvement both to the Trust and parish roads, they solicited the sum of six pounds towards the expense of making the same, the total estimated cost being twelve pounds. The surveyor to the Trust reported that he had examined the spot; and his having expressed an opinion that the alteration proposed would be advantageous to the Trust, it was agreed that the sum asked for should be contributed."

The July discussion was continued, and the question mooted was the advisability of placing a bar or chain on the

south side of Thornwood Common turnpike gate, across a
parish road or highway there, leading from and out of the turnpike road by the "Blacksmiths' Arms," to and into the parish
of North Weald Bassett, and also a bar or chain on the north
side of Thornwood gate across a parish road or highway
leading from and out of such turnpike road by the side of the
brook or watercourse to or into Duck Lane, in North Weald
Bassett. It was also ordered that the same tolls should be
taken at the bars or chains as are now taken at the Thornwood
gate, and that the ticket given at the one should clear the
others. It was moreover provided that the inhabitants and
bonâ fide occupiers of land in North Weald Bassett should be
exempted from the payment of tolls at either of the said side
bars or chains, on paying the lessee for the time being, annually,
the sum of 10s., by way of composition in lieu of the tolls, but
at the next meeting it was moved that the composition be
reduced to 5s. per annum.

February, 1866.—Measures were taken for carrying out
the resolution of September in last year. Mr. George Hine,
land surveyor, Epping, was instructed to value the disused
toll-house and buildings and land at Duck Lane, distinguishing
the value of the land from that of the building materials;
and at the same time it was ordered that both be offered to
Mr. Matthews, the owner of the adjoining property; and that
if he declined purchasing, the materials were to be offered
at public auction, and the land sold subsequently in the same
manner. The surveyor was ordered to provide sufficient road
sand to make a footpath on the Ongar Road from its commencement to the end of the new house built by the side of
it on the "Plain."

CHAPTER VIII.

Continuation of the Proceedings of the Trustees.

ั 1790 the roads in the vicinity of the town again came
nder the notice of the Trustees. In January the surveyor,
Ir. Powers, was ordered to bring in an estimate of the cost of
utting the road across the " Plain " in a proper state of repair,
d in August Mr. Conyers complained, on behalf of the
habitants of Epping, of the turnpike road leading into the
wn being so narrow—in some parts not more than 28 feet
ide ; when it was ordered that it should be widened under his
rections. This was done by filling up a ditch at a cost of
irty-five pounds. But the work was improperly finished ; for
June, 1792, Mr. Doubleday reported that the road at
pping Place, being improperly sloped down, had been the
casion of several accidents, carts, &c., having been over-
rned ; also that a boy had lost his life through the upsetting
the cart in which he was riding. In consequence of these
cidents, and with the desire of preventing their recurrence,
re had been made an outlay of fifteen guineas without having
st obtained the consent of the Trustees to the expenditure.
was explained that Mr. Conyers and Mr. Abdy, two of the
ustees, on hearing of the accident which occasioned the death
the boy, had at once taken steps, by contracting with
r. Parker, to have the road put in a safe condition, suitable
the traffic passing over it. The claim was duly admitted,
d the amount ordered to be paid.

The duties of the Trustees comprised much more than
iking and keeping in repair the roads put under their control.

M

In order to secure men of position in the county, there is the following clause in the Act George II, 8th ch. :—" And whereas great mischief hath arisen from mean persons acting as trustees in execution of such Acts of Parliament made for repairing publick roads, in that part of Great Britain called England, as do not direct and require that the trustees thereby appointed shall be qualified to act as such, by the possession of real or personal estate to a certain value ; be it therefore enacted by the authority aforesaid, that from and after the said fourth day of June, no person shall be qualified or capable of acting as a trustee in the execution of any such Act as aforesaid, unless he shall, in his own right, or the right of his wife, be in the actual possession or receipt of the rents and profits of lands, tenements, or hereditaments of the clear yearly value of £40 ; or possessed of, or entitled to, personal estate alone, or real and personal estate together, to the value of £800 ; or shall be heir apparent of a person possessed of estate in land of the clear yearly value of £80 ; and unless he shall (not being such heir apparent as aforesaid), before he acts as such trustee, take and subscribe the oath as following before any two or more of the trustees appointed or to be appointed by or in pursuance of such Act, who are hereby authorized and required to administer the same in the words or to the effect following, that is to say :—

" ' I, A. B., do swear that I truly and *bonâ fide* am in my own right, or in the right of my wife, in the actual possession and enjoyment or receipt of the rents and profits of lands, tenements, or hereditaments, of the clear yearly value of forty pounds, or possessed of or entitled to a personal estate alone, or real and personal together, to the value of eight hundred pounds. So help me God.' "

The Trustees had control over all matters relating to the turnpike road. They appointed the surveyor, who had previously been chosen by the Justices of the Peace at Quarter Sessions, and they were empowered to prosecute any one transgressing against either of the clauses of the " Highway Acts."

The using narrow wheels had been considered to be

injurious to roads (George II, 30), and to be a practice which required careful watching. In subsequent Acts the wish to put a stop to their use is very evident.

It being reported at the meeting in December, 1798, that an inhabitant of Chelmsford had, contrary to the 13 George III, drawn his waggon with two horses abreast on the Ongar turnpike road, notice was sent to him that his conduct in so doing was an infringement of the Act. He appears, however, to have paid no attention to the warning, for at a meeting of the Trustees in September, 1799, his persisting in harnessing his horses two abreast was again brought before them, when he was informed that he would be indicted at the next Quarter Sessions for his offence.

March, 1801, found him to be still persisting in the objectionable mode of harnessing his horses, for there is an entry in the Minute Book—"The owners of the waggon from Chelmsford, which travelled from Chelmsford through the Ongar gate, having done great damage to the turnpike road by drawing with horses abreast, and thereby destroying the horse path; and, notwithstanding they had been twice written to on the subject, they persisted in so doing, the clerk had orders to prepare a bill of indictment against them, to be preferred at the next Quarter Sessions." In April the following year, 1802, it is stated "The owners of the waggon with narrow wheels drawn by two horses abreast on the turnpike road having been indicted, and pleaded guilty, and were fined five shillings on their promising not to offend again, being reported as continuing to harness the horses two abreast, contrary to law, it was ordered that if they repeated the offence they would be again prosecuted."

The owners of the waggons had apparently used the road from Chelmsford to Ongar for several years, before it had been made into a turnpike road, and probably felt aggrieved when they found that changes had to be made, for which they did not see the necessity, and so offered the resistance to the alteration in the manner of harnessing their horses, which brought the firm of carriers before the magistrates at Quarter

Sessions. It may be supposed that the defendants, when pleading guilty, gave plausible reasons for their conduct, as the magistrates inflicted so small a fine. The objection to two horses travelling abreast in narrow wheel carts or waggons is not very clear. It may, however, have been observed that two horses abreast, travelling in the same line with the wheels, wore the roads away much more at the sides than in the middle, and that by putting the horses one in front of the other they were maintained in a better and more uniform condition.

The construction of the wheels of carts, waggons, &c., using the Epping and Ongar turnpike roads evidently had the careful supervision of the Trustees; for in the winter of 1800, complaints having been made of the injury done to the roads by the wheels in use, the surveyor was ordered to give his attention to them.

At the next meeting, February, 1801, he reported that he had measured the broad wheels of the waggons belonging to several persons travelling on the road, and he found some of them to have the middle tire higher than the Act allowed— more than one inch from a flat surface; and on expressing a wish to examine the tires in a more particular manner, he was ordered to do so, and to bring in a report at the next meeting; he was also instructed to have the waggons he found in default charged with the same toll as that charged for narrow-wheel waggons.

The Trustees showed great liberality in numerous instances by making a grant of money to those servants who had had extra work put upon them, or those who had shown great diligence in the performance of their duties. In 1798 a gratuity of ten guineas was given to John South, the surveyor, and to Clark, the toll collector, for having given satisfaction. Similar liberality appears to have been frequent, as pecuniary grants are often mentioned in the Minute Book. On application by the collector at the Ongar gate, one shilling and sixpence per week was allowed him for oil, candles, and firing.

The first collector appointed at the Ongar gate was paid seven shillings per week. He, however, obtained employment in London as clerk a few months after his appointment, and resigned the situation. A labourer succeeded him, having offered to collect the tolls and work on the roads for nine shillings a week, assisted by his wife, who was to take the tolls whilst he was at work on the road. The arrangement appears to have been satisfactory, for the collector at the Root gate was appointed on similar terms; but if they worked to the satisfaction of the Trustees they were to be paid ten shillings and sixpence per week. At the meeting of the Trustees in January, 1700, the order was made that they should be paid one shilling and sixpence per week from the time they were first employed by the Trustees, "as it appears they have now worked on the road, as well as collected the tolls;" and the allowance was again made at the September meeting, and repeated at subsequent meetings.

The Trustees having the power to put a stop to nuisances affecting the high roads, "the surveyor was instructed to give notice to persons who permitted hogs to run loose on the turnpike roads, and damage them, that they would be prosecuted." At the same meeting directions were given for painted boards to be put up at the two Forest gates, offering one pound reward "to such person as shall give information of any person that shall be convicted of carrying away posts or rails belonging to the turnpike road." The depredations must have been frequent to render such a notice desirable. One hundred years ago there were no railroads to distribute a supply of coal over the country, and the carriage by road must have raised the price beyond the labourer's means. The bringing woods, and waste lands into cultivation, must have made wood for fuel only procurable by purchase; and turf also, which at one time was available for firing, and a means of adding to the winter store, could not have been easily obtainable. It is not, therefore, surprising if posts and rails, on an unprotected highway, became as tempting as hares and rabbits to the father of a family almost perishing from cold and hunger. There is no entry of the reward having been paid, so it may be concluded that the guilty parties were not discovered, or supposed that the magistrates had pity on the culprit, and taking the circumstances into consideration, dismissed him with a caution.

The practice of compounding for tolls at the turnpike gates on the Epping road had been carried on for 20 years.

In 1781 there were 45 compounders
In 1782   ,,   48   ,,
In 1783   ,,   45   ,,

—the lowest composition being fixed at 5s. 3d., except for the two surgeons, John Harrison and Edward Griffin.

The amount paid in 1784 is not mentioned, but in 1785 the composition money to be paid by the two surgeons was raised to 5s. 3d. each.

In July, 1789, there is the following minute :—" And the Trustees, being of opinion that it will be very beneficial to the Trust not to permit any person to compound for their tolls in future," and notice of their decision having been inserted in the Chelmsford paper, there is no list of compounders in that year. But there is, the next year, a minute, entered March, 1790 :—" Ordered, that at the next meeting the notice of — Conyers, Esq., for applying to the Trustees to revoke the order that restrained him from compounding for his tolls, be taken into consideration, and that the clerk do cause proper notice to be placed on all the gates accordingly."

At the meeting in May, there not being an account produced of Mr. Conyers' tolls, the further consideration of that business was postponed.

August, 1790.—The decision of July in the previous year was revoked, and it was ordered—" That such persons as chose to compound for their tolls may be permitted so to do on paying double what they formerly did."

The following entry in the Minute Book gives the names of those who compounded, and the amounts they paid :—

List of Compounders on the Epping Turnpike Road.

	£	s.	d.
Burrell, James	0	10	6
Burrow, John	1	1	0
Binches, Hannah	0	10	6
Conyers, Rev. Mr.	1	1	0
Conyers, John, Esq.	2	2	0
Cowlin, Williams, Esq.	2	2	0
Chaplin, Henry, Jun.	0	10	6
Doubleday, Joseph	0	10	6
Finchlin, Ben	0	10	6
Hatchway, Jun.	1	1	0
Healy, Sam. Esq.	0	10	6
Lambert, Simon	0	10	6
Parrish	0	10	6
Parker, Thomas	1	1	0
Walkley, John	0	10	6
Hewart, Charles	0	10	6
	£13	13	0

List of Compounders on the Ongar Road.

	£	s.	d.
Burrow, John	1	1	0
Clarence, Edward	2	2	0
Elsom, John	1	1	0
Lewis, Jonathan	2	2	0
Miller, Thomas	1	1	0
Stokes, Jonathan	1	1	0
Walker, Thomas	0	10	6
	£8	18	6

At the meeting held on the 20th of December, 1790, Mr. Conyers reported that " he had made a contract for the cartage of gravel with William Welch, of Epping, to provide and lay on the turnpike road stones from Four Want Way, leading from Thoydon to Waltham, to the lower turnpike, at two shillings and sixpence per load gauged : and from thence to Potters Street, at three shillings per gauged load. And he hath also agreed with Joseph Adams, of Loughton, for to do the like from the said Four Want Way, from the end of the turnpike road next to Woodford, at three and sixpence per load, and they are to furnish carts made exactly to hold a gauged load."

The Epping Highway Trust had been in existence twenty-four years, during which time the Trustees had appointed the toll collectors at the different gates, and had had the money collected paid to their treasurer at stated times ; but each payment was small in amount, and the money they had at their disposal uncertain, so rendering it difficult for the Trustees, whose views were progressive, to have their plans accepted by their more cautious fellow Trustees. A stated annual sum would remove any uncertainty as to the amount of money at their disposal. They had the power of borrowing money on the security of the tolls, of which they appeared to have availed themselves to a large amount. The gentlemen in the neighbourhood lent the money very freely at $4\frac{1}{2}$ or 5 per cent. per annum, as the interest was a first charge on the amount of tolls taken at the various gates. The security was, no doubt, very good, but the uncertainty as to the amount of the balance, or the sum at the disposal of the Trustees for maintaining the highways and making alterations where necessary in the levels, or breadth, or direction of the roads under their care, must have often given rise to disagreement at the meetings. There is not, however, mention made in the Minute Book of there having been any difference of opinion amongst the Trustees, as the result of a deliberation only is recorded. They, however, January 28th, 1793, contemplated making an important change in the manage-ment of the tolls ; for they appointed a committee, consisting of

Trustees, ordinary trustees in the commission of the peace, commissioners of land tax, and the mortgagees of the tolls, to consider "how far it will be for the interest of the trust to let the tolls by auction," and to report at the next meeting.

There not being, in April, sufficient number of Trustees present to compose a meeting, the report was not received until May. It was in favour of leasing the tolls, and letting them at auction to the highest bidder. The clerk was, therefore, ordered to give the required legal notice, by advertising in the Chelmsford paper, of the Trustees' intention to lease the tolls for three years, at an annual rental; and in the following August they were let to Mr. Joseph Usherwood for the yearly sum of £1,140, in four quarterly payments. There was to be made a deposit, so as to secure the first quarter's payment, and securities offered and approved of, before the contract was signed by a committee appointed for that purpose. It was ordered that notice be given to the toll collectors to leave the service of the Trustees at the end of September, when Mr. Usherwood's lease would commence, and to give up possession of the turnpike gates to him.

At the meeting in September, when Mr Usherwood should have been prepared to accept the lease and sign the counterpart, he attended without his sureties, and requested that the lease might be for one year only. The lease had been drawn, and the Trustees appear to have declined making any alteration, for they tendered it for his acceptance and finally left it with the clerk to be handed to Mr. Usherwood on his complying with the terms on which it was to be granted.

It may be assumed that the business was concluded to the satisfaction of the Trustees, but there was no further mention made of any matter relating to it until the meeting, July, 1794, when "Mr. Usherwood, the lessee, by Mr. Clark, the collector of the tolls, applied to be released from this contract, alleging that it would be his ruin if the Trustees insisted on his abiding by the same; whereupon Mr. Clark was desired to state what the Epping turnpike gate had produced for the last three-quarters of the year, and what the Ongar gate had produced for

the same time." For answer he stated that from Michaelmas
to Midsummer last the Epping turnpike gate had produced
only five hundred and seventy-nine pounds seven shillings, and
the Ongar gate ninety-four pounds ten shillings and ninepence.

The matter having been fully discussed, it is stated that
"it appearing to the Trustees *_to be improper for a publick trust
to profit by the ruin of an individual_, it was resolved that the
benefit of the clause in the Act 9th George III, which gives the
Trustees a power of revoking former contracts, be taken ; and
that at the next meeting of the Trustees it be taken into consideration whether the order made in August last for leasing
the tolls for three years should not be revoked, as the lessee is
desirous of it, and to be released from his contract." In the
following August it was agreed that Mr. Usherwood should be
released from his contract at Michaelmas, one year having then
expired.

The amount of tolls taken at the turnpike gates having
been brought under the notice of the meeting by Mr. Clark's
statement, the Trustees, who had to pay interest on borrowed
money, and also to keep the highway in good condition, thought
that some measure should be taken for increasing the sum
received from the tolls. The advantages the traffic between
Woodford and Loughton obtained from the road, which had
previously run in front of the "Roebuck," being made straight,
and from the steepness of the incline having been considerably
reduced, by cutting through the top of the hill and filling up
the bottom, probably led to the proposal by one of the members
that a turnpike should be erected near to Woodford. But
another member of the Trust having expressed the opinion that
the Trustees had no legal powers, by which they were enabled
to carry out the proposal, a committee was appointed to draw
up a case for the opinion of counsel, to be submitted to the

---

* The words are not underlined in the Minute Book, but the expression of
such an honourable feeling deserves especial notice, as it is characteristic of the
highmindedness which prevailed among the country gentry at the end of the
last century.

consideration of those members of the Trust who chose to attend.

The opinion of counsel was produced at the meeting in August, 1794. It said the Trustees had full power to erect a turnpike gate near to Woodford, or any other place on the old road except between the two Epping turnpikes—namely, between Epping and Thornwood Common gates.

In consequence of counsel's opinion, it was ordered that an advertisement should be put in the Chelmsford paper for an estimate (tender) for erecting a turnpike gate, &c., and the surveyor was directed to ascertain if there was any house in a suitable position which could be used for a toll house.

In this he appears to have been unsuccessful, for at the meeting, 15th August, 1794, held at the "Roebuck," Buckhurst Hill, the Trustees decided that the spot near a cottage beyond the "Baldfaced Stag" to an "oak spear" on the opposite side of the road, would be suitable for the erection of the new turnpike gate, the tender for which was £188 3s. 7d. "But a memorial being presented by several of the inhabitants of Woodford and other parishes against the resolution for erecting a gate between Woodford and the 'Baldfaced Stag,'" it was ordered that an advertisement be inserted in the Chelmsford paper, stating that the memorial would be taken into consideration at the next meeting.

The meeting was held 20th September, 1794, and the memorial from the inhabitants of Woodford, &c., having been read, and also the opinion of counsel as to the powers conferred by the Acts of Parliament on the Trustees, Mr. Hamilton moved that "The resolutions and order made at the meeting, 1st of August last, for erecting a turnpike, &c. near to Woodford, be rescinded," which motion was lost. Mr. Allen then moved that the order for erecting the turnpike should be immediately acted upon. This motion was carried by a majority of thirty, with only four dissentient votes. It was, however, moved by Mr. Conyers that the surveyor should be directed to put up a temporary fence and toll house at as little expense as possible, and postpone the erection of a more permanent building, until he received instructions to do so from the Trustees. For the purpose of carrying out the above resolution, a Committee was appointed ; they purchased of John Freshwater a structure for £16 5s. 6d., which would answer the purpose, and had it set up near to the "Baldfaced Stag" as a temporary toll house. A collector of tolls was duly appointed, and began his collection at midnight on September 30th. During the first twelve days he received at the rate of 20s. per day, which was duly reported to the Trustees, who were satisfied, and ordered the tolls to be taken until further orders to the contrary.

There seems to have been some desire to divide the Trust, as the clerk had orders given him at the meeting, 1794, to oppose the division. The tolls at the turnpike gate recently erected near the "Baldfaced Stag," were not to be collected when fairs were held in the town or parish of Epping, Latton, Harlow, and Sawbridgeworth, at which times the Epping and Sawbridge gates were always left open. On January 23rd, 1795, the compounding for tolls occupied the attention of the Trustees, and it was agreed that the inhabitants living within the parishes of Chigwell, Loughton, and Waltham Holy Cross, be permitted to compound by the year for their tolls at the "Woodford" or "Baldfaced Stag" turnpike gate, in case they chose to do so. But at the meeting in March it was suggested that a less sum than 20s. might be taken ; and in April following the composition was fixed as follows :—"A person keeping a four-wheeled carriage could not compound for less than one guinea, and for a carriage with two wheels, both vehicles paying Government duty, not less than ten and sixpence, and a person keeping a horse or saddle-horse, five shillings, the money to be paid to the collector." But the composition did not exempt persons having carts or waggons with wheels or fellies having less breadth than six inches from paying the tolls. The toll gate by the "Baldfaced Stag" must have been a source of vexation to many of those who had to pass through it ; on February, 1796, there is the following entry in the Minute Book :—"The Trustees, taking into consideration the trouble and pain Mr. Thomas Clark, the collector of the tolls, had at all times taken to secure the tolls at the new gate near the "Baldfaced Stag," and the insults he had received (words obliterated), and has at all times been abused for doing his duty, do, as a reward for his faithful services, order that a gratuity of five guineas be paid to him by the treasurer." The donation was, no doubt, very acceptable, and acted as balm to his wounded feelings.

It can easily be imagined that toll keepers had occasionally to put up with improper behaviour from travellers ; for turn-pikes were always vexatious obstructions to the traffic on the road, more especially so in bad weather, when the horseman, or the occupant of a vehicle, had to unbutton his coat, take off his glove, and with wet and benumbed hand seek in his pocket for the money with which to pay the toll, and wait, trying to keep a restive horse quiet, whilst the collector went into the toll house for the change and ticket. The ticket was a flimsy piece of paper about 1½ inch square, with a letter or number on it, and, being the receipt for the toll, had to be preserved : for the collector could demand its production on the return journey, or repayment of the toll. A collector could be very disagreeable, within the limits of his duties ; he might compel the production of the ticket although he knew the person had passed through the turnpike the same day—so that a traveller, however inclement the weather, in rain or snow, with driving wind, had to find the ticket. If he had put it into his waistcoat pocket for safety, his wraps had to be displaced ; and when he had found it, and the collector, having ascertained it had not been lost, returned to his toll house and warm fire—it is no wonder if, at times, he was followed by harsh words from a traveller, rendered cold and uncomfortable through what seemed to him to be, on the part of the toll collector, an unnecessarily strict attention to his duties.

Although no mention is made of the appointment of toll keepers ; a reward of five guineas for his "extraordinary care and trouble" having been paid to one of them, it is evident that the Trustees had resumed the management of the tolls, and the collectors.   They continued to do so until 1801, when in July it was proposed that the tolls taken at the three gates, from the north part of Harlow Bush Common to Woodford, including the Buckhurst Hill gate, should be let for three years by auction to the highest bidder, subject to the right of the compounders to pass through the gates free.   The amount of the compositions was stated to be thirty-six pounds fifteen shillings.

The intention of the Trustees having been advertised, as required by the Act of Parliament, in the Chelmsford paper, and in the " Morning Herald " and the " Chronicle," they met, as arranged, at Epping Place on the 21st of September.   The minute of the meeting begins thus :—" Whereas, in pursuance of the order made at the last meeting of the Trustees for letting the tolls at the three gates on the Epping Turnpike road, notice has been given that the same would be let to the best bidder, this day, from Michaelmas Day next, for three years, subject to the lessee permitting the present compounders to continue to compound for their tolls on the payment of the same compositions as are now paid by them, according to the list now produced."—It was agreed that Thornwood Common bye gate should be let with the others.

The highest bidder was to be the purchaser, on his producing sufficient security for the payment quarterly of the money due.

The tolls were put up at eight hundred and thirty-two pounds.   There were four competitors, who made twenty-four bids.   The lowest bid was £832, and the highest £1,055. " And the glass having been turned three times and no person advancing, Mr. Billbeam, together with Mr. Usherwood, were declared the highest bidders at the sum of £1,055."

A committee, as usual, was appointed to complete the transactions and sign the lease, but in consequence of Messrs. Billbeam and Usherwood, who had been bidding against each other, coming forward to lease the tolls conjointly, the Trustees had suspicion of there having been underhand proceedings which prevented their getting the full value of the tolls, and on a requisition being signed by five of the members of the Trust, a meeting was convened in September, 1801, "to consider how far the contract made at the last meeting is binding on the Trustees." There were present ten Trustees, and they came to the conclusion, from the information they had received, that there had been collusion between those who were bidding for the tolls, and that they were not, therefore, bound to carry out the agreement with Messrs. Billbeam and Usherwood.

A letter had been received from Messrs. Billbeam and Usherwood, as follows :—

"We understand that insinuations have been flung out against our character, as having been concerned with Mr. Handly in preventing the tolls of the Epping gates being fairly let by auction last Monday. To convince you of the contrary, we beg to request that the tolls may again be put up to the best bidder, unless you choose to accept £1,100 a year for them, which we understand Mr. Everitt meant to give; and which we know to be as much or more than they are worth."

(Signed)   "EDWARD BILLBEAM.
"WILLIAM USHERWOOD."

It was admitted by Mr. Usherwood and Mr. Carter, Mr. Billbeam's agent, both of whom were present, that there was a private agreement between themselves by which the tolls did not fetch so much as the parties would otherwise have given,* but that no person would have given more than £1,200 per annum ; they now offered to enlarge the term of their agreement and pay a rental of £1,201 a year for the three years, instead of the sum of £1,055, at which they were declared to be the highest bidders.

"It appearing to the Trustees that the sum was beyond what either of the other parties had offered, it was ordered and

---

* The admission has an interest, as it shows that the system known as a "knock out" was in existence at the time, and not unusual, for it is not likely the Trustees would have had further dealing with them if they had considered their conduct actually fraudulent.

agreed that the contract should be carried out in accordance with their offer."

The lease of tolls granted to Messrs. Billbeam and Usherwood did not include the Ongar gates and side bars or gates belonging to it. At the meeting on the 15th March, 1802, it was proposed to let them by auction. The further consideration of the proposal was, however, postponed to the next meeting, which was held on July 5th, when it was decided that it would not be advisable to let them. At this meeting the amount of tolls collected at the Ongar gates from April 4th to June 17th was produced. It amounted to £29 7s., from which had to be deducted the toll collector's salary of five guineas. The average takings as above was a little under £150 per annum, but the balance of receipts from December 12th, 1782, to June 26th, 1783, handed to the treasurer was only £51 13s.

Until the 25th of April, 1803, the practice had been to open both the Epping and Thornwood Common gates when fairs were being held at either Epping, Latton, Harlow, or Sawbridgeworth; but the custom was ordered by the Trustees attending this meeting to be discontinued. The minute is as follows :—" Mr. Billbeam, the lessee of the tolls, this day applying to the Trustess, and requesting that when the fairs are held in the town and parishes of Epping, Latton, and Harlow, in the county of Essex, and Sawbridgeworth, in the county of Hertford, both the Epping turnpike gates may be shut and tolls collected at both the said turnpikes, it was ordered that the gates be shut at those times and tolls collected accordingly at both the said gates."

The toll collectors at gates being employed by the contractors, were not under the control of the Trustees; but as a complaint was laid before them at a meeting on the 25th June, 1804, by John Horsley, Esq., who complained of having been insulted by Thomas Brett, the collector of tolls, at the " Bald-faced Stag " turnpike, as he passed through the gate on the 22nd of May, the Trustees took some action in the matter, for they ordered the clerk to write [*the rest is so obliterated by time as to render it impossible to make out what further instructions were given to him*]. At the next meeting, the collector having attended and made such an apology for his conduct as satisfied John Horsley, Esq., the matter thus terminated.

The three years' lease of the tolls expiring Michaelmas, 1804, orders were given to the clerk to advertise the Trustees' intention of again letting them. A difficulty appears, however, to have arisen as to the right of the collector to take tolls at two gates when a person had changed horses between them; for it was ordered that the question should be submitted to counsel for his opinion. Counsel's opinion is not entered on the Minute Book.

In accordance with the advertisement the tolls were put up to auction in the following September, when those taken at the gates on the Epping high road were let to Mr. Billbeam for £1,010, and those taken between Epping and Ongar for £165 per annum.

At the expiration of the three years' lease, the tolls had increased considerably in value. The Epping gates yielding £1,335, and the Ongar gates £228.

The tolls of the road from Woodford to Harlow Bush Common, which had been put up to auction in August at £1,335, and the Ongar at £228 per annum, without finding a bidder, were again put up September 29th, when they were leased for three years at a rental for the Harlow and Woodford gates, £1,465, and Ongar £280. The Trustees very liberally ordered that six guineas should be paid by the treasurer towards the expenses of those who attended and bid at the letting of the tolls. A committee was appointed to meet at the "Black Lion," Epping, on the 30th inst., at 11 o'clock in the forenoon, to sign the lease.

A difficulty arose soon after the commencement of the tenancy with the compounders. In December the toll keepers were brought before the Trustees and reprimanded for demanding toll from the compounders. The first meeting in January, 1809, was a special meeting for the consideration of the tolls and to decide whether the lessee might take double

N

tolls from narrow-wheel waggons. The Act 7 George III was read and fully discussed (the minute is nearly obliterated), but the decision arrived at was to take the opinion of counsel; and at the next meeting the opinion of counsel, Mr. Shephard, was read, according to which the lessee of the Ongar toll gate had a right to take double tolls on waggons, carts, &c., having wheels of less width than six inches. There is also a minute thus :—"Ordered that in future instead of the Trustees paying one shilling each, when they do not stay to dinner, for the use of the room, the clerk do pay Mrs. Stoakes (*sic*) at each meeting ten shillings, and charge it to his account."

The objectionable practice of harnessing horses two abreast, which had given rise to a prosecution at Quarter Sessions in 1801, was still persisted in, for at the meeting, October, 1809, the Trustee residing at Blake Hall complained that there were several waggon owners drawing with two horses abreast contrary to the Act. The surveyor, however, reported at the meeting, March, 1810, that he had not been able to find out the persons who had drawn carts on the turnpike road with narrow wheels and horses abreast.

As early as the year 1807 there was apparently some idea of obtaining a new Act of Parliament; for there is the following entry in the minute book : " The Clerk produced a letter from Thomas B. Bramston, Esq., in answer to that which he had written in pursuance of the order made at the last meeting (minute obliterated), wherein he says that before he can consult his neighbours in the parish of Writtle with respect to the extension of the proposed new Bill into that parish, he must be informed what is intended to be done with respect to any new gates. It was ordered that Charles Smith, Esq., Capel Cure, Esq., and others, be appointed a Committee to meet Mr. Bramston, and such of the inhabitants of Writtle as may be appointed by that parish, to confer together on the subject, *i.e.*, the extending the roads through that (words obliterated) parishes, or such of them as be eligible."

The result of the deliberation is not mentioned ; nor does the proposed Act again appear on the minutes until March,

1810. When, there having been some dispute at the Epping turnpike gate (the nature of which cannot be made out, as the minute is not legible), it proceeds to say: " But as no summary remedy is given by the Turnpike Acts, it was ordered that Mr. Jessop do prepare a clause, to be inserted in the Act at the time of the renewal thereof, to give the Magistrates a power in case any such offence should again be committed, to punish the collectors in a summary way ; and also a clause to punish persons travelling with horses abreast, with narrow wheels on the turnpike road."

May 28th, 1810.—The Clerk was ordered to give notice of the Trustees' intention to apply to Parliament for a renewal of the Turnpike Acts, and to produce a draft, at the next meeting, of such clauses as he thought should be added to prevent the nuisances which had been complained of : but neither clauses nor the nuisances are mentioned. In December the draft was submitted for the approval of the Trustees, when a Committee was appointed to examine it, and also a proposed alteration in the tolls to be demanded. In June Mr. South, the surveyor, was paid seven pounds, and the lessees of the tolls ten shillings and sixpence each, for their attendance at the House of Commons to give evidence on the Bill. In July the bill for passing the Act through Parliament was produced and ordered to be paid.

The Act 51 George III. chap. 29: date April 11th, 1811. It commences with a preamble, as usual, reciting the previous Acts of Parliament relating to the trust, and continues as follows :—

" Whereas the Trustees appointed to put the said Acts in execution have, in performing the Trusts thereby in them vested, borrowed a considerable sum of money on the credit of the tolls granted by the said Acts, which is still unpaid, and have applied the same, together with the tolls collected by virtue of the said Acts, in amending the roads in the said Acts mentioned ; and although great progress hath been made in repairing thereof, the same are not sufficiently amended, nor can the same be effectually repaired, and the money repaid, unless the term and powers granted by the said Acts be further continued, and the said Acts be made more effectual. May it therefore please your Majesty, that it be enacted, ' That the powers contained in the previous Acts be continued (except what are hereby altered or varied, and also except such as relate to exemption from stamp duties), shall be in full force and effect, and shall extend to the repairing and widening the said roads.' "

Five or more of the Trustees, who had been appointed by the Act, or any persons they might appoint, were to receive the tolls then payable until September the next, when the tolls as follows were to be demanded, unless the Trustees at any time thought proper to reduce the amounts :—

For every Chaise, Carravan or Calash, drawn by one Horse, Mare, Gelding, or Mule, Sixpence.

For every Coach, Chariot, Chaise, Berlin, Landau, Carravan, Calash, Hearse, and Pleasure Carriage, drawn by more than one Horse, Mare, Gelding, or Mule ; *videlicet,*

If by Two Horses, Mares, Geldings, or Mules, Eightpence.

If by Four Horses, Mares, Geldings, or Mules, One Shilling.

If by Six Horses, Mares, Geldings, or Mules, One Shilling and Sixpence.

For every Cart drawn by only One Horse, Mare, Gelding, Mule, or Ass, empty or laden, Sixpence.

And if drawn by more than One Horse, Mare, Gelding, Mule, or Ass, if abreaſt, One Shilling and Threepence.

Or if at length, One Shilling.

For every Dray drawn by One or more Horse, Mare, Gelding, or Mule, Eightpence.

For every Cart drawn by Three or more Horses, Mares, Geldings, Mules, or Asses, One Shilling.

For every Waggon or Wain, One Shilling and Sixpence.

For every Timber Carriage, drawn by more than Three Horses, Mares, Geldings, or Mules, Two Shillings and Sixpence. And if less, Two Shillings.

For every Horse, Mare, Gelding, Mule, or Ass, laden or unladen, and not drawing, One Penny Halfpenny.

For neat Cattle, by the Score, One Shilling and Sixpence; and so in proportion for a greater or less Number:

For Calves, Swine, Sheep or Lambs, by the Score, One Shilling; and so in proportion for any greater or less Number:

And for every Waggon, Wain, Cart or Carriage, having the Fellies of the Wheels thereof of less Breadth or Gauge than Six Inches from Side to Side, at the least, at the Bottom or Sole thereof, and for the Horses or Beasts of Draught drawing the same, double the Tolls or Duties which are above directed to be paid for the same respectively: which respective Sums of Money shall once a Day only be demanded and taken at such Gate or Gates, which are or may be erected on the Road called the *Epping* Turnpike Road, and the like Sum and Sums of Money at the Gate erected or to be erected on the *Ongar* Turnpike Road as aforesaid, in the Name of or as a Toll, and shall be vested in the said Trustees, and applied as hereinafter is directed; and such Tolls to be paid at the Gates now erected or to be erected on the Road called the *Ongar* Turnpike Road, shall not exempt any Person or Persons from Payment at the Gates erected or to be erected on the Road called the *Epping* Turnpike Road leading from *Woodford* to *Harlow*.

Then are mentioned the numerous exemptions, relating to waggons and carts loaded with agricultural produce "not sold or disposed of," or carrying manure, or gravel for mending the roads—which appear in previous Acts. It also states that no toll shall be demanded or taken from any inhabitant of a parish going to, or returning from, their place of worship, on any day on which divine service is ordered by authority to be celebrated, nor when attending the funeral of any person dying, and to be buried in either of the parishes through which the road passes. Nor from any clergyman going to, or from visiting a sick person; or to perform his parochial or ministerial duties on the day mentioned.

Clause 6 says—"And whereas great inconvenience has arisen for want of a discretionary power being vested in the said Trustees, occasionally to shut or open said gates :". It is enacted that the Trustees may, during the weeks when fairs are held at Epping, Latton, Harlow, or Sawbridgeworth, or either of them, or at any other time, cause both gates to be shut and tolls collected at both the turnpikes ; but no person having paid at one gate should be liable, on the production of his ticket, to pay at the other gate.

Clause 9 was intended to put a stop to a very objectionable practice :—"And whereas accidents happen to passengers and travellers by means of persons loading their carts and waggons with trusses of straw and hay across the same, so as to project over the fellies of the wheels of such carts and waggons in the narrow parts of the road, thereby forcing coaches, chaises, and such like carriages off the road ; and also great damage is done to the roads by waggons, carts, drays, with narrow wheels, drawn by more than two horses in pairs ; be it further enacted that waggons or carts drawn by more than two horses abreast, or loaded with hay, straw, or wood, projecting over the fellies of the wheels, to the annoyance of any one passing along the high road, the person so offending shall be liable to a penalty not exceeding five pound, at the discretion of the justices, before whom such offender shall be convicted." The fine was to go towards the repair of the roads, "and if any lessee of such tolls, or the person or persons appointed by him to collect the same, shall take a greater toll from any person than is authorised or directed by this Act, or shall give any false tickets, or by any ways or means attempt to take from any person or persons passing through the said gates any other or larger toll than is authorised by this and the said Acts, he or they shall, for every such offence, forfeit and pay a sum not exceeding five pounds, to be paid on conviction before any one of Her Majesty's justices of the said county."

The Act was to be in force for twenty-one years.

The tolls were leased for three years to the highest bidders, from Harlow Bush Common to Woodford, for £1,470, and from Epping to Writtle for £280. Very soon after (December, 1811) there was a dispute with the lessee, on account of his demanding double tolls on narrow wheel waggons, which was contrary to his agreement. On appearing before the Trustees to answer the complaint, he maintained that he had a right to do so; he was, however, given fourteen days in which to reconsider the question before they took further proceedings, and at a subsequent meeting he agreed to discontinue the practice.

In 1812 a special meeting was held in consequence of an Act passed through Parliament in July, through which the lessee lost some of the tolls; when it was the unanimous opinion of the Trustees present that he should have some reduction made in the rental. Notice was given of the Trustees' intention to put up a toll bar near to Weald Church, provided the lessee chose to pay the cost. Two carters were each fined fifteen shillings for evading the tolls at the Forest (" Baldfaced Stag ") Gate. Complaints had been made at a previous meeting of injury having been done to trees in Garnish Wood, through digging gravel for the roads. A Committee was appointed to assess the damage. The amount was forty shillings, and an order was given that it should be paid.

May 21, 1813.—Some objection, being reported by the surveyor, Mr. South, as being made by the owner of property from which he desired to remove gravel for the use of the road, an order was issued by the Trustees empowering him to do so, and to tender the owner the fair value of the gravel taken, and also to include the value of injury to his property, should there be any. At the same time the clerk was directed to write to the owner to "inform him that the Trustees felt themselves necessitated to make such an order, but flattered themselves he would not oblige them to enforce the same." At the next meeting Mr. South reported he had taken what stones he required by the permission of the owner

No further business of importance came before the Trustees until August 15th, 1814, when the tolls were again put up to auction. The amount offered and accepted cannot be stated, as a large portion of the leaf in the Minute Book on which they

were written has perished.   There remains, however, the entry
that £10 should be given for a dinner for those who came to
bid for the lease of the tolls.

In October following the late lessee of the Ongar Gate,
stating that he had lost £40 by his contract, the Trustees
thought some compensation should be made to him; and on
his mentioning that he should be satisfied with one month's rent,
£23 6s. 8d., the treasurer was ordered to pay him that sum.

July, 1815.—The lessees of the tolls applied to have their
lease cancelled, saying that otherwise they should be ruined.
They seem to have been behindhand with the rent, for the clerk
was directed to write to their securities, stating that unless the
amount due was paid proceedings would be taken against them.

The lessees again came before the Trustees at the meeting
in January, 1816, when it was mentioned by them that they had
lost £192 13s.   A suggestion was therefore made that the tolls
should be increased.

The clerk was directed to give notice of the Trustees'
intention to consider the question at the next meeting, when it
was agreed that the tolls should be as follows :—

	s.	d.
" If drawn by more than two horses	1	0
For every waggon or wain drawn by six horses or less	1	6
For every waggon or wain drawn by more than six horses	2	0
Every limber carriage drawn by three or more horses or mules	2	0
and if with less	1	6
For every mare, gelding, mule, horse, or ass not drawing	0	1
For neat cattle by the score	0	10
For calves, swine, sheep, or lambs by the score	0	5

"And for every waggon, wain, cart, or carriage, except carts
drawn by one horse only, having the fellies of the wheels

thereof of less breadth or gauge than six inches from side to side at the least at the bottom, and for the horse or beast of draught drawing the same, double the tolls, which are above decided to be paid for the same, shall be charged."

March 28, 1816.—The lessee brought in a list of tolls, which he submitted to the Trustees as being capable of increase without being oppressive; but as no calculation was supplied, and there being but few Trustees present at the meeting, the further consideration of his suggestion was postponed.

May 16, 1816.—It is stated the lessee attended on that day, to renew his application for an increase of the tolls; but as it appeared that, notwithstanding what had taken place at the last meeting, he had been taking more tolls on coaches, post chaises, &c., than he was entitled to, whereby he had been guilty of gross imposition, the clerk was ordered to take proceedings against him without delay for breach of covenant, "and that an advertisement be inserted in the 'Morning Post,' 'Morning Herald,' 'Morning Chronicle,' and the county paper as under, viz. :—

"EPPING TURNPIKE.—The Trustees of these roads hereby give notice that they have taken every method in their power to prevent the exactions of double tolls at the three toll gates on their road, and actions have been taken against the lessees of the tolls for taking more tolls than they were authorised to do by their lease, as well as informations laid against the collector. Therefore, persons who have, or shall, be imposed upon by the collector, exacting from them double tolls, are requested to give notice thereof and the particulars of such double tolls as have been paid by them, to Mr. Jessop, clerk to the Trustees, at his office at Waltham Abbey or Clifford's Inn."

June 11, 1818.—The opinion of Mr. Marryat was read; and it appearing that the lessees had continued to take larger tolls than were let to them, it was ordered the action should proceed; but the Trustees were of the opinion that if the lessees would comply with the following the proceedings might be suspended.

Owing to the condition of the Minute Book the terms cannot clearly be made out; but there was to be some compensation made for breach of contract, and the lessee was to put an advertisement in the papers above mentioned, acknowledging his error,—the form of advertisement, and the day of its insertion, to be settled by the Chairman.

The question as to whether his lease should be cancelled, and also the consideration of making some alterations in the tolls, was referred to the next meeting, June 18th, when it was ordered that application should be made to the mortgagees for their consent to the reduction of the tolls; and it was to be advertised in the Chelmsford papers that a meeting would be held to take into consideration the reduction of some tolls and increasing others. In August, Mr. Pooly and Mr. Mayne having given it as their opinion that the notices required by the Act had been given, the Trustees drew up a fresh schedule of tolls. But the paper has perished, and the amount of toll cannot therefore be given.

The lessees of the tolls could not have acceded to the terms on which the action against them for breach of covenant was to be suspended; for there is an entry amongst the minutes, "and it appearing that it is necessary that Counsel should be retained for the Trustees, it is therefore desired that the clerk do retain Mr. Gurney and Mr. Marryat; and should they be engaged for the defendant, then such other Counsel as the Chairman and Treasurer should appoint."

At the meeting in November, 1816, a letter was read from the lessee, which seems to have given rise to a proposal then adopted, viz., that a Committee should be appointed, and that they should, as soon as the defendant had pleaded to the action, attend the consultation of the Counsel retained in the cause, and report the result at the next meeting.

September, 1816.—The mortgagees having consented to a reduction, the tolls were reduced to the amounts mentioned in a schedule attached to the lease granted in October, 1814, the same as had been previously (in March) settled as fair and reasonable, but there is no mention made of the items. The action pending against the lessees appears to have caused some anxiety; for, at a meeting held the 29th day of November, Mr. Jessop, the clerk, was ordered to see Mr. Marryat immediately, and appoint an early day for a consultation with Mr. Gurney:—"The Replication in the action brought against the lessee of the tolls was read, and it was ordered that it be recommended to the solicitors to conduct the prosecution against them with the utmost care and caution, and that if any doubt or difficulty should occur between the present time and the next meeting of the Trustees, the solicitor do take the opinion of Counsel should he think it necessary," and that an advertisement should be inserted in the papers enumerated; but as the papers and advertisement are the same as has been already mentioned, they are not repeated. The case did not come on for trial.

At the meeting held December 30th, the Committee to whom the action was referred having made the following report, "The lessees were called in before us at Mr. Jessop's chambers, and made a proposal that they would pay the full costs and charges of the suit (to be taxed by the master as between attorney and client) in three weeks from that day, and that they would not take any other tolls in future than what were let to them by their lease, and that they would surrender up their lease and the toll-houses at Lady Day next, and that an advertisement should be inserted in the newspaper usually circulated in the county of Essex stating the same, and that judgment should be entered up to secure their compliance therewith, and a penalty of £200 settled as the damages in case default was made therein." On the recommendation of the Committee, these terms were agreed to by the Trustees.

They ordered that an advertisement should be put into the papers stating that the tolls would be let to the best bidder on March 31st next, and then would be taken into consideration whether, previous to putting the same, tolls should not be advanced on stages drawn by four horses and on narrow-wheeled waggons. At the next meeting the following tolls were ordered to be advanced, viz. :—

On stage-coaches drawn by two horses, from 6*d*. to 9*d*.
On stage-coaches drawn by four horses, from 1*s*. to 1*s*. 6*d*.
On stage-coaches drawn by six horses, from 1*s*. 6*d*. to 2*s*.

The tolls were put up to be let to the best bidder at the sum they were last let for, viz., £2,025, but no sale took place, so that the Trustees had to appoint toll-collectors; when it was ordered that the collector and all those he employed for the Norton Heath, Root Street, and Ongar gates should be paid £1 7*s*. salary per week, and at the "Baldfaced Stag" £1, and the Epping Gate £1 per week. And the clerk to advertise that the tolls were to be let May 5th, when the collectors produced their accounts as follows; and the tolls were leased to Mr. Everitt for £2,170 for three years.

An Account of the Tolls received by the Trustees' Collectors.

1817.	Epping.	Thorn-wood.	Stag.	Ongar.	Norton Heath.	Weald.
	£ s. d.	£ s. d.	£ s. d.	£ s. d.	£ s. d.	£ s. d.
1st April ...	...	1 14 6	3 4 0	0 7 0	0 4 4	...
2nd ,, ...	...	2 4 0	1 16 0	0 6 0	0 4 0	...
3rd ,, ...	...	1 19 6	2 10 0	0 3 6	0 3 6	...
4th ,, ...	...	3 2 6	2 11 0	0 1 3	0 11 0	...
5th ,, ...	...	1 15 0	4 13 0	0 8 0	0 3 2	...
6th ,, ...	...	1 16 0	1 13 0	0 1 3	0 10 6	...
7th ,, ...	...	2 18 0	11 4 0	0 8 0	0 2 6	...
Coach money ...	...	5 15 0	3 1 6	...	...	...
...	...	20 14 6	30 12 6	1 15 0	1 19 0	2 1 0

An Account of the Tolls received by the Trustees' Collectors.
—(continued.)

1817.	Epping.	Thorn-wood.	Stag.	Ongar.	Norton Heath.	Weald.
	£ s. d.	£ s. d.	£ s. d.	£ s. d.	£ s. d.	£ s. d.
8th April...	...	1 12 0	3 15 0	0 6 0	0 7 7	...
9th „ ...	...	2 19 0	2 1 6	0 5 0	0 3 4	...
10th „ ...	...	1 15 0	3 3 0	0 7 0	0 8 0	...
11th „ ...	...	3 6 6	1 16 6	0 9 0	0 7 7	...
12th „ ...	..	1 16 0	3 14 0	0 8 0	0 13 0	...
13th „ ...	...	1 9 6	0 16 6	0 3 6	0 6 6	...
14th „ ...	...	2 5 6	1 14 0	0 5 6	0 2 0	..
Coach money	...	6 9 0	3 15 0	...	...	...
...	...	21 12 6	20 15 6	2 4 0	2 8 0	1 17 0
15th April	...	1 11 6	3 9 6	0 6 0	0 6 4	..
„	...	2 15 6	1 15 6	0 6 6	0 3 2	...
„	...	1 10 6	2 0 6	0 7 0	0 4 0	...
„	..	3 0 6	1 9 0	0 8 0	0 4 6	...
„	..	1 11 6	4 5 0	0 10 0	0 6 6	...
„	...	1 2 0	1 6 0	0 3 6	0 6 2	..
„	...	1 14 0	1 5 6	0 6 0	0 1 10	...
Coach money	...	6 9 0	3 15 0	..	..	.
...	...	19 14 6	19 6 0	2 7 0	1 12 6	1 15 0

Dates obliterated.

An Account of the Tolls received by the Trustees' Collectors.
—(continued.)

1817.	Epping.	Thorn-wood.	Stag.	Ongar.	Norton Heath.	Weald.
April	0 16 6	...	...	...	...	...
,,	0 11 0	...	...	...	..	...
,,	1 10 6	1 7 0	1 12 6	0 3 6	0 5 7	...
,,	1 3 6	1 18 0	1 5 0	0 6 6	0 5 1	...
,,	1 1 6	1 7 0	1 10 6	0 5 0	0 3 2	...
,,	1 7 0	3 1 6	1 3 0	0 8 0	0 8 0	...
,,	1 13 6	1 14 6	2 6 6	0 9 0	0 8 6	...
,,	...	0 19 0	1 3 0	0 3 0	0 6 8	...
,,	...	2 3 0	1 19 6	0 8 0	0 2 0	...
Coach money ...		6 9 0	3 15 0	...	...	...
...	8 3 6	18 19 0	14 15 0	2 3 0	1 19 0	1 14 0
1st week ...	...	20 14 6	30 12 6	1 15 0	1 19 0	2 1 6
2nd ,, ...	...	21 12 6	20 15 6	2 4 0	2 8 0	1 17 0
3rd ,, ...	...	19 4 6	19 6 6	2 7 0	1 12 6	1 15 0
4th ,, ...	8 3 6	18 19 0	14 15 6	2 3 0	1 19 0	1 14 0
...	8 3 6	80 10 6	85 10 0	8 9 0	7 18 6	7 7 6
Salary ...	0 14 0	4 0 0	4 0 0	1 16 0	1 16 0	1 16 0
...	7 9 6	76 10 6	81 10 0	6 13 0	6 2 6	5 11 6
...	76 10 6	...	...	6 2 6	...	...
...	81 10 0	...	...	5 11 6	...	...
Epping gates ...	165 10 0	Ongar gates ...		18 7 0	...	...

Dates obliterated. (vertical label at left)

Excavating gravel, for the roads in the forest, was the cause of the decay of the trees near to the pits; and in June, 1817, the Lord of the Manor of Theydon Garnon was paid £12 3s. 9d for 75 trees which had been destroyed through digging gravel.

At the meeting of the Trustees in August, a toll-keeper was paid £1, the amount of a forged one pound note which he had taken from a traveller, and retained in payment of his weeks' wages.

In the following December, 1817, important business came before the Trustees.

No mention is made of a misunderstanding between the Trustees and Mr. Nelson, a large coach proprietor. But there is entered the following minute :—" And Mr. Nelson's solicitor was heard on his behalf, and a proposal was made, that the opinion of another counsel should be taken, if the solicitors could agree upon one; but if not (words obliterated) counsel on each side. And the Trustees agree if such opinion should be in favour of Mr. Nelson, that they would at the next meeting recommend the Trust to take the matter into consideration."

Mr. Jessop, the clerk, was directed to prepare a case; he, however, stated at the meeting, January, 1818, that he and the solicitors for the coachmasters could not agree upon a case; and that Mr. Clarke, the solicitor for the coachmasters, had informed him "they would not abide by any other opinion than Mr. Marryat's." A letter was also read from Mr. Clarke, addressed to the Trustees, demanding that the money which had been taken by the toll-collector should be returned, and his own costs paid; also that their answer should be sent to him by the following Wednesday. The Trustees were not, however, to be hurried, for there is an entry as follows :—" It is ordered that Mr. Jessop do inform him that the Trustees are not at present prepared to give an answer to his letter; but will lose no time in letting him know when they come to a decision." It appears there had been a similar claim made on the Trustees of the Cheshunt roads, as Mr. Jessop was ordered to enquire if they had given up a claim of the same nature. A letter from the clerk of the Cheshunt Road Trust was read at the next meeting (February, 1818), in which he stated, that no legal decision had been attained respecting the change of horses, to justify the taking of double tolls.

The Trustees of the Epping roads had not waited for the answer from the clerk of the Cheshunt Trust, for there is on that day the following minute :—"And a case which (by the direction of the Committee named and appointed at the last meeting) had been laid before Mr. Tidd Pratt ; and his opinion also being read, and four opinions of counsels having been taken on the question mentioned in such case, and two of them differing in most points from the others, it was proposed and ordered, that all the said opinions be laid before Attorney-General Shepherd, and his decision obtained, as well as his advise how the Trustees ought under the present circumstances to act." At the following meeting (March 2nd, 1818) Mr. Jessop reported he had laid the case and opinions before counsel as directed; "but Mr. Attorney-General had informed him, by his clerk, that he should not be able to answer for a fortnight or three weeks." The further consideration of the question before the Trustees was postponed until April 6th, as they were of the opinion the business could not be proceeded with without his answer. The advisability of increasing the tolls was also to be brought forward at the next meeting, as well as the offer of the lessee of the tolls to surrender his lease, the consideration of which was, however, postponed until the opinion of the Attorney-General had been received.

In April, 1818, the clerk reported :—" He had repeatedly applied to the Attorney-General for his opinion on the case laid before him, but his clerk had informed him he could not answer any case for a month or six weeks."

The clerk was then ordered to lay the case "before the Solicitor-General, with copies of all the opinions which had been taken, in case he thought it would be in his power to answer the same within one month, but if not, before Mr. Gurney, the counsel."

At the next meeting held the following month, as the

Solicitor-General said he would send an answer the following week, the clerk was directed to call a special meeting of the Trustees, giving them not less than ten days' notice.

July 6th.—The opinion of the Solicitor-General was read. (It is not entered in the minute-book.) At the meeting a proposal was made to raise the tolls, and for the schedule to be submitted for consideration to the next meeting. "The matter was fully debated, but the Trustees differing in opinion on the subject, and the opinion of Mr. Serjeant Shepherd not yet obtained, it was agreed that the matter should stand over to the following meeting."

Tenders for repairing the roads were handed in.

To repair from the 13th mile-stone to the 16th, including trunk arches, bridges, &c., at per mile, £80.

To repair the road from Epping Plain to Tyler's Green, per annum £95.

To repair from Bald-faced Stag to the 13th mile-stone (but not carpenters' or bricklayers' work), per mile, £48 10s.

To repair from Norton Heath to the 7th mile-stone, 3¾ miles, £120.

To repair from the 3rd to the 7th mile-stone on the Ongar road, 4 miles, at per annum, £140.

To repair the whole Epping road, exclusive of the tradesman bills, at per mile, £66 3s.

And there was a verbal offer to do the work at £50 per mile.

The Trustees, however, did not approve of the offers, and decided that the surveyor should continue to keep the road in repair.

At a meeting which had been summoned for the 4th day of September at Mr. Jessop's offices, "It was taken into consideration by the said Trustees the expediency of giving notice in the usual manner of their intention at the next meeting of Parliament to apply for an Act to explain and amend the last Act made and passed relative to the said roads, and the Trustees being of opinion that it would be as well to give the Trustees a power in case they shall hereafter choose to do so.

It is ordered that the clerk to the said Trustees do cause a motion to be given accordingly, but therein also give notice of their intention to apply for the repeal of the last Act, and grant a new term of twenty-one years, or extend the same as they shall judge proper."

Up to the 26th October the coachmasters had not commenced an action against the Trustees, who were evidently expecting them to do so, for there is the following entry :—

"And as no action has as yet been brought by the coachmasters, and in case one should, it will be necessary a Committee should be formed to conduct the defence."

There were seven Trustees appointed, and any other Trustee was at liberty to attend their meetings, three to form a Committee to conduct the defence, "and also to prepare a new Bill to bring into Parliament in case it should be thought necessary." It was decided at this meeting not to advance the tolls.

The intention of the coachmasters was soon made evident, for at a special meeting held November 13th, 1818, there was made the following minute :—

"The clerk having received a copy of a latitat from William Everet, the lessee of the tolls, which had been served on him in an action brought by Robert Nelson, Anne Nelson, Joseph Alcock, and James Waterhouse, it is ordered that he do cause an appearance to be entered, and in case a declaration is delivered immediately to call a meeting of the Trustees (who are on the Committee) to consider of the defence necessary to be made therein, but previous thereto that he do write to William Everet that unless he pays up the arrears due from him within one week, they will not pledge themselves to defend the action ; it was further ordered that in case the venue should be laid in Essex Mr. Gourny should be retained for the defendant, the lessee of the tolls."

The lessee, who was behindhand in his payments, ultimately made a composition of five shillings in the pound, and his sureties had to make up the balance. There was, however, a concession to be made in their favour, provided they paid the amount due from them within a week. On 27th September, 1819.—The treasurer reported he had received the dividend, and also the sum due from the securities.

No further mention is made of the coachmasters until February, 1821, when there is a minute :—" The coachmasters having again complained of the hardship of paying tolls on change of horses passing the same day, and given notice that they would bring an action against the Trustees if they persisted in the practice, the matter was fully debated, and on condition of their waiving their claim to any return of what had been received, it was agreed the same should be discontinued in future."

In the new Act of Parliament at the time under the consideration of the Trustees, there is a clause regulating the tolls on stage coaches, &c., so the amicable arrangement with the coachmasters is probably due to neither party being certain of their legal position.

At the meeting in June, 1821, the Trustees, having given the matter careful consideration, decided to apply to Parliament for the new Act, proposed at a previous meeting ; and they gave orders that proper notices should be given in the month of August or September, of their intention to apply at the next Session for a new Act of Parliament, " to extend the powers of the last Act, and alter and amend the same." In September it was arranged that the Bill should be drawn by the Committee appointed for the purpose, and to settle the various clauses. The Committee meetings were to be open to any of the Trustees who chose to attend. The clerk having submitted the draft of the Bill to the members of the Committee in January, 1822, they reported they approved of the draft, and recommended that it should be adopted, with the schedule of tolls as altered.

The clerk was, however (January, 1822), requested to re-examine the draft of the proposed Bill, and to " leave out so much thereof as the General Turnpike Act had provided for." He was to make the alterations pointed out, and to send a copy for the Committee's perusal. He was also ordered to

O 2

"immediately prepare and send the Petition for the Bill: and send it at the same time to the treasurer to get it presented, at the meeting of Parliament, by Admiral Harvey."

February 11th, 1822.—There is entered as follows :—"At this meeting the minutes of the last meeting were read and confirmed, and the Petition for the House of Commons was examined and signed, and the Bill was also read over, altered, and approved of ; and it is ordered that the same be taken to Mr. Dorrington, the Clerk in Parliament, to peruse and settle, so as to make it conformable to the Rules of the House, and then that he do all acts necessary to carry the same into a law."

In April it was ordered that 200 copies of the new Act should be printed, "with the index which Mr. Jessop has prepared, and if the alteration of printing them in the octavo form does not exceed ten pounds, then to be so printed."

June, 1822.—Mr. Jessop, the clerk, informed the Trustees that the new Act had passed both Houses of Parliament, and had been signed by his Majesty on the 15th of May.

The printer having told him the expense of an octavo edition of the Act would exceed the sum which had been mentioned, he had the 200 copies printed in the same form as the Bill. He was directed to send a copy to each Trustee. Amongst the Bills ordered to be paid was that of Mr. Dorrington, the Clerk to the House of Commons, as under :—

	£	s.	d.
The bill of fees in the House of Lords and Commons	295	5	0
John Shaw, the printer's bill	74	11	0
Mr. Jessop, Mr. Smith, and Mr. Doubleday's expenses, and coach hire, as witnesses attending in the House of Lords and Commons, and at the Chelmsford Sessions	12	12	0
Mr. Jessop's bill as solicitor	140	0	0
	£522	0	0

Title—3 George IV, cap. 44. An Act for more effectually repairing the road from Harlow Bush Common, in the parish of Harlow, to Woodford, in the county of Essex, and then from Epping through the parishes, &c., &c., to the parish of Writtle, in the said county, 15th May, 1822.

Although from the instruction to Mr. Jessop to leave out the clauses appearing in the General Turnpike Act of the same year—3 George IV, cap. 126, 6th August, 1822—it consists of forty-five pages and eighty-three clauses, and was to continue in force for twenty-one years.

It commences with the usual preamble, mentions the Acts which it repeals, and re-enacts those powers conferred on Trustees by previous Acts thought suitable. It appointed a new list of Trustees—about fifty, with power to appoint additional—who must have the property qualification mentioned in previous Acts. They were not to be concerned in any contract, nor hold any place of profit under the Trust, nor keep victualling houses, or other houses of public entertainment. But mortgagees might act as Trustees, and Trustees might act as Justices of the Peace, unless personally interested. The Trustees were to pay their own expenses, excepting the hire of the room for their meetings, for which ten shillings were allowed. The office of treasurer and clerk were not to be held by the same person.

The tolls then payable were to cease from and after 30th of September, and the following tolls to be substituted :—

	£	s	d
For every horse or beast of draught drawing any chaise, caravan, or pleasure carriage or calash, with two wheels, if drawn by one horse or beast of draught..	0	0	6
If by two horses or beasts of draught	0	1	0
For every horse or beast of draught drawing any coach, chaise, Berlin landau, landaulet, caravan, calash, hearse, and pleasure carriage with four wheels—if drawn by one horse or beast of draught	0	0	9

	£	s.	d.
If by two horses or beasts of draught..	0	1	0
If by three ,, ,, ...	0	1	6
If by four ,, ,, ...	0	2	0
If by six ,, ,, ...	0	3	0
For every cart or dray, if drawn by one horse or beast of draught, empty or laden	0	1	0
If drawn by two horses or beasts of draught, if abreast	0	2	6
If ,, ,, ,, at length	0	2	0
If drawn by three or more horses or beasts of draught	0	2	6
For every horse, mule, or ass, laden or unladen ..	0	0	2
For every drove of oxen, cows, or neat cattle, per score	0	2	6
(And so on in proportion for any greater or less number.)			
For every drove of calves, hogs, sheep or lambs, per score	0	1	0
(And so on in proportion for any greater or less number.)			
For every waggon or wain	0	3	0
For every timber carriage drawn by less than three horses or other beasts of draught	0	3	0
If by three or more horses or beasts of draught ..	0	4	0

And for every waggon, wain, cart, or dray, or timber carriage, having the fellies of the wheels thereof of less breadth or gauge than six inches from side to side at the least, at the bottom or sole thereof; and for horses and beasts of draught drawing the same, one-half more than the tolls or duties which are above directed to be paid for the same respectively.

No person was required to pay the tolls more than once in the day for the same horses and carriages passing through a turnpike cleared by the ticket that the toll collector was bound to give, gratis, excepting for those travelling on hire. For them there is a special clause as follows—the result, no doubt, of the Trustees' dispute with the coachmasters.

"XXVI.—Provided nevertheless, and be it further enacted,

that the said tolls shall be payable for or in respect of all horses or mules drawing any stage coach, for all and every time of passing and repassing on the said roads on the same day, to be computed as aforesaid (*i.e.*, from 12 o'clock at night), on a ticket being produced denoting a new hiring: Provided always, that all horses travelling for hire, and drawing or having drawn any chaise or other carriage, for which any toll shall have been paid at any turnpike erected or to be erected on the same roads, shall, on returning without a ticket denoting a fresh hiring being produced, be permitted to pass toll-free although such horses, chaise, or carriage shall not have passed through such turnpike on the same day."

Any person evading the toll in any manner was for "each offence to forfeit and pay any sum not exceeding five pounds, over and beside such damages or punishment as he, or she, or they, shall be otherwise liable by law."

There was continued the power to the Trustees to lessen and again raise the tolls, if they thought it to be necessary to do so; but they had to first obtain the consent in writing of the person or persons who were entitled to five-sixth parts at least of the money then due on the credit of the tolls. There was also a special meeting of the Trustees to be called, of which ten days' notice of the time and place had to be given.

The General Highway Act, to which reference was made, when the Trustees instructed their clerk to leave out of the draft he was preparing "So much as the General Turnpike Act provided for"—was passed August 6th, 1822 (Anno Tertio, George IV, Cap. 126) "An Act to amend the general laws now in being for regulating Turnpike Roads in that part of Great Britain called England."

It deals especially with the wheels of the vehicles; but as the clauses regulating their fellies, &c., were not to come into operation until 1826, four years were allowed to make the alterations required by the Act.

By Clause 5, wheels exceeding 6 inches in width were not

to have their diameters at the inner and outer edges, differing more than half an inch; and wheels less than 6 inches in width more than one quarter of an inch. Clause 6 does not permit waggons or carts to have wheels of less breadth than 3 inches; Clauses 7, 8, 9 regulate the amount of tolls payable; and Clause 10 mentions the carriages, &c., &c., which do not come under the regulations as to the breadth of wheel.

The Clauses referred to above are copied in full, as follows, and Clause 12, regulating the weights of waggons, carts, &c., being given in a tabulated form, is so copied:

Clause 5. "And be it further enacted, that from and after the first day of January one thousand eight hundred and twenty six, if the tire or tires of any wheel or wheels of any waggon, cart, or other such carriage which shall be used or drawn on any turnpike road shall not be so made or constructed as not to deviate more than half an inch from a flat or level surface in wheels exceeding six inches in breadth, or more than one quarter of an inch from a flat or level surface in wheels less than six inches in breadth, or in case the several nails of the tire or tires of every such wheel or wheels shall not be so countersunk as not to project above one quarter of an inch above the surface of such tire or tires, then and in every such case the owner of every such waggon, cart, or other such carriage shall for every such offence forfeit and pay the sum of five pounds, and every driver thereof the sum of forty shillings."

Clause 6. "And be it further enacted, that from and after the first day of January, one thousand eight hundred and twenty six, no waggon or other such carriage shall be allowed to travel or be used on any road with the fellies of the wheels thereof of a less breadth than three inches; and from and after the day and year last mentioned, if any waggon or other such carriage having the fellies of the wheels thereof of less breadth than three inches shall be used or drawn on any turnpike road, the owner of every such waggon or other such carriage so used shall for every such offence forfeit and pay any sum not exceeding five pounds, and every driver thereof, not being the owner, any sum not exceeding forty shillings."

Clause 7. "And be it further enacted, that from and after the said first day of January, one thousand eight hundred and twenty three, the Trustees or Commissioners appointed by virtue or under the authority of any Act or Acts of Parliament made or to be made for making or maintaining any turnpike road shall and they are hereby required to demand and take or cause to be demanded and taken, for every waggon, wain, cart, or other such carriage having the fellies of the wheels thereof of less breadth than four and a half inches at the bottom or soles thereof, or for the horse or horses or cattle drawing the same, one half more than the tolls which are or shall be payable for any carriage of the same description having the wheels thereof of the breadth of six inches, and for every waggon, wain, cart, or other such carriage having the fellies of the wheels thereof of the breadth of four and a half inches and less than six inches at the bottom or soles thereof, or for the horse or horses or other cattle drawing the same, one fourth more than the tolls or duties which are, or shall be, payable on any carriage of the like description, having the wheels thereof of the breadth of six inches, by any Act or Acts of Parliament now in force or hereafter to be passed for making or maintaining any turnpike road, before any such waggon, wain, cart, or other carriage respectively, shall be permitted to pass through any turnpike gate or gates, bar or bars, where tolls shall be payable by virtue of any such Acts."

Clause 8. "Provided always, and be it further enacted, that where any particular Act or Acts of Parliament now in force for the making, repairing, or maintaining any turnpike road shall direct an higher rate of toll or tolls to be taken on any waggon, wain, cart, or other such carriage having the fellies of the wheels thereof of less breadth than six inches, and such higher rate is more than the addition which is herein before directed to be taken, such higher rate of tolls in and by such Act or Acts imposed shall continue to be levied and collected on the road or roads to which the said Act or Acts relate in the proportions therein fixed."

Clause 9. "And be it further enacted, that where any waggon or cart shall have the sole or bottom of the wheels thereof rolling on a flat surface, and the nails of the tire of such wheels countersunk, and be cylindrical, that is to say, of the same diameter on the inside next the carriage as on the outside, so that when such wheels shall be rolling on a flat or level surface the whole breadth thereof shall bear equally on such flat or level surface, and shall have the opposite ends of the axletrees of such waggon, cart, or other carriage, so far as the same shall be inserted into the respective naves of the wheels thereof, horizontal, and in the continuance of one straight line, without forming any angle with each other, and in each pair of wheels belonging to such carriage the lower parts when resting on the ground shall be at the same distance from each other as the upper parts of such wheels, it shall and may be lawful for the trustees or commissioners of any turnpike road, at a general meeting, if they shall think fit so to do, to make an order for every such waggon and cart to pass, through any toll gate or bar under the superintendence of the trustees or commissioners making such order, upon paying only so much of the tolls and duties as shall not be less than two-thirds of the full toll or duty payable by any Turnpike Act on such waggon, cart, or other carriage, and the horse or horses or cattle drawing the same."

Clause 10. "Provided always, and be it further enacted, that nothing herein contained relating to the breadth of the wheels of carriages, or to the tolls payable thereon, shall extend or be construed to extend to any chaise marine, coach, landau, Berlin, barouche, sociable, chariot, calash, hearse, break, chaise, curricle, gig, chair, or taxed cart, market cart, or other cart for the conveyance of passengers or light goods or articles."

The Act also regulates the weight of waggons when loaded, and furnishes the following :—

"TABLE of weights allowed in winter and summer to carriages
    directed to be weighed (including the carriage and loading)
    by the Act of the third of George the Fourth"—being
    Clause 12 tabulated—

	Summer. tons. cwt.		Winter. tons. cwt.	
To every waggon with nine-inch wheels	6	10	6	0
To every cart ,, ,,	3	10	3	0
To every waggon with six-inch wheels	4	10	4	0
To every cart ,, ,,	2	15	2	10
To every waggon with wheels of the breadth of four and a half inches ..	4	5	3	15
To every cart with wheels of the breadth of four inches and a half	2	12	2	7
To every waggon with wheels of three inches ,.	3	15	3	5
To every cart with wheels of three inches .. .. .. ,.	1	15	1	10

For the several purposes of the Act the summer was
reckoned from the first day of May to the thirty-first day of
October, both days inclusive; and winter, from the first of
November to the thirtieth day of April, both inclusive.
Additional weights were allowed for carriages used for the
conveyance of goods, if constructed with springs. And in
London, or within the Bills of Mortality, the drays with two
wheels drawn with three horses, and having wheels of not less
width than four inches, were allowed 2 tons 16 cwt., both
summer and winter. The regulations as to weight did not
extend to carts or waggons loaded with manure, or agricultural
produce not for sale.

Clause 15 enacts, that for overweight, the following sums,
in addition to the tolls, shall be charged. viz. :—for the first and
second hundredweight, excess weight, threepence; for each
hundred above two hundredweight and not exceeding five
hundredweight, sixpence for each hundredweight over and above
the weight allowed; above five hundredweight, and not exceed-

ing ten hundredweight, two shillings and sixpence for every hundredweight in excess of the weight allowed; and above ten hundredweight, five shillings for each hundredweight.

There were made the usual exemptions in favour of agriculturists, and for carriages carrying military stores, &c. Horses travelling for hire under the Post-horse Duties Act, were not to be charged for tolls, if returning, or returning with empty carriages the next day before nine o'clock in the morning. If horses, which had paid toll, passed through a turnpike drawing a carriage, on the same day, or within eight hours after first passing through the gate, the toll paid on the horses was to be deducted.

The General Turnpike Act, which consists of eighty-one pages and one hundred and fifty-three clauses, also treats of matters relating to the Highway Trusts, and confers powers on Trustees to enable them to deal with such difficulties, as experience had taught the legislature, were likely to arise.

Clause 80 enacts, " that the said trustees or commissioners, shall, immediately after the accounts and statements have been examined, audited, and signed, cause a sufficient number of copies of such statements to be printed, and direct their clerk to transmit a copy thereof to each acting trustee or commissioner of such road."

Clause 88 enacts, that when a new road is made, it shall be in lieu of the old one, and " the old road shall be stopped up ; and the land and soil be sold by the trustees to some person or persons whose land adjoins. But if from the new road, access cannot be conveniently given to any lands, houses, &c., in the old road, then it was to be sold subject to the right of way to the lands and houses so situated."

At the end of the Act there is given Forms of Proceedings as follows :

No. 1.—Order of trustees for erecting a weighing machine.

No. 2.—Table of weights allowed in winter and summer to carriages directed to be weighed.

No. 3.—Agreement between trustees of different turnpike roads, for erecting one weighing machine for the use of such roads.

No. 4.—Notice of a meeting of trustees for ordering a side gate to be erected.

No. 5.—Order of the trustees for erecting a side gate.

No. 6.—Notice for letting tolls.

No. 7.—Order of trustees for reducing the tolls.

No. 8.—Agreement between the trustees of a turnpike road and a person liable by tenure to repair some part of it.

No. 9.—Magistrates' summons.

No. 10.—Notice to be given to surveyors of highways.

No. 11.—Justices' order apportioning statute labour.

No. 12.—Order of justices at a special sessions to take part of the statute duty from turnpike roads, for the benefit of other highways in the said parish, &c.

No. 13.—Certificate of the above order to the justices of the peace at their quarter sessions.

No. 14.—Agreement by subscription for advancing money to make and repair a turnpike road or highway.

No. 15.—Warrant from a justice of the peace to enter the toll-gate house, and remove the persons therein.

No. 16.—Bond from the surveyor.

No. 17.—Summons for any person or persons to attend a justice or justices.

No. 18.—Information.

No. 19.—Form of conviction.

No. 20.—Warrant to distrain for forfeiture.

No. 21.—Return of the constable to be made upon the warrant of distress where there are no effects

No. 22.—Commitment for want of distress.

No. 23.—Notice of appeal to the quarter sessions.

Clause 80, already mentioned, orders statements to be printed, and a copy sent to each Trustee. In the schedule is given the form, headed.

No. 24.—General statement of the income and expenditure of the [*insert the name of the particular road*] between

day of   and the   day of   on which the
amounts are to be made out.

The accompanying plate, copied by photo-lithography, from one amongst the Trust papers, shows the form on which the accounts were to be rendered each year; there is entered in the minute book a similar statement of the year's receipts and expenditure. But it is thought better to print them in a tabulated form, which will be found further on.

In accordance with a motion, made by Mr. Conyers and seconded by Mr. Young, at a former meeting, that the Epping turnpike gate should be done away with, it was ordered, July, 1823, that the Epping toll gate should be kept open for six calendar months, from the first of August next; and, that the Thornwood gate should be shut during that period, except at fair time, and then it was to be open as usual.

The arrangement was much in favour of Mr. Conyers, Mr. Young, and those who lived on the London side of the Epping gate, but unjust to others; and particularly to those who lived on the Harlow side of Thornwood gate, as they, on coming into Epping, would have to pay toll every month instead of alternate months.

A petition was therefore presented (at the meeting held January, 1824) "from the inhabitants of the parishes on the north side of Thornwood Common complaining of the order that was made, on the 28th of July last, for shutting the Thornwood turnpike gate and opening the Epping turnpike gate for six calender months." The Trustees postponed the consideration of the Petition, as they wished to have a statement of amount of tolls taken, and the consequent increase, if any.

The Petition again came before the Trustees at the meeting held March, 1824. It is stated that the Petition was fully discussed, when it was moved and seconded, that the alternate opening and shutting the gates be resorted to as before. On the question being put the votes were in favour of the motion.

It was reported, at the meeting, October, 1823, by the Trustees "that the whole of the turnpike roads under their care

are in a good state and condition ; and that 2,241 loads of gravel have been, by their direction, laid by the side of the said roads, ready to put on during the winter ; all of which are paid for ; and also 1,250 loads of gravel that has been once sifted lying at Buckhurst Hill, Monk Wood, Forest Pits, Epping Plains, and Coopersale Pits, all of which have also been paid for. And that the length of the turnpike road from the commencement of Harlow Bush Common to Woodford is eleven miles, and the length of the branch road from Epping to Norton Mandeville is also eleven miles."

The order was given for the payment of a gratuity of twenty pounds to the surveyor, his conduct having been satisfactory.

LOUGHTON HILL.—Between Buckhurst and Golden's Hill, a very short distance from the latter, is another hill, Loughton Hill. On Mr. Powers stating (January, 1824) that complaints had been made by the stage coachmen and others, of the sharpness of the hill at Loughton, opposite the blacksmith's shop, leading to the " King's Head ;" and an estimate of the cost of lowering it having been produced, the Trustees assembled at the meeting held that day, gave orders to lower the hill : but the cost was not to exceed £120. The work on the hill was completed in June, at a cost of £117 2s. 2d., besides a bill in addition of £10 19s. 6d. for incidental expenses.

From some cause, unexplained, the inhabitants of Loughton had not been permitted to compound for their tolls. In March, 1824, they sent a memorial to the Trustees pointing out the injustice to which they were subjected. But it was September before it received attention, when there is the minute—

"The Petition, from the inhabitants of Loughton, for permission to compound for their tolls, having been taken into consideration, the Trustees decided that the best method to be adopted would be lowering the tolls ; which were accordingly settled as follows :—

	s.	d.
"Broad wheel waggons	o	9
Narrow wheel ,, ...	I	$1\frac{1}{2}$
Broad wheel carts with 3 horses	o	6
,, ,, 2 ,, ...	o	4
,, ,, I ,, ...	o	2
Narrow wheel cart with 3 horses	o	9
,, ,, 2 ,, ...	o	6
,, ,, I ,, ...	o	3"

During the next four years there was nothing of importance connected with roads, to engage the attention of the Trustees. The occupier of a house having put his garden fence too far forward, within thirty feet from the centre of the road, had orders to remove it, June 13th, 1825. But he begged he might not be compelled to do so until he could with safety move the "quick set hedge," and his request was granted. The same year Mr. Benjamin Doubleday was appointed treasurer. He had to give a bond for £1,000, and find two sureties for £500 each. There was a dispute with a carpenter, the Trustees not being satisfied with his charges, and also an alteration of a road, relating to which is the entry—

October 10, 1825.—At the previous meeting, it having been stated that the road near to Mr. Elliot's new house* might be shortened, and the road made straight, the plan produced was adopted. At the meeting of the Trustees, January, 1826, Mr. Powell reported that the intended new piece of road had been staked out, the gravel pits filled up, and the ground made level, also that two ditches had been made, to drain off the water on each side of the road. The sum of £8 had been paid to the contractors for doing the work. Mr. South, the surveyor, was directed to produce, at the next meeting, an estimate of the expense of stocking and relaying the road to the depth of two feet, and also to the depth of three feet. Robert Cowel agreed to cart the gravel at 9d. per load, and he was ordered to do

---

* It is not mentioned on which road the new house was built.

EPPING AND ONGAR
TURNPIKE ROAD.
28th April, 1828.

THE Trustees propose to lower the Hill near the Bull and Horseshoes Public-house at Latton, and to raise the lower part of the Road towards Epping, and to contract for the same as follows:

The Contractors will be required to dig out the Gravel on the surface of the Road the whole length of the proposed alteration, and sift the same with Sieves of thirty-five wires in twenty-two inches width, to be used as hereafter specified.

The highest point of the Hill is to be dug out nine feet nine inches; extending five hundred and forty-one feet towards Harlow, and five hundred and sixty-nine feet towards Epping. The Sub-soil to be removed to the lower part of the Road towards Epping, and there spread, (after the Gravel has been removed,) raising the lowest part nine feet six inches, and leaving a new Road of six hundred and seventy-five yards in length, nearly on one level. The Screenings of the Gravel to be spread evenly over the whole surface, and Stones in a thickness of nine inches over the Screenings.

The width of the Road to remain at thirty feet, along the whole length. The sides, where cut down, to be sloped at an Angle of 45 degrees, and, where raised, the Base to be extended in the same proportion.

A new Water Tunnel is to be built, six feet wide, and Six feet high in the centre, of sound, hard Stock Bricks, well laid in sound Mortar, and grouted throughout every second Course, two Bricks thick, with proper Footings and Foundations; to be forty feet in length, and to be Paved in the Waterway, laid in Cement.

Proper Fencing, with Watchmen and Lights during Night must be vided during the time the Work is in hand.

The Work to be commenced on or before the 19th day of Ma be continued uninterruptedly till the whole is completed. through the whole line at a Width of twelve feet, and, whe s passable Carriages, the remainder to be proceeded with and contin all completed.

One Fourth part of the Contract Money to be paid when the First l has been found passable for the Public.

One Fourth more when half the Second Line is completed; and remainder within Fourteen Days after the whole shall have been found in proper state, and used by the Public.

Good Security will be required of the Contractors, to begin, continue, and complete the whole in a Workmanlike manner, under the directions of the Surveyor, according to the Contract. To be completed in Three Month.

Tenders to be sent in to the Meeting of the Trustees, which will be held at Epping Place Inn, the 5th day of May next.

BENJAMIN DOUBLEDAY, *Treasurer.*

Reproduced from old Print by Photo-Litho
THOS TURNER & SON, 18, SHERBORNE LANE, CITY

the work in the spring, according to his estimate. The disputed carpenter's bill amounting to £29 9s. 9d., which had, at a previous meeting been laid before the Trustees, again came under their notice, January, 1827. When, thinking the amount too high, they offered £25 17s. 9d. The carpenter attended, and objected to the proposed reduction. The bill and also a previous bill of £15 3s. 6d. was consequently referred to Mr. Hubert of Lambeth, surveyor, to settle the same on the part of the Trustees and the carpenter. He decided that £44 should be paid to the carpenter by the Trustees for work done at the gate house of the "Baldfaced Stag"; and the expense of the arbitration to be shared. So that in reality he certified the correctness of the carpenter's bill.

J. Jessop, Esq., the clerk, having died, at a special meeting of the Trustees, held the 24th of March, 1828, John Windus was unanimously elected clerk in his stead. And at the same meeting it was moved that the long services of the late lamented John Jessop, Esq., deserve the warmest acknowledgment of the Trust; the motion was carried unanimously.

THE HILL AT LATTON.—The highway from Harlow Bush Common to Woodford, under the management of Trustees, appointed in accordance with the provision of the Act of 1769, had been greatly improved; Golden's Hill, Buckhurst Hill, and Loughton Hill had been lowered; and the entrances, at each end of the town of Epping, had been altered so as to render them suitable for the traffic passing through the town into Cambridgeshire and Norfolk.

There was, however, at Latton a difficult hill, but capable of considerable improvement. At the meeting of the Trustees held April, 1828, the clerk was instructed to mention, when giving notice for the next meeting, that the proposal for altering the road at Latton, near the "Bull and Horseshoe" public-house, would be taken into consideration, and to give public notice that the estimate for making the alteration would also be examined.

At the next meeting, the plan suggested for improving the hill having been accepted by the Trustees, and John Thurlow's estimate and specification being satisfactory, a formal contract was ordered to be prepared, and securities, to be approved of by the chairman, given, for the completion of the work in a satisfactory manner.

The work on the hill must have been carried on with energy and under the careful supervision of the contractor; for there is an entry made September, 1828, "The Committee for superintending the work at the Bull and Horseshoe Hill whilst in progress, reported that John Thurlow had completed his contract, and, that the old line of road made by him is passable for, and used by, the public." He had received the first and second instalments, and a further sum of £262 15s., the third and last instalment, was ordered to be paid to him; and, also £42 10s., an additional sum due to him, most likely, for work done, and not included in his contract.

The lowering the hill by the "Bull and Horseshoe" was, it may be considered, the last alteration or improvement made in the old road. At the meeting, instructions were given to the surveyor "to produce at the next meeting" a table, showing "the length of road maintained by the Trust, distinguishing the extent of the road in each parish; also the number of bridges and arches on such roads maintained by the Trust, the size thereof, and in what parish they are situated." The surveyor, in October, produced the document, as instructed at the last meeting. It was ordered to be entered on the minute book; and the accompanying plate is a fac-simile of the entry, reproduced by photo-lithography.

January 5th, 1829, "In consequence of the representation of Mr. Henry Gilby, the proprietor of the Stortford coach, stage coaches were in future to be relieved from payment of the additional tolls, taken three days before and three days after the fairs in the neighbourhood, at which times both gates were shut and tolls taken."

TRUSTEES

F THE

EP   NG & ONGAR

Turnpike Roads

DO HEREBY GIVE NOTICE,

THAT THEY WILL BE READY AT THEIR

Adjourned Meeting at Epping Place,

On MONDAY, the 5th DAY of MAY NEXT,

To receive Tenders from Persons willing to contract for lowering the Hill at and near the Bull and Horse Shoes Public House, Latton.

Particulars may be known from Mr. John South, Surveyor of the Roads, Latton, who will point out the proposed Alteration.

Signed by order of the Trustees,

JOHN WINDUS,

Clerk to the said Trustees.

EPPING,
7th April, 1828.

WAKE ARMS INN

NEW ROAD.

TO LOUGHTON

TO
EYDON DOG

CHAPTER IX.

New Road—Wake Arms to Woodford.

At the meeting, April, 1830, in consequence of the death of the late surveyor, a new appointment to this office had to be made. There were three applicants—John Thurlow, Thomas Smith, and Mr. McAdam. The two first applied for the situation at the previous salary of £50 per annum; Mr. McAdam expressed his willingness to undertake the office at the same salary, but pointed out to the Trustees that 100 guineas would not be more than an adequate remuneration for the services required. The show of hands was in favour of Mr. McAdam, and he was duly elected. A motion was then made and carried, that a salary of £100 per annum be allowed him, without any stipulation as to his place of residence, and with power to appoint his own assistant surveyor.

The object of the Trustees in electing Mr. McAdam, the celebrated maker of roads, at a salary so much in excess of what had been previously paid, is not here mentioned; it is, however, made manifest at the meeting held Monday, June 14, 1830, when the following minute was entered:—" Mr. McAdam having reported that a great improvement might be made in the road between Epping and Woodford, by adopting an entire new line between Epping and Woodford Wells:—Resolved that measures should immediately be taken for ascertaining which line would be most desirable for effecting the object. That Mr. McAdam do prepare a correct survey or surveys, to be produced at the next meeting, and that notice shall be given by the clerk to the Trustees, that a motion will then be made for adopting the best plan, in order that the work, if determined upon, may be begun as soon as possible."

At the following meeting, June 30th, sixteen days after Mr. McAdam was appointed surveyor, he produced his plan, and Lord Braybrook moved, and Mr. Roland Austin seconded, that the line proposed by him should be adopted. The motion was carried by a majority of 14 to 4. It was also agreed that £7,000* should be borrowed towards the expense of constructing the line of road proposed.

Mr. McAdam was then instructed to prepare the plans, sections, and specifications of the proposed new line of roads, to be left at the office of the clerk, as well as at the office of Mr. McAdam, Whitehall.† It was also to be advertised, that the Trustees were ready to receive tenders for the completion of the said work.

August 23rd, 1830. The tenders were submitted as follows :—By Messrs Bough and Smith.

For performance of the work in making the new line of road from near Woodford Wells to the Keeper's Lodge, viz. :—

First Division	..	..	..	.. £2,750
Second Division	..	..	..	.. 2,665
		Total	..	.. £5,417

which tender was accepted; it being, however, understood that a trifling deviation, made at the suggestion of General Grosvenor, near his residence, should be adopted.

Mr. McAdam's charge for surveying, &c., the new line of road amounted to £99 15s. Good progress was being made with the work, for, 3rd January, 1831, the contractors were paid £400 on account of work done, and the treasurer ordered

---

* This was borrowed at 4½ per cent. per annum, but the interest was soon after increased to 5 per cent.

† The plans are probably at Chelmsford.

to make up the amount of the first instalment, *i.e.*, one-fourth part of the contract, as soon as he received the surveyor's certificate, that a third part of the road had been completed. 11th April. " The treasurer reported, he had paid up the amount of the first instalment due to Messrs. Bough and Smith, amounting to £1,354 5s., the surveyor having certified to him 'that a third part of their contract had been completed.'" September, 1831. The authority was given for "the payment of £200 to Messrs. Bough and Smith, the contractors, and a further sum on the 26th inst; one month hence, £100, and six weeks hence, £100; provided the work was done to the satisfaction of Mr. McAdam," who was at the same time authorised to advance the contractors any sum or sums of money, not exceeding £50 per week, until the next meeting. It was also ordered that £150 be paid on account of brickwork.

February, 1832. The treasurer was ordered to pay the contractors the sum of £154 5s., to make up the amount of the second instalment. The surveyor was to continue to make advances of £50 to the contractor, as arranged at the previous meeting. In May £150 was paid to them and directions given that the weekly advances of £50 should be continued.

The accompanying map shows that the new road, by running straight to the corner of the road leading to Copt Hall Park, left a short distance between it and the termination of the road from Waltham Abbey.

The parish of Loughton having made a request that the approaches of the Waltham Abbey and the Loughton parish roads to the new road, should be made as staked off; and the contractor consenting to complete the same for the additional sum of £45, it was ordered to be done.

The old road ran in front of, and parallel with, the " Wake Arms," and the land between the two roads has been built upon. But a portion of the old road can still be traced by the bushes at the side, when looking from the Epping end of it. A barn is now built across it ; and as the gravel has been removed, it would scarcely be noticed unless attention was directed to it. The new portion can easily be recognised in Autumn by the quantity of fresh gravel on it ; and in Winter by its very bad condition.

July 18th, 1831.   In the proposed Act of Parliament which had been under consideration, provisions were to be made for the insertion of "a clause giving the Trustees power to make a new line of road from Fairmeade Bottom to Tottenham Mills, so as to join the Stamford Hill Road ; and also power for the increase and alteration of the tolls."   The conditions being, "provided the Metropolitan Trust will meet the said proposed road of junction on the Essex side of the river Lea."

The clerk was to prepare a copy of the proposed Act, to be submitted to the next meeting, and to forward a copy of the resolution to the Trustees of the Metropolitan Roads, and the Trustees of the Middlesex and Essex Roads.   The surveyor was directed to prepare plans and sections, and a book of reference of the proposed new line of road from Fairmeade Bottom.

As the costs of making the proposed road, and incidental expenses, would amount to a considerable sum of money, means of procuring it had to be considered.   The tolls belonging to the " Trust " were heavily mortgaged ; it was therefore " Resolved that the clerk be directed to apply in the proper quarter, for the loan of £15,000 from the Commissioners appointed under an Act of Parliament, passed in the second year of the reign of His present Majesty, for authorising the issue of Exchequer Bills, and the advance of money for carrying on public works, and fisheries, and employment of the poor, and to authorise further issue of Exchequer Bills for the purpose of the said Act."

November 14th, 1831.   In reply to the applications for the loan just mentioned, a letter was received from the Secretary of the Exchequer Loan Commissioners, stating that no step could be taken until the Act had passed.   No communication having been received from the Metropolitan Trust, it was decided to postpone for the present the application to Parliament.

May 7th, 1832.   At this meeting the Bill proposed and adopted October 10th, 1831, was duly considered ; when, the clerk was desired to take the necessary measures to secure its reception by both Houses of Parliament at the next session; and it was moved that a Committee be appointed, and attended by Mr. McAdam, to visit the new line of road, and to report at the next meeting.

The Committee appointed to view the road from Fairmeade Bottom to Tottenham Mills, viz.:—The Right Hon. Lord Braybrook, Rolan Alston, Esq., Capel Cure, Esq., Hatch Abdy, Esq., and others, met at Tottenham Mills, according to appointment, on Monday, June 18, 1832, and made their survey. They reported at the meeting held at Epping Place, on August 6th, 1832, as follows:—

"That the said proposed new road would be a great acquisition to the public, and that in the event of its being carried into effect, the line delineated on Mr. McAdam's plan would be the best line to adopt, but the Committee are of opinion that the Trustees of the Epping and Ongar Turnpike Roads are not, at present, in a situation to undertake a work of so great magnitude."

In consequence of this report the resolution passed at the last meeting relative to the proposed new Act of Parliament was necessarily suspended; and the clerk was directed not to take further steps therein until further orders. Mr McAdam's bill for surveying and specification of the new line of road, amounting to £172 12s. 0d., was brought in and ordered to be paid.

An extensive landslip having taken place [reported   ]* a question arose as to who was liable for the cost of repairs—the contractors or the Trustees. The clerk was directed to prepare a case to be submitted to Mr. Thesinger; and the contractors were to be allowed to peruse such case previous to its being submitted to Counsel, and to consult their professional adviser thereon, and to state additional facts and put additional queries, subject to the approval of the clerk.

* The writing being defaced, the report cannot be made out.

The Counsel's opinion is not mentioned. But it must have been in favour of the contractor; for, April, 1833, Mr. McAdam "was authorised to effect a contract, for the Trustees, with any qualified person, to repair the slips at his or Mr. McAdam's estimate, according to his specification, at any sum not exceeding £540."

The contractors' account having been regularly paid on the certificate of Mr. McAdam, it might be supposed that the work had been carried on to the satisfaction of the surveyor, Trustees, and the Committee appointed to overlook it; so that the following minute must cause some surprise :—"January, 1833. The clerk was ordered to write to Messrs. Bough & Smith, and to state to them the dissatisfaction of the Trustees at their not having attended at the present meeting, and at their having left the works of the new road in their present unfinished state, and unless they satisfied the Trustees as to their intentions with reference to the completion of the work, the Trustees would commence proceedings against them and their sureties." In consequence of the clerk's communication, Mr. Bough having died, Mr. Smith, his co-contractor, attended the meeting previously mentioned (April, 1833) and asked permission to engage a person to complete the road now in progress, and to pay him £300 upon the certificate of Mr. McAdam.

At the next meeting, in May, 1833, which was an especial meeting, called for the purpose of considering his request, it was decided that the Trustees would take into their own hands the unfinished works of the new road, in order to get the same completed. The Trustees, deducting from the (alleged) balance due to Mr. Smith, the estimated cost of completing such unfinished work. They did not, however, admit Mr. Smith's pecuniary claim, but offered, without prejudice, £300 to be paid to Mr. Smith and the administrator of Mr. Bough on their executing a deed of release to the Trustees.

A new specification having been prepared by Mr. McAdam; Mr. William Watkins offered to complete the new road, including the slips, for the sum of £2,200; his tender was accepted, and a surveyor during the progress of the work was to be appointed by Mr. McAdam, at a salary of 25s. per week.

By July, 1833, the work was so far advanced that the treasurer was ordered to pay £250, first instalment due to Mr. Watkins under his contract, and he was authorised to pay the remainder of the first, and the whole of the second instalment, on receiving the surveyor's certificate. In 1834 the work was finished, for Mr. McAdam produced the account of Mr. Watkins, the contractor, and certified that "he was, on a final settlement of his account, entitled to the sum of £1,104 2s. 11d." This the treasurer was ordered to pay, as he was in funds. Some time after, January, 1835, Mr. Walker's account "for procuring 4,802½ cubic yards of gravel delivered at the different stations in different quantities on the new road, as per contract at 2s. 6d. per yard, being £600 1s. 3d.; and 1,153½ yards of flint, delivered on the same road at 3s. 3d. as per contract, being £188 5s. 1½d.: in all £788 6s. 4d., was passed." The sums were ordered to be paid to Mr Walker.

The lord of the manor at Chigwell was paid £14 for 2,000 bundles of wood, and the lord of the manor of Loughton £11 1s. 8d., for trees used on the new road, in addition to the £16 18s. 6d. which he had received in 1833.

But no money appears to have been paid as compensation for the manorial rights over the land taken from the forest for making the road. Manorial rights are usually guarded with great care, even in small matters. January, 1834, the lord of the manor of Chigwell having complained that certain trees had been lopped and carried away on the Chigwell Manor under Mr. McAdam's authority, he was summoned to attend the meeting on February 10th, when the Trustees, being of opinion that the surveyor had exceeded the power of the Turnpike Act, he was ordered to desist in future from lopping trees in the waste, without the consent of the owners; and it was further ordered that Mr. Abdy be paid the sum of sixpence for each tree thus lopped.

The road was completed in 1834 to the satisfaction of

Mr. McAdam, the eminent road-maker, whose name, turned into an adjective—Macadamized—is associated at the present time with roads. But the work could not have been so well done, as might be expected from the certificates which had been handed to the treasurer.

June, 1835.—"Sir James McAdam reported that the brick arch, under filling at Long Valley on the new road, had broken in and become useless." A new drain was ordered to be made; and, July, 1836, it having been reported that a land slip had taken place, rendering the road unsafe for travellers, Sir James McAdam, who was in attendance, was authorised, in accordance with his recommendation, to expend a sum not exceeding £180 in repairing the slip.

Some portion of the road into Woodford belonging to the Middlesex and Essex Trust had evidently been made over to the Trustees of the Epping and Ongar Roads, although no mention is made of such an arrangement in the Minute Book; for in July, 1836, there is the following entry:—

"A letter from Mr. Dacre, the clerk to the Trustees of the Middlesex and Essex Trust, requiring to know whether the Trustees of the Epping Road would purchase the four pumps and the materials of the wells in the newly adopted piece of road, having been read; the clerk was ordered to answer the same, by stating the opinion of the Trustees of the Epping Road, founded upon the known practice on other roads, that they were entitled to them by virtue of the Act of Parliament. But the Trustees of the Epping Road will be responsible for watering under the present contract until the 31st of October next, and without prejudice to the question of property in the pumps and materials of the well."

16th January, 1837, another letter was received from Mr. Dacre relating to the Woodford pumps, when it was ordered that the clerk do write to Mr. Dacre and state the willingness of the Trustees of the Epping Road to submit the question in dispute to Mr. Tidd Pratt, or any other barrister whom they agreed upon, and be guided by his opinion, upon a case to be settled between Mr. Dacre and Mr. Windus, on behalf of the Trustees respectively; "and that in case of refusal the clerk of the Trust do take Mr. Tidd Pratt's opinion on a case to be submitted by himself."

A further correspondence must have taken place of a very unsatisfactory character, for there is the entry (July 3rd): "Ordered that a letter be written by the clerk to the Trustees of the Middlesex and Essex Roads, stating that the Trustees of the Epping and Ongar Roads will not do otherwise than they proposed—that is, take the opinion of a barrister on the question at issue, and if this plan be not agreed to, the Trustees of the Middlesex and Essex Roads will take their own course."

The pumps at Woodford, which in July, 1836, had been the subject of correspondence between the clerk of the Trustees of the Epping roads and the clerk of the Trustees of the Middlesex roads, were brought under notice again in September, 1850. Mr. Skelton attended a meeting on the 9th, and stated he wished to become a purchaser "of the rights and interests of the Trustees in a certain well belonging to them, and situate at Woodford." The surveyor having stated that the well had not been used for a number of years, nor was it, in his opinion, likely to be of any use at any future time to the Trustees, the clerk was instructed to ascertain the Trustees' interest, if any, in the well, and to report at the next meeting whether they had power to dispose of it.

From the clerk's report, made March 8th, 1851, it appears that the "Trustees could not convey the soil of, but had merely the right to dispose of, the materials therein, and that he had ascertained from the surveyor that the materials were of the value of £25, which sum Mr. Skelton had paid for the same, as will appear on reference to the treasurer's account book."

July 4th, 1836. As there was no toll-gate at the end of the New Road, it was thought advisable to remove the turnpike by the "Baldfaced Stag" (called the Stag Gate) to some spot near the junction of the old and new lines of road into Woodford on the London side, to be selected by a committee which should be appointed for that purpose.

It was finally settled that a toll-house and gate should be placed at the junction of the New Road with the old Epping Road through Loughton.

The land occupied by the "Baldfaced Stag" gate and gardens was sold to the lord of the manor for the nominal sum of £5, and the materials of the toll-house and turnpike gate were sold for £15.

At the same meeting it was decided that "the Epping gate, Thornwood gate, and Duck Lane gate should be continued, and be opened and shut alternate months as at present; but that these gates shall in no case clear the Woodford gate or be cleared by it."

August, 1837.—Fences were ordered to be put on the road at places most requiring them; the outlay was not to exceed £200. Subsequently orders were given that fencing should be erected south of Warren House, and finally that the surveyor should report what part of the road more particularly required fencing, and what the cost would be.

The report was furnished to the Trustees at the meeting in November, 1838, when, by the advice of Sir James McAdam, about 150 rods of embankment was also ordered to be made by the side of the road, where it was to be carried across the valley to prevent accidents occurring to travellers passing along it; the estimated cost was seven shillings per rod

The contractor not having rendered an account of the money due to him for putting up the fence or railing, the surveyor was directed to apply for a statement of work done, and to ascertain the correctness of the measurements. His examination resulted in his stating that fifteen pence per rod ought to be deducted from the amount of contract, as the work was not done according to the specification.

The construction of the New Road seems to have been completed, as it is not again mentioned, excepting the contracts for gravel, until January, 1860, when permission was given to enclose a small piece of waste land by the side of it, as it had been satisfactorily proved to the Trustees that the enclosure

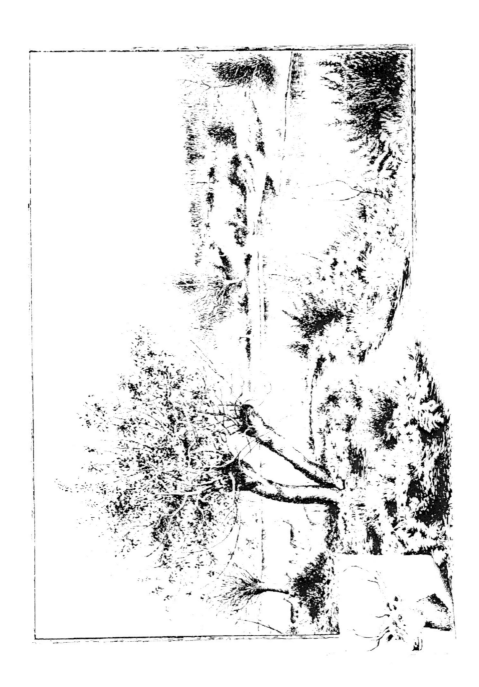

would not in any way be detrimental to the Trust. The Minute does not mention where the piece of land was situated, nor to whom permission was given.

In September, 1865, a letter was received from the lessee of the tolls complaining of the state of the New Road near the upper end of the Trust, and a committee was appointed to examine its condition, and also the material —(gravel ?)—placed by the side.

At the annual meeting in February, 1866, the members of the committee furnished a report, in which they stated that they considered the road, on the whole, to be satisfactory, but it was resolved on their recommendation that " portions of the New Road be under-drained with three-inched pipes under their supervision, and that practical hands be employed to execute the work."

CHAPTER X.

CONTINUATION OF THE PROCEEDINGS OF THE TRUSTEES.

AUGUST, 1830.—The expenses incidental to making the new road through the forest led to the clerk being directed to give notice, as required by the Act of Parliament, that a special meeting would be held at Epping Place, on the 6th of October, for the purpose of increasing the tolls; also that they would on the same day be put up to auction, and leased to the highest bidder.

It was agreed that the tolls enumerated in the following schedules should be demanded until further notice :—

"For every horse or beast of draught drawing any chaise, caravan, pleasure carriage, &c., with two wheels, if drawn by one or two horses or beasts of draught .. .. each horse $4\frac{1}{2}d.$

For every horse or beast of draught drawing any coach, chaise, &c., &c., with four wheels, if drawn by one horse or beast of draught .. $6d.$

If drawn by two horses .. .. each horse $4\frac{1}{2}d.$

If drawn by three or more horses or beasts of draught .. .. each horse $4d.$

For every cart or dray, if drawn by one horse or beast of draught, empty or laden .. .. $3d.$

If by two or more horses or beasts of draught, the same being laden with hay or straw .. .. $4d.$

All other carts drawn by two or more horses or beasts of draught .. .. $6d.$

Should the said carts so exempted return with any other

load except that of manure, such carts are to be liable to pay the extra 2*d*.

For every horse, mule or ass, laden or unladen, and not drawing .. .. 1½*d*.

For every drove of oxen or cattle, per score .. 10*d*. and so in proportion for any greater or less number.

For every drove of calves, hogs, sheep, or lambs .. 5*d*. and so in proportion for any greater or less number.

For every waggon or wain .. .. 1*s*.

For every timber carriage drawn by less than three horses or beasts of draught .. .. .. 1*s*.

If by three or more horses or beasts of draught .. 2*s*.

"And for every waggon, wain, cart, dray, or timber carriage having the fellies of the wheels thereof of less breadth or gauge than six inches from side to side, at least at the bottom or sole thereof, and for the horses or beasts drawing the same, one-half more than the tolls or duties which are above directed to be paid for the same respectively.

"The above tolls having been paid for the passage of any horses or mules drawing any stage coach shall be sufficient for every time of passing and repassing of the same horses or mules, on the same day through the same gate.

"But it shall not be lawful to take toll on the same day at more than one gate on the Epping road, or at more than one gate on the Ongar road for the passings, and only at one gate for the re-passings of the same horses or mules drawing any stage coach."

And the tolls, as above, were payable for all horses or mules drawing any post-chaise or other carriage travelling for hire on a fresh hiring.

The tolls were put up to auction at the sum of £1,753 —Mr. Louis Levy, as agent for Nathaniel Levy and Elisha

Ambler, was the highest and last bidder at the sum of £2,420. They were, therefore, declared the renters of the tolls.

The tolls—let in 1830 for £2,420 to Messrs. Levy and Ambler for one year, and continued to them the following year for £2,420, theirs being the highest bid—were knocked down in 1832 to the highest bidder at £2,515; but as he failed to comply with the conditions on which they were to be leased to him, the twenty pounds he had deposited became forfeited, and were carried to the credit of the Trust.

The tolls were again put up at auction, and leased to Elisha Ambler. Then there arose a question whether proceedings should be taken against the defaulting lessee, to recover the difference, between the sum he tendered, and that at which they were leased to Mr. Ambler. After due consideration the Trustees concluded it would be advisable for no further action to be taken. The next year, 1833, the tolls were put up at £2,355 —the price given for them the previous year, but there was no bidding. A tender, however, was received, and the offer of £3,372 for the tolls was accepted by the Trustees. But it appears by a minute made September 7th, that the proposed lessee refused to execute the contemplated lease, and to find securities. His reason for so doing is explained at the meeting in November, when there is entered in the minute-book: "One of the purposes of the meeting being the consideration of the tender of £3,372, which the lessee alleges to have been a mistake for £2,372."

The Trustees decided, after due consideration, to cancel his offer, and to repay to him £201, part of the sum of £281 which he had deposited with them as security, and to retain the £80, "being a forfeiture of £50 deposit and £30 towards *certain* expenses."

In April, 1831, it was resolved by the Trustees, "That application be made at the next Session of Parliament for a new Local Act to enlarge the powers of the present; and that in such Act a clause be inserted to enable the Trustees to keep up the old line of road through Loughton, as well as the new road now in progress; and that notice be given to the bondholders of such intended application." This was duly done, as appears by the clerk's report at the meeting in July. In the following September—the form of notice of the intended application to Parliament having been produced and approved—the Trustees ordered that it should at once be inserted in public newspapers circulating in the counties of Essex and Middlesex, and in the *London Gazette*; copies were also to be given to all parties entitled to notice, and otherwise, pursuant to the Standing Orders of the House. It was moreover ordered that this draft Act of Parliament, produced pursuant to the order of the last meeting, be submitted to Roland Alston, Esq., and Robert Bodle, Esq., for their consideration; who are requested to make their report thereon at the next meeting. In October the committee, to whom the draft new local Act was submitted, "reported that they had read the same, and, with a few alterations approved of it, and proposed its being adopted." But at a meeting in November (1831) it was resolved, that the proposed application to Parliament at the next Session be deferred for the present. This resolution appears to have been taken in consequence of no answer having been received from the Metropolitan Road Trustees, in reply to a letter which had been sent respecting the road proposed to be made from the new road, then being made across Fairmead Bottom towards Tottenham, as far as the River Lea.*

A determination was, however, exhibited in May, 1832, to proceed with the new local Act; for at a meeting in that month there is the following minute: "Resolved, that the clerk of the Epping and Ongar Trust be desired forthwith to take all proper and necessary measures so as to secure the reception of that proposed Bill, which was adopted at a general meeting of the said Trust held at Epping Place on the 10th October, 1831, by both Houses of Parliament at the next Session."

But nothing further was done until November, 1835, when the draft notice of the intended application to Parliament having met with the unanimous approval of the Trustees present, the

* See Chapter on New Road from "Wake Arms to Woodford."

clerk was ordered to advertise the notice in compliance with the standing orders of both Houses of Parliament, and to take the necessary steps for obtaining such new Act. There was however a motion made at the meeting January 15th, 1836, by C. Phillips, Esq., and seconded by Daniel R. MacNab, Esq., that the foregoing resolution be rescinded ; whereupon an amendment was moved and carried, that the Bill be proceeded with according to the former resolution, and Thomas William Branston was requested to present and take charge of the Bill in the House of Commons, and Lord Braybrook to protect it in the House of Lords. The arrangement for procuring the new local Bill was now pushed forward : at the meeting in the following April it was ordered :—

"That the clerk be directed to proceed with the new Turnpike Bill, settled by the Committee appointed for that purpose, with the clause empowering the Trustees to keep in repair, without restriction, the Loughton Road, as well as the new one. If this cannot be effected, then the clerk is to get the Bill passed with Lord Shaftesbury's branch road clause, and leaving out such part of the Bill as relates to taking the pieces of road at present belonging to the Middlesex and Essex Trust."

In June "the clerk reported that he had succeeded in getting the new Bill, as settled by the committee of Trustees appointed for that purpose, passed into an Act, with the additional clause, termed the Branch Road clause, which the Committees at both Houses of Parliament said should be inserted."

The Act which had been for so long a time under the consideration of the Trustees was not passed until 1836—after the completion of the new road. Across the margin of the copy of the Act amongst the Trust's papers there is written in pencil : "The act passed for the purpose of allowing the heavy charges on the tolls to be paid off." The memorandum suggests the supposition that there was a doubt as to whether the Acts of Parliament then in force, authorised the construction of the road through the forest.

The title of the Act is : "Anno sixto Gulielmæ 4to Regis

19th May, 1836—an Act for more effectually repairing roads from Harlow Bush Common to, and into, the parish of Woodford, and from Epping to Writtle, and other roads therein mentioned, all in the county of Essex."

After naming the previous Act and its object it proceeds :—

"And whereas the Trustees for executing the said recited Act have proceeded to put the same into execution, and great improvements have been made in the said roads, and by virtue of the recited Act, and money still remaining due and owing, and cannot be paid off, nor can the said several and respective roads mentioned and described in the said recited Act, nor the new line and pieces of road hereinafter mentioned be effectually maintained, improved, and kept in good repair, unless the term granted by the said recited Act be further continued * * * Also for maintaining and keeping in repair the new line of road or deviation from the present road from Harlow Bush Common to Woodford aforesaid, near the Wake Arms in the parish of Waltham Holy Cross, and passing through the parishes of Waltham Holy Cross, Loughton and Chigwell, to Woodford, all in the said county of Essex, and for adopting and taking upon themselves the care and management of another piece of road or continuation recently made (by and at the expense of the Middlesex and Essex Trust), connecting the said last mentioned new line or deviation with the Middlesex and Essex Turnpike road near Woodford Wells, and also such other part of the said Middlesex and Essex Turnpike road as lies between the bounds of the parish aforesaid, where the present Epping road terminates, and the north end of the new branch of the metropolis road called the Woodford Cut, near Higham House, and for maintaining and keeping in repair the said last-mentioned pieces of road."

It further states that it is advisable to repeal the above recited Act ; and then proceeds to enumerate again the roads above-mentioned, as being those under the jurisdiction of the newly-appointed Trustees. It also provides that the repeal of the Act recited shall not revoke former Acts, nor prevent the recovery of penalties incurred, previously, to the Act coming into operation.

By it the Trustees of the Middlesex and Essex roads appointed by 4th and 5th William IVth, chap. 89, were discharged from the cares of a certain portion of the road.

Fresh Trustees were appointed; about fifty large landed proprietors and others; including Daniel Robert McNab and Thomas Loft, the two medical men practising in Epping, and James Windus, solicitor, with powers to appoint additional Trustees.

Clause 9 says :—" And whereas a map or plan describing the said new line and pieces of road hereinbefore mentioned, and the lands, &c., over which the same are carried or made, together with a book of reference containing the names of the owners and occupiers of the land, have been deposited at the office of the Clerk of the Peace for the county of Essex"; it was enacted that they should remain in his custody, and that any person, at seasonable times, might take copies or extracts, on paying the sum of 5s. for each inspection, and at the rate of 9d. for every one hundred words, of such copies or extracts of such map or plan and book of reference.

The tolls to be taken as scheduled :—

	s.	d.
For every horse or other beast drawing any coach, chariot, barouche, chaise, curricle, phaeton, &c., &c.	0	6
If with four wheels and drawn by one horse only ..	0	9
For every horse or beast drawing any waggon, wain, or cart, dray, or caravan, &c., having the fellies of the wheels of the breadth or gauge of six inches, at the least, any sum not exceeding	0	4
And in case the fellies of the wheels shall be of less breadth than six inches, but not less that four inches and a-half, any sum not exceeding ..	0	5
And if of less breadth than four and a-half inches, any sum not exceeding	0	6
For every horse, mule, or ass, laden or unladen, not drawing	0	2

	s.	d.
For every drove of oxen, cows, neat cattle, any sum not exceeding, per score	2	6
For every drove of hogs, calves, sheep, or lambs any sum not exceeding, per score, and so in proportion for any greater or less number ..	1	0
For every carriage propelled or moved by steam, gas, machinery, or any like means, any sum not exceeding for each..	0	6

And the same and every part thereof shall be paid, applied, and disposed of in manner hereinafter mentioned."

Clause 13 enacts :—"That in case the tolls hereby authorized to be taken shall have been paid by any persons for the passing of any horse, mule, &c., &c., or any carriage through any toll-gate in the Trust: upon the production of the ticket denoting the payment of toll on that day, they were to be exempt from the payment of further toll."

Clause 14 :—"Provided always, and be it further enacted, That no more than two full tolls shall be taken for, or in respect of the same horses, beast, or cattle, or carriages in any one day." This last clause seems to contradict the one before. But the first appears to apply to persons continuing to drive their vehicles during the day, and the second to a vehicle passing through turnpikes, but occupied by a different person or member of a family: except they were hired;—for the regulation of these there are separate clauses.

Clause 15 :—"Provided always, and be it furthur enacted, That for and in respect of the horses or other cattle drawing any stage-coach, stage-waggon, van, cart, and for the conveyance of passengers or goods, for payment, hire, or reward (except hay carts returning empty) for which toll had been paid, and returning on the same day, through the same turnpike, toll-gate, or bar the tolls hereby made payable shall be paid for every time of passing and repassing through the same turnpike, toll-gate, or bar, in like manner as if no toll had been paid thereat." Horses let out to hire, and drawing a post-chaise, or other carriage, for every time of passing and repassing, had also to pay toll if travelling with a fresh party, *i.e.*, on a new hiring. Carriages propelled by steam, gas, or machinery had to pay tolls every time they passed or repassed along the road.

Clause 18 :—"And whereas it has of late become a practise for low carts, trucks, carriages with narrow wheels, and drawn by a dog or dogs, and heavily laden to pass and repass along the said road to the injury thereof, and to the great inconvenience and danger of persons travelling thereon, it is therefore expedient that the same should be subject to the payment of the tolls by this Act granted; be it therefore enacted that for every dog or goat drawing any low cart, truck, or other carriage there shall be paid the sum of one halfpenny at each turnpike, toll-gate, side-bar, or chain on the said road."

Clause 20 provides :—" That no money arising from any of the tolls mentioned in this Act shall be applied in or towards the repair of any line of road authorized to be made or repaired by this Act, unless some toll-gate, turnpike, or toll-bar shall be erected or continue upon such line of road, or along the side thereof, nor unless the said tolls shall be demanded or taken thereat pursuant to the powers and provisions of this Act; provided also, that no more money shall be expended by the said Trustees in or towards the repair of any such line or road than shall be collected thereat or borrowed on the credit of the tolls collected thereon."

After the schedule of the tolls is the provision that they "should be paid, applied, and disposed of in manner hereafter mentioned" (Clause 21). It runs as follows :—

" And be it further enacted, That out of the monies already received by virtue of the said Act hereby repealed on account of the said road, and now in the Treasurer's hands, or out of the first money which shall arise or be received from the tolls by this Act granted or otherwise, the said Trustees shall, in the first place, and in preference to all other payments whatsoever, pay and discharge all the costs, charges, and expences relative to the obtaining and passing of this Act; and the remainder of all such monie shall, after payment of the necessary expences of erecting or repairing toll-gates, toll-houses, weighing engines, and other buildings, milestones, or posts and fences, and for books, advertisements, salaries of officers, and other expences incidental to the execution of this Act, be applied, in the next place, in keeping down the interest of the principal monies advanced or borrowed on the credit of the tolls arising on the said roads by virtue of the said Act hereby repealed, in preference to the interest of any monies to be borrowed on the credit of this Act; in the next place, in keeping down the interest of the principal monies which may hereafter be borrowed on the credit of this Act; and afterwards on amending, widening, diverting, improving, repairing, and preserving the said roads, and in otherwise putting this and the general turnpike Acts into execution, and then in repaying the principal monies already borrowed on the credit of the tolls arising on the said roads by virtue of the said Act hereby repealed; and lastly, in repaying the principal monies to be borrowed on the credit of this Act, and to and for no other use or purpose whatsoever."

In many cases discontent or inconvenience may have been felt by the owners of the lands purchased by the Trustees for the making of the road in pursuance with this and other Acts. It is therefore provided that the freehold and inheritance of lands should remain and be vested in the persons of whom they were purchased. But, as indicated in the following, this was not to interfere with the Trustees' right of way, except when the lands were no longer wanted for the road, the rights of way then ceasing.

"The said Trustees shall, by means of such purchase and conveyance, be entitled to a perpetual right of way in or upon the lands purchased by them in pursuance of this Act and the Acts, or any of them."

Acts of Parliament show annoyances to which people were subjected, by inserting clauses which gave legal power to suppress them.

Clause 27 has, therefore, an interest indicating that the

practices thereby forbidden were so common on the Epping highways, as to become a serious source of annoyance, and probably a danger to persons passing over them, on horseback or in carriages.

Clause 27 :—"And be it further enacted, that if any person or persons shall exercise three horses at the same time upon any part of the said roads by riding one of them and leading the others abreast, or if any person shall hang out any linen or other clothes within forty feet from the centre of the said roads, or any of them, every person so offending shall for every such offence forfeit and pay any sum not exceeding forty shillings."

With the Act there are no plans, but there is the following table of particulars relating to the land taken :—

No. on the Plan.	Description of Property.	Owners or Reputed Owners.	Occupiers.	Parish.	County.
1	Part of new road through and over Forest Waste and common land.	Sir William Wake, Baronet, as Lord of the Manor of Waltham Holy Cross, and the Trustees of the Epping and Ongar Turnpike Roads.	The persons having right of common-age and the public.	Waltham Holy Cross.	Essex.
2, 4, and 6	Ditto	William Whitaker Maitland, Esq., as Lord of the Manor of Loughton, and the said Trustees.	Ditto . .	Loughton.	Essex.
5	Ditto	Charles Sotheby, Esq., as Lord of the Manor of Seward-stone, and the said Trustees.			
7	Ditto	John Rutherford Hatch Abdy, Esq., as Lord of the Manor of Chig-well, and the said Trustees.	Ditto ...	Chigwell .	Essex.

No. on the Plan.	Description of Property.	Owners or Reputed Owners.	Occupiers.	Parish	County.
8	Part of new road through and over Forest Waste and common land.	William Pole Tylney Long Wellesley, Esq., as Lord of the Manor of Woodford, and the Trustees of Middlesex and Essex Turnpike Roads.	The persons having right of commonage and the public	Woodford	Essex.
9	Part of the turnpike road through Woodford.	The Trustees of the Middlesex and Essex Turnpike Roads.	The public	Woodford	Essex.

A few years later the introduction of railways was about to change the means of locomotion throughout the country. There was consequently great necessity for economy in keeping up the roads, so that the interest on the money borrowed, and finally the principal, might be paid out of the anticipated diminished income. It is evident, by the following minute made in April, 1839, that the Trustees of the Epping and Ongar highways were fully alive to the probable loss of income, and were anxious to make such provision as would enable them to meet the annual expenses:—"That in consequence of the precarious nature of the security for the money borrowed upon the Epping and Ongar turnpike roads, in anticipation of the Northern and Eastern Railroad, it is deemed necessary to economize, with a view to paying off a portion of the existing debt. Resolved that the expenditure be reduced to the rate of twenty-five pounds per week for material and labour, that sum being considered by Sir James McAdam to be sufficient, with care and management, to maintain the road." The allowance for the tickets was reduced to five pounds. The attention which was being given to lessen expenses as far as possible, enabled the Trustees to pay by the end of the year, £500 off the loans, and to continue the reduction of the debt.

Two years and a half later, in September, 1841, the

tolls were put up to auction at £3,000, but there was no
offer. The Trustees had therefore to undertake the collection
of the tolls at the various gates on the Trust. A Committee,
appointed to attend to the management of the tolls and other
incidental matters, took possession of the toll-houses at 12 p.m.,
October 11th, and appointed toll collectors. But the question
arose as to whether a superintendent should not be appointed to
look after the interests of the Trust; the general opinion being
in favour of the proposal, a superintendent was appointed at a
salary of twenty shillings per week; and in November the wages
of the toll collectors were fixed at one guinea per week on the
Epping turnpike road, and nine shillings per week on the Ongar
road. At the same meeting, as contracts had been made with the
lessees of the tolls to receive a certain sum annually in place of
payment being made each day, the Trustees, considering the
payments to be fair and reasonable, permitted such compositions
to be renewed.

	£	s.	d.
Henry John Conyers, Esq., for the Epping gate only	2	2	0
Daniel Robert McNab, for the whole of the gates	2	10	0
Thomas Loft, Esq., for the whole of the gates..	2	10	0

The two last mentioned were medical men, practising in
the town and neighbourhood, and as they were constantly
passing and repassing through turnpike gates and side bars, the
paying their tolls in one sum must have saved them much
trouble, and so have been of great advantage to them.

In June, 1842, the treasurer was ordered—"Out of the
receipt from the tolls, to each month set apart the interest upon
the existing debt; and then the rate of three pounds per
centum per annum, to be applied in reduction of the principal
sum borrowed, and that the remainder of the receipts, as far
as is necessary, to be applied towards the maintenance and
repair of the roads under the care and management of the
Trustees."

In September, 1842, the tolls were put up at a reduced price, viz., £2,540; there was no bidding, but an offer was made to take a lease of the tolls at the price named, and the Trustees thought it advisable to accept it.

The great reduction in the value of the tolls must have caused much anxiety to the clerk, and to the Trustees, who took an active part in the proceedings; they appointed a Finance Committee to consider the state of the expenditure, and to offer any suggestions which might arise, and were capable of being carried out, for the improvement of the pecuniary position of the Trust.

At the next meeting of the Trustees (in November), the Finance Committee gave it as their opinion, that it would be advantageous to the Trust to enter into a contract for keeping the Epping roads in repair, suggesting that there should be one contract for the whole line of road, or in such portions as may be most favourable to the interest of the Trust; pointing out at the same time, that the contract for repairing the Ongar road was working satisfactorily. It was also advised, except in cases of emergency, that tradesmen should contract for any work required to be done; and, that the treasurer and surveyor's salary should be reduced.

The Finance Committee was requested to put the proposal into the form of a report, to be submitted at a meeting of the Trustees, to be held on the 21st instant, for their consideration; when it was resolved that the recommendation of the Committee should be adopted and acted on to the extent, viz., "that Sir James McAdam be consulted thereon, and requested to advise as to the form of advertisement for contract, stipulating what work and what quantity of material might be required, and into what portions it will be proper to divide the said road."

The clerk was directed to immediately communicate with Sir James McAdam, and, with the sanction of the Finance Committee, "make the proposal public, and also the particulars of the work expected, in such manner as thought to be advisable." The proposal that the work to be done by tradespeople should be submitted to contract was adopted; but the consideration of

the reduction of the treasurer and surveyor's salaries was postponed to the next meeting.

November, 1842. In consequence of Sir James McAdam
having stated that the plan proposed had been frequently tried,
and had failed, and had consequently been given up on all the
Trusts with which he was connected, the plan was abandoned ;
but the Committee considered it would be advisable to advertise
for contracts to procure, and lay up stones and gravel in the
separate depôts to be provided, and set apart by the surveyor.
They recommended that two hundred yards of stones or gravel
per year should be provided for each mile of road.

In consequence of the information and opinion obtained
from Sir James McAdam, the proposal to keep in repair
the Epping high road by contract was abandoned, and the
plan of employing milemen as labourers at a certain sum per
mile, and to contract for the material required was adopted.

December, 1842.—The clerk was directed "to select fit
and proper labourers as milemen, and to bring them before the
Finance Committee for instruction, at a meeting to be appointed
for that purpose." There were two tenders for supplying the
materials for the road ; one for the first six miles, from Harlow
Bush Common, and the other for the remainder.

The prices are not mentioned, but the tenders were accepted
on certain conditions. The contractors were to be under the
control of the road surveyor; they were not to work any
gravel pit before the place had been shown to him, and
inspected, and approved. The pits were to be sufficiently
filled up, and the ground left level, after the material had
been exhausted. The surveyor was directed to give particular
attention to the instructions, and to see that they were carried
out.

The salaries were taken into consideration ; and it was
resolved that Sir James McAdam's salary should be reduced
to £80, and the treasurer's to £40 per annum. The clerk's
salary appears not to have been reduced, as it is not mentioned.

The contractor for the repairs of the Ongar road was
ordered to discontinue the practice of cutting down the sides

of the road. Complaints had been made to the Trustees, and it was stated that his so doing was injurious to the highway.

The revenue from the tolls was decreasing. In 1842 they had been let for £2,540. In February, 1843, the lessee of the tolls made application for a reduction of his rent on account of the great falling off in the sum collected. The consideration of his request was deferred to the next meeting, at which the whole of the mortgagees were requested to be present. The meeting was fixed for the 27th of the following month, when there is entered the Minute as follows:—

"The application of the lessee of the tolls for a reduction in his monthly payments having been taken into consideration and fully discussed, it was resolved that the Trustees have no legal power or authority to abate any portion of the rent reserved in his lease."

A notice was sent to John Windus, the clerk, dated July 21st, 1843, and signed, as required by the Act of Parliament, requesting him to call a special meeting of the Trustees, to be held at "Epping Place Inn" on the 28th of August, for the purpose of putting up the tolls to be let by auction.

At the meeting the tolls were put up to be let for £2,540. There being no advance on that sum the tolls were not let.

At the meeting of the Trustees held on the 9th day of October, 1843, the tolls were again put up to auction, but at a reduced sum, viz., £2,200, with the same result; so a further reduction was made, and they were put up at the sum of £2,000, when Elisha Ambler, being the highest bidder at £2,060, they were leased to him, the Trustees agreeing to pay £5 towards the expense of the tickets required. But, on the tolls being put up at the same sum in September, 1844, there was no offer to take them at that price. They were again put up in October, and leased to William E. Bottle for one year for £2,145.

There was again a decline in the value of the tolls; they were in 1845 (August 25th) put up to auction at £2,145; but there was no bid for them, and they were put up at £2,050 with the same result. But, a further reduction having been made, they were leased to William Bottle at £2,005 for one year. Although there was annually a less sum received for the tolls, the Trustees continued to pay off each year a portion of their liability on mortgage. The account to December, 1838, shows an indebtedness on mortgage bonds of £12,000, and in December, 1845, it had been reduced £8,500.

In 1847 the Trustees had to take the collection of the tolls under their own management.

They had been put up to auction in August at £1,915; again in October at £1,880, and as there was no bidding they were again put up the same day at £1,810 per annum. But as no offer was made they were not let. The railroad to the eastern counties had been opened for traffic in 1845. The rapidly decreasing amount of toll taken, and the uncertainty as to the future, were the probable causes of the unwillingness of turnpike toll contractors to offer a sum likely to be accepted by the Trustees for the tolls on the Epping and Ongar roads. As the Trustees appointed the toll collectors, they became parties to the action referred to in the following Minutes in December (1847):—

"The clerk reported, that the collector at the Woodford Wells Gate, since the last meeting, had been summoned to the Ilford Bench for taking tolls for horses drawing stage coaches, the property of Mr. A. McNamara, who claimed exemption by reason that such coaches and horses were employed in conveying the mails, which claim of exemption the collector had been directed not to allow, because no letters were ever carried through the gate, but were deposited, and taken up, a mile on the London side of the gate. So that the horses and coaches when passing through the gate were not, in fact, then employed either in conveying, fetching, or guarding, or in returning back from conveying, or guarding such mails; and that in consequence of such summons he, the clerk, had attended the Ilford Bench on behalf of the collectors, when the Justices dismissed the summons, declaring their opinion that under the circumstances the complainant was not entitled to exemption."

In February, 1848, Mr. Henry Doubleday, the eminent

naturalist, was appointed treasurer in place of his father, deceased. And in August there is the following Minute :—

"The Trustees learn with deep regret the demise of their late respected clerk, Mr. John Windus, on the 17th instant; and they desire to record their high sense of his valuable services, and his prompt attention to all the interests of the Trust, for a period of upwards of twenty years. And William Coxhead Marsh, Esq., proposed, and Daniel Robert McNab, Esq., seconded the proposal, that Mr. John William Windus be appointed clerk *pro tempore.*"

The proposal was unanimously accepted, and a meeting was appointed to be held the 9th day of October to elect a clerk, and also for putting the tolls up to auction. Mr. Windus was then appointed clerk, and the tolls were let to Elisha Ambler for £1,645.

A Finance Committee was appointed by the Trustees at a meeting held 8th March, 1852.* The duties of the Committee were to examine all accounts of receipts and expenditure, and also the annual general statement. The clerk, treasurer, and surveyor were instructed to be present at the meetings.

The Finance Committee consisted of only three members, and two were to form a quorum.

The meetings of the Trustees were not well attended. There were seldom more than five members present, often only three, so it was probably considered useless to appoint a larger number than three as a Finance Committee.

June 28, 1852.—There was a proposal to reduce the interest on the loans or mortgages to 4½ per cent. per annum : and if the bondholders would not consent to the reduction, to give them notice that their bonds would be paid off.

In August the clerk reported he had, in pursuance of the directions received by him at the last meeting, applied to the different bondholders, and that they had severally agreed to the

---

* The business before the Trustees during the intervening years consisted in letting the tolls and making arrangements for the supply of gravel; they are not here entered, as they will be given further on in a tabulated form.

reduction of 10s. per annum from the interest of their respective mortgages.

The Trustees having had their attention called to the nuisance arising from swine being turned out on the side of the highroads, and the injury they did to the Trust, "Resolved that the parties so offending be warned, and in the event of their continuing the nuisance that proceedings would be taken under the Turnpike Act."

In August, Sir James McAdam having died, Mr. James McAdam was unanimously appointed surveyor, at a salary of £80 per annum. But he did not long enjoy the benefit of the appointment, for it is stated the next year "Mr. James McAdam, who had been appointed surveyor in August of the previous year in place of Sir James McAdam, having died, Thomas Wilson, the deputy surveyor, was appointed in his place at the same salary, viz., £80 per annum."

Although the introduction of gas into a town is only incidentally connected with the highways, the intention of erecting works to supply the town of Epping with gas shows a spirit of enterprise amongst the promoters, and first shareholders worthy of being noticed, and the following Minute is therefore copied. When it was made there was neither a canal nor a railway, so the coals had to be brought some distance by road, Harlow being the nearest station, to Epping: "23rd August, 1852.—Mr. James John Stevens, of Darlington Works, having applied to the Trustees for permission to open the turnpike roads, for the purpose of laying gas mains and service pipes; and, having undertaken to reinstate the said roads, to be answerable for all damage during the operation of the works, and to perform and complete the same under the direction and to the satisfaction of the Trust surveyor, the question was fully discussed, when it was resolved that such permission, so far as the Trustees of the road were concerned, should be granted upon payment of one shilling per square yard for consequential damages, with which Mr. Stevens expressed himself satisfied."

February 28th, 1853.—"It appearing by the treasurer's

account book that a balance, amounting to £435 0s. 8d., was in hand, it was resolved that the clerk be instructed to insert an advertisement in the county paper stating that a meeting of the Trustees would be held on Monday, the second day of May next, for the purpose of receiving proposals in writing from any creditor who may offer to accept the lowest composition in respect of the moneys due to him, and secured upon the said Trust; and that, in the event of no such proposal being made, they would proceed to apply the said sum, or such other sum as should then appear to be in hand, according to the directions contained in the Acts passed respectively on the 12th and 13th, and 13th and 14th years of the reign of her present Majesty, intituled 'The Turnpike Continuance Act.'"

The interest on the money borrowed now being 4½ per cent., in May, 1853, there was a motion made to the effect that the interest to be paid to the bondholders in June, 1854, and for the future would be at the rate of 4 per cent. per annum, and that should they decline to accept the reduced rate of interest, six months' notice be given, that the principal would be paid. But in the following year, 10th April, 1854, the rate of interest again came under the notice of the Trustees in consequence of the increased value of money, when it was agreed that the interest payable in June following should be at the rate of 4 per cent. per annum, as already settled, but that the future payment should be at the former rate, 4½ per cent. per annum. February, 1856, a bondholder applied to the Trustees, upon behalf of himself and other bondholders, to have the interest raised upon their respective bonds from 4½ to the original rate of interest, 5 per cent. per annum, upon the grounds of the scarcity of money, and its increased value. The Trustees present declined to accede to the proposed increase; whereupon the bondholder served the Trustees with notice calling upon them to pay off the amount due to him, and at the same time intimated that he should insist upon the increased rate of interest. At the meeting held August 25th the question of again raising the rate of interest on the bonds to 5 per cent. was discussed; when it was determined that, as the Trustees were not in a position to pay off the respective amounts due to the different bondholders, the increased rate of interest should be paid; that is to say, the interest which the bonds respectively carry, the first payment of such increased interest to become due and be paid at Christmas, 1856.

WATERING THE ROADS. April, 1854.—The surveyor of the Trust having applied for instructions relative to watering the portion of the Trust passing through the town of Epping, "It was resolved that, taking into consideration the expense of watering, coupled with the difficulty in procuring a sufficient supply of water, the consideration of the question should be postponed to the next meeting."

But the subject of watering the road through the town does not appear to have been again brought before the Trustees until February, 1859, when it is stated that, with reference to the application for a water-cart by the Epping parishioners, "the Trustees determine that until the water is forthcoming they could not entertain the question."

It may be concluded that during 1859 a supply of water had been obtained; for at the meeting, February, 1860, there was discussed the question of giving a donation to the surveyor of the parish of Epping, in aid of the expense of watering that portion of the turnpike road which passed through the town. It having been stated by the surveyor that the expenditure would be in some measure beneficial to the Trust, it was arranged that a donation of £25 should be given in June following.

At the meeting February, 1855, is a Minute as follows:—"A letter from Office of Woods and Forests of the 16th instant, addressed to the surveyor of the Epping and Ongar Turnpike Trust, upon the subject of forestal rights of the Crown in and over Epping Forest, and requesting to be informed whether the Trustees of the said Trust were prepared to negotiate for the purchase of such rights in, and over, a certain encroachment, stated to have been made by them on a portion of the forest situated in the manor of Woodford, was read; when, the question having been well considered, it was resolved that the clerk be directed to reply to the said letter stating, that the Trustees, not being aware of having encroached in any way, were wholly at a loss to conceive upon what grounds a claim for compensation by the Crown could be made. The land referred to is not more definitely mentioned.

Oct. 6th, 1856.—A memorial, which had been received at the meeting in August from the inhabitants of Epping, praying for a reduction of the tolls, was again brought forward, when, "The Trustees present were unanimously of opinion that, under existing circumstances (the tolls having fallen from £3,256 in 1838 to £1,465) it would be impolitic at present to comply with the memorialists' request."

The notice which had been given, as ordered at a previous meeting, respecting persons allowing swine to be at large on the highways, appears to have received no attention, for in November, 1856, is the following entry:—"The Trustees, having received information that various parties were in the habit of turning swine and other animals upon the Turnpike Trust, to the annoyance and injury of parties using the roads; resolved that the surveyor be now instructed to order all pigs or swine and such like animals to be seized and impounded; and to detain the same until the sum of two shillings be paid to such surveyor, over and above the reasonable charges and expenses of impounding and keeping the same, the said sum of two shillings to be applied to the use and in aid of the tolls of such road, pursuant to the directions contained in the General Turnpike Acts."

On August 17th, 1857, a letter mentioned as having been received on the 12th inst. from the valuer of the North Weald Enclosure, reporting the width of the main road and the Ongar road, as set out by him for the purpose of inclosure, was read and discussed, when the Trustees were of the opinion that the width proposed, viz., 40 feet for the main road, exclusive of the culverts or ditches on either side, and 30 feet for the Ongar road, exclusive of the culvert or ditch on either

side, would be amply sufficient, and the clerk was instructed
to reply to the valuer to that effect. Nothing, however, is
mentioned in the Minutes to show to what waste land the above
relates.

The following December "the Chairman called the attention of the meeting to the Resolution (above mentioned) passed
at the last meeting, with reference to the width of road to be
retained by the Trustees, through that portion of the Trust
lying within the parish of North Weald Bassett (the width
having at the last meeting been unanimously determined upon
and reported to the valuer), and he also referred the clerk to
the 118th section, 3rd of George IV., cap. 126, and instructed
him, should he consider it advisable, to call the attention of the
proper officers to the matter."

No further mention of the matter is made in the Minutes,
so it may be concluded that the widths of the road were fixed
according to the Resolution.

At the meeting in February, 1858, it having been reported
that the objectionable and illegal practice still continued, of
hanging gates in various parts of the Trust so as to open
outwards on to the turnpike road; it was resolved, "That the
surveyor be directed to give notice to parties thereof, where
he should deem it necessary, and that in the event of their
non-compliance he be empowered forthwith to put the law in
force."

At the same meeting the question of repairing and keeping
up the footpath throughout the Trust, was discussed at some
length, and it was decided that a special meeting should be
called for the 15th of March "for the purpose of taking the
matter into consideration, with a view to the maintenance of the
footpath by, and at the expense of, the Trustees of the road,
if the same could be legally done." At the next meeting,
March 15th, it is stated, that as regards the footpath, the
motion, of which notice had been given, was ordered to stand
over, it having been virtually withdrawn in consequence of
the practice adopted by turnpike trusts generally throughout
England. It was however, at the meeting determined to

empower the Trust surveyor to provide pipes to carry the surface water from the roads into the adjoining ditches.

February 7th, 1859.—There is a Minute—"The question of a slight deviation in the Loughton road opposite to the station having been discussed, resolved, that the surveyor be instructed to watch the interest of the Trust, and see the work carried out free of expense to the Trust, with the concurrence of Mr. Williams." But nothing more relating to the question is mentioned until the meeting August 10th, 1861, when it is stated, "A long conversation took place respecting a proposed deviation in the turnpike road at or near the Loughton Railway Station, and a suggestion was made that the Trustees should not only go to a considerable outlay, but that the requisite quantity of land should be purchased, &c., when the meeting was of opinion that it could not entertain the question at present.'

Two years later, in February, 1863, the subject again occupied the attention of the Trustees, for there is the following entry :—

"A certain deviation in the road opposite the Loughton Railway Station ; Resolved, that the Trust surveyor be instructed to communicate with the Lord of the Manor's surveyor respecting, and report at the next meeting."

Accordingly, the question of altering the corner of the turnpike road opposite the railway station at Loughton was brought forward at the meeting in June of that year, when a letter was received from the surveyor of the Manor offering the ground required for £30, free of all expense to the Manor. It was then unanimously resolved "that the offer be accepted, and that the necessary steps be immediately taken."

It appears to have resulted in the Great Eastern Railway purchasing the portion of the old road thrown out of use, for there is the following Minute made September 28th, 1863 :—

"A letter from Mr. Adams, on behalf of the Great Eastern Railway Company, offering £40 for the disused turnpike road fronting and adjoining to the railway station at Loughton, when it was resolved that the offer of the Company be accepted, and that the clerk be instructed to take the necessary steps for completing the sale to the Company on the above-mentioned terms."

15th August, 1860.—The Trustees proceed, pursuant to due notice, to the appointment of a general and superintending surveyor of the Trust, in the room of the late surveyor, Mr. John Wilson, deceased; when the different testimonials delivered in, having been opened and read and their respective merits discussed, Mr. John Harding was proposed, and no other person having been nominated he was elected, at a salary of £80 per annum, with the understanding that, as he could not reside within the district of the Trust, he would undertake to place his son in some convenient suitable locality; and, further, that he would be responsible to the Trustees for the due performance of the entire duties of the surveyorship by such son in his absence."

At the meeting in August it is stated, "It having been again represented to the Trustees that the tolls were sustaining a loss in consequence of the opening of a certain road or highway into the main road, enabling parties to evade the tolls at the Woodford Gate, the clerk was instructed to give notices summoning a meeting for the purpose of ordering a side bar or the placing a chain on the side of the new road." And at the meeting September 24th, 1860, is the following entry, "That the Trustees of the said turnpike roads, in exercise of the powers of the general laws relating to the turnpike roads, do judge it necessary forewith to erect, and do hereby order the erection of, a bar or the placing of a chain on the side of the said turnpike road known as the New Road, at or near a certain parish road or highway there leading from and out of such turnpike road to and into the parish of Chingford; and do further order the same tolls to be taken at such bar or chain, as are now taken at the main gate, known as the Woodford Wells Gate." But it was provided the one should clear the other, and that persons residing within 500 yards of the said proposed bar on the west side, and being *bonâ fide* inhabitants and residents shall be exempted from payment of the said toll on paying annually on 16th day of October to the lessee a sum of one shilling by way of compensation.

In February, 1861, a complaint was made on the part of the inhabitants of Chingford concerning the recently erected side bar, when the Chairman pointed out that the matter could not be entertained until the expiration of the existing lease. The complainant then gave notice that he would at the meeting for letting the tolls in the ensuing year, bring before the notice of the Trustees the propriety of excluding *bonâ fide* parishioners of Chingford from the payment of tolls at the said bar.

This question accordingly came before the Trustees in August, 1861, when it was determined "to insert a special clause in the conditions of letting, to the effect that owners or occupiers residing within the limits of Whitehall Lane, in the parish of Woodford, and in the houses known as Whitehall and Heron's Nest, in the parish of Chingford, be exempted from payment of tolls at the said bar on payment to the lessee of the tolls, annually, in advance, the sum of 10s. by way of compensation and in lieu thereof; provided, however, that the foregoing resolution shall in no way affect or make void the resolution, past on the 24th day of September, 1860."

At the same meeting a notice of the intention of the London and Bury Railway Company to cross the turnpike road in the parish of Chipping Ongar was produced and laid upon the table; also a similar notice of their intention to cross the said turnpike road in the parish of High Ongar.

The plan for a London and Bury Railway Company was abandoned, and the Great Eastern Counties undertook to construct the present line through Epping to Ongar.

At the annual meeting 2nd of February, 1863, the question of reducing the tolls was brought forward, when it was moved and seconded that, in consequence of the trifling amount of the existing bond debts, coupled with the heavy rate of tolls compared with those of the neighbouring Trusts, the clerk be instructed to prepare and publish the proper legal notice summoning a meeting of the Trustees. The proposal was adopted; and at the meeting in the following June the clerk reported that he had, pursuant to the provision of the Act of Parliament, caused advertisements to be inserted in the county papers, and notices to be affixed to the turnpike gates or bars throughout the Trust stating the purport of the meeting; and that he had also procured the consent of the bondholders to the proposed reduction, as required by the Turnpike Acts.

The subject before the meeting, it is stated, was fully discussed, and it was "Unanimously resolved that a uniform reduction of one-third be made from the tolls throughout the Trust, subject, however, to the following exceptions, viz.; that goat and dog carriages pay as at present; and in cases in which the present toll amounts to 4*d.*, the reduced scale be taken at 2½*d.*" At all future lettings the extra toll taken during fair weeks at the price specified in the old schedule be discontinued.

The schedule of tolls, as follows, signed by the Chairman, was ordered to be entered on the day's proceedings, and to come in force on the 16th October, 1863.

For every horse or other beast drawing any coach, chariot, barouche, chair, curricle, phaeton, landau, Berlin, calash, break, hearse, or other carriage of like description with two wheels—if drawn by one or two horses or beasts of draught, for each .. .. 3*d.*

If with four wheels and drawn by one horse or beast of draught .. .. 4*d.*

If drawn by two horses or beasts of draught each 3*d.*

If drawn by three or more .. .. .. each 2½*d.*

For every horse or other beast drawing any wain, waggon, cart, dray, caravan, or other like carriage .. .. 2½*d.*

For every horse or other beast, laden or unladen, and not drawing.. .. .. 1*d.*

For every drove of oxen, cows, neat cattle, per
 score   ..   ..   7*d*.
     (And so in proportion for a less number.)
For every drove of calves, hogs, sheep or lambs,
 per score 3*d*
     (And so in proportion for a less number.)
For every carriage propelled or moved by steam,
 gas, machinery or other means, for each wheel   4*d*.
For every dog or goat drawing any kind of carriage   ½*d*.

In August, 1863, although the tolls were so much reduced, they were put up at £2,100, the sum for which they were then let, but no bid was made. At the next meeting (in September) they were put up at the same price; but as no one bid for them, they were put up at £1,000, and ultimately let for £1,605.

At the first meeting in 1864 (on February 15th) the question of increasing the treasurer's and clerk's salaries was discussed, when it was unanimously agreed that the treasurer's salary should be at once increased to £40 per annum, and the clerk's salary raised to the same amount.

There was brought forward by the clerk a claim of £7 against the lessee of the tolls, for the expenses of a prosecution instituted by him for evading the toll at Duck Lane Gate, which he thought should be borne by the Trustees; the question of upholding their rights being solely concerned. The matter, it is said, was briefly discussed, and it was unanimously agreed that the account should be paid out of the Trust funds.

It appears also that the surveyor got into trouble. The following is the Minute made at the time: "It appearing that sundry notice boards, stating that horses, cattle, &c., straying upon the turnpike road would be impounded, had been placed by the surveyor on the waste lands contiguous to the Trust roads, and that such boards had been so placed without the order of the Trustees, and were in reality illegal," it was therefore resolved that the same be forthwith removed.

The tolls were put up at the sum for which they had been

let the previous year, but there was no bidding, so the clerk was instructed to call a meeting for the 3rd of October. The tolls were then put up again at £1,605. No bidding in advance of that sum having been made, they were offered at £1,200, and subsequently let for the sum at which they were at first put up, viz, £1,605. The Trustees, being very satisfied with the result, they resolved, "In consequence of the competition for the tolls, and the satisfactory sum realised by such competition, that the sum of 10s. should be allowed towards the expense of each *bonâ fide* bidder."

In consequence of a report before the meeting "that the contractor for the purchase of the road sands had been in the habit of breaking up and cutting away and removing from the sides of the turnpike road the sands, stones, &c., the surveyor was instructed, in the event of a repetition of the offence, to summon the party or parties so offending."

At this time it appears that sundry encroachments on the waste were commenced, and the Trustees' attention having been called to several by their surveyor, at the meeting held February 13th, 1865, they gave instruction in the following Minute :—

"The Trust surveyor having reported that, in the Loughton and Woodford Division of the Trust, large tracts of common or waste land were being daily enclosed, and that the boundary fences in many instances were so placed by the sides of the turnpike roads as to reduce the breadth, or confine the limits thereof within the distance of thirty feet and twenty-five feet respectively from the middle or centre of such roads, contrary to the provisions of the General Turnpike Acts, it was unanimously resolved that he be instructed to ascertain by admeasurement from the centre of the said roads in different localities between the 'Wake Arms' and the Woodford Wells Gate, on both the Loughton and the new roads, what encroachments had taken place; and that he submit to the Trustees at their next meeting, to be holden on the 13th day of March next, a written report, setting out such encroachment, if any, and the reduction in the legal width of the roads occasioned thereby."

Accordingly, the surveyor brought in his report relating to the alleged encroachments on the upper division. As the first encroachment mentioned did not appear to be injurious in any way to the Trust, it was allowed to remain. A pond which had been made in Buckhurst Hill was ordered to be emptied or filled up, as it was considered to be injurious to the adjoining road; and a newly erected fence on another property was ordered to be removed back to the original Trust fence.

The wishes of the inhabitants of the town of Epping were again brought before the meeting in February, 1861, when it was resolved that a contribution of £25 be granted towards the watering of the town. The subject is not further mentioned until 1865, when (March 13, 1865), the question of watering the town of Epping came before the meeting of the Trustees held on that date. After much discussion it was determined " to do so, upon the condition that the parishioners would contribute £15 towards the expenses, such sum to be paid to the treasurer by or before the 1st of June, the sum to be expended by the Trust surveyor not to exceed £25 in addition to the said sum of £15."

In August, 1866, the tolls arising from the several gates and bars in the Trust were put up to auction at the sum at which they had been leased the previous year, £1,555. But as Duck Lane Gate had been done away with, and exemptions from tolls made in favour of the inhabitants of North Weald Bassett, the Trustees could not have been disappointed when they found that there was no bidding.

The clerk was ordered to summon a special meeting for October 1st. On the Minutes of the last meeting having been read and signed by the chairman, he moved and carried the resolution that, to the conditions on which the tolls were usually let, should be added the following : " Whereas it is contemplated to include in the schedules to the Turnpike Continuance Act of the next Session of Parliament such Trusts as shall then be found to be free from debt, the Trustees therefore reserve to themselves the right of determining this present or any future letting in the event of the above Trust being included ; or in the event of the cesser of the same Trust from any cause whatsoever, and should any such letting be so determined before its expiration, the rent per diem throughout the year shall be ascertained, and a proportionate reduction made at that rate." The tolls were put up at £1,555, but there being no bidding above that sum, they were again put up at £1,000. Mr. Thomas Bowers being the last and highest bidder, they were let to him, subject to the conditions above mentioned for one year, for £1,175.

Although the chairman made no mention, in the resolution, of any cause for believing the Epping and Ongar Trust was about to cease, it is quite clear that at the time there were sufficient reasons for supposing there was an intention, on the part of Government, to terminate the Trust, if possible, with due regard to its liabilities. For there is on the same date entered the Minute as follows : " A letter from the Right Honourable the Secretary of State, inquiring what portion of the balance in the treasurer's hands at Christmas last had been applied in liquidation of the existing mortgage debt, was read ; when the clerk was instructed to state, in reply, that no portion had been so applied, the Trustees being of opinion that such balance would be required for the repair of the roads ; but that at the meeting this day holden, they had determined to order their treasurer to pay £200 forthwith from the fund in hand towards the liquidation of the existing debt."

Complaints having been made by one of the Trustees and others of the condition of a portion of the roads under their management, owing, it was said, partly to the want of efficient drainage, it was resolved that a sum not exceeding £50 should be judiciously laid out, by a Committee appointed for that purpose, on the hills on the old Loughton road, and on a portion of the new road,—all being within the parish of Loughton.

The year 1866 terminated with two alterations in the roads, one at the top of Golden's Hill and the other near to Woodford Wells.

The first was not of much importance.

By the Minute it appears that at the top of the old road up Golden's Hill there was a small frontage, formerly a portion of the turnpike road, which the proprietor of the premises abutting upon it was desirous of adding to his property.

The alteration by which the fence would be made to run in a straight line was considered to be beneficial to the Trust. So it was agreed that the applicant should be allowed to purchase the strip of land referred to for £20; which price was considered to be more than its value. The legal expenses were, however, to be borne by the Trustees, and the clerk consequently was instructed to prepare the deed necessary to complete the purchase.

The other alteration was one of great importance. It was the alteration of the old Loughton road, near to Woodford Wells, before it joined the new road from the "Wake Arms." The business commences with the entry in the Minute Book as follows :—

"The meeting for letting the tolls and transacting other general business being completed, the Trustees proceeded to hold a special meeting, duly called and advertised, for the purpose of considering an application for the alteration of the old road through Loughton, pursuant to the notice given at the last meeting; where it is stated that, the Trustees had received an application for the diversion and alteration of the portion of the old Loughton road, at or near the Woodford Wells Gate, in the parish of Woodford, and the instituting of a new line of roadway near there, according to a plan then exhibited."

The notice calling the meeting was read.

The clerk reported he had duly caused notice of the meeting to be affixed at different gates throughout the Trust, and to be advertised in the county papers, as required by the Act of Parliament.

The Committee appointed to examine the proposed deviation of the road and the substitution of a new line of roadway reported that they had done so, and that, in their opinion, the alteration would be beneficial to the Trust and to the public generally.

The plan mentioned is not amongst the Trust papers. It may, therefore, be stated that it consisted in the enclosing within the boundaries of the estate known as Knighton's, a portion of the old road, and making through the waste land a road in place of the one to be enclosed. It appearing by the report of the Committee appointed to examine the plans, &c., "that such diversion and alteration would be beneficial to the Trust, by decreasing the elevations, and shortening the existing mileage, it was resolved to divert and alter the line of the said road accordingly, and to substitute a new line of roadway in accordance with the plan produced."

The surveyor to the Trust was desired to cause the necessary alterations to be made. "The cost, charges, and expenses, however, both legal and otherwise, including the thorough underdrainings of the substituted road, and the cost of all necessary fencings, be borne and paid by the owner of the estate, the application being entertained by the Trustees at his special request, and for his benefit."

December 3rd, 1866.—The owner of the estate proposed a further slight deviation of the existing road, and a removal of the present toll-house and gates to a site on his land more convenient to him. This proposal met with the approval of the Trustees, provided the sanction of the present lessee could be obtained, and compensation rendered him for any injury he might sustain. Further stipulations were made, that the alterations should be carried out free of all cost to the Trustees, and that the old road should remain open for traffic until the new portion was available and safe for use by the public.

The question of the value to be put on the disused road-way was discussed. The Trustees determined, so far as they could legally do so at the meeting then held, that the existing roadway, together with the site of the present toll-house, should be valued in accordance with the requirements of the Turnpike Acts ; and that the new roadway to be substituted for it should be valued at the same time ; and that having arrived at the value of the site of the toll-house and present roadway, the value of the proposed new roadway should be deducted, and the balance only paid by the owner of Knighton's.

At the meeting held April, 1867, the Committee which had been appointed to examine its condition reported that the new piece of road was hard and suitable for use. It was consequently ordered to be opened to the public, and that the piece of ground thrown out of use should be conveyed to the owner of Knighton's, in accordance with the agreement which had been made.

In August the tolls were put up to auction at £1,175, the sum they had realised the previous year; and, in order to prevent their being let under their value, a reserved price was fixed at £1,400; the bidding, however, reached £1,630. The deputy surveyor was appointed surveyor at a salary of £80 per annum, subject to the appointment being terminable by a three months' notice.

There was in 1868 some thought of endeavouring to procure an extension of the powers of the Trustees; for it is stated, July 21, "The proposed new Turnpike Bill was laid before the meeting, but its further consideration was postponed."

August 27th.—A letter, dated the 12th, from the Home Secretary was read. The letter is not copied into the Minute Book. But it evidently related to the termination of the Trust, for there is entered, "The opinion was unanimously expressed, that the tolls could not be abolished until 1870." There appears to have been some inquiry made by the Home Secretary respecting the state of the roads, to which no answer was given.

September, 1869, the proposal to endeavour to obtain a new Highway Act was brought before the meeting. The clerk was instructed to institute inquiries as to the probability of success if application were made to Parliament to renew the Trust; and the probable expense. There being no further mention of the proposal in the Minute Book, it may be concluded that the information he obtained was such as did not justify further proceedings. In October the tolls were again let, but for £870 only.

The Trust was approaching its end, and the Trustees seemed to have been anxious as to their financial position. The surveyor and treasurer had evidently been ordered to make a careful examination of business entrusted to them; for, January, 1870, there is the following entry made in the Minute Book, on the statement of the surveyor and treasurer having been examined, "The Trustees were unanimously of the opinion that the state of their finances was far more satisfactory than, at their last meeting, they had reason to hope." February 7th, 1870, a letter was read from the Secretary of State relating to the course to be adopted in winding up the Trust, and enclosing extracts from the various Turnpike Acts bearing on the subject. Its further consideration was postponed until the following meeting, to be called at the end of March; when the sale of the Trust property was also to be taken into consideration, and arrangements made for its disposal.

March 30th, 1870, the special meeting assembled at the "Cock Inn," according to notice, for the purpose of receiving the official report of the surveyor appointed to value the Trust property, and to determine upon the mode of proceeding in reference to the sale and disposal of such properties.

"The report of Mr. Hine, the surveyor, containing the estimate of the respective values set upon the different Trust properties having been read and approved, it was resolved that such properties should be offered to the several parties having the right of pre-emption at such estimated value; and that, in the event of their declining to avail themselves of such right, the said properties, or such of them as shall not be taken, or sold, shall be submitted to public auction at the 'Cock Inn,' at Epping, on Friday, the 13th day of May; and the reserved price to be fixed on each property to be finally determined at a meeting of the Trustees, to be held on the 20th day of April next, for that and other purposes."

June 24th.—The clerk reported to the Trustees then assembled that the sale of the Trust property had taken

place according to their instruction. The amount realised was
£957 6s., as is shown by the following statement copied from
the account book :—

ACCOUNT SALES of the entire Trust property on the expiration of the Trust and
removal of the gates.

1870, July	£ s. d.	1870, July.	£ s. d.
Paid Mr. Hine his charge for valuation and sale of property, as per account	41 4	Received the purchase money for Woodford Wells toll house and premises	415 0 0
Messrs. Windus and Amys expenses of, and incidental to, the sale of the entire Trust properties, the conveyance to the purchasers as required by the Turnpike Act and the winding up of the Trust, and distribution of the balance in hand amongst the several parishes	75 16 2	Epping toll house and premises	175 0 0
		Road Street	150 0 0
		Thornwood	175 0 0
		Norton Heath	71 0 0
The expenses of pulling down and removing High Ongar toll house, as per agreement	1 10 0	Materials of High Ongar toll house	15 0 0
		Norton Heath gate posts and fencing	1 2 0
		" High Ongar	1 15 0
		" Road Street	0 15 0
		" Thornwood	1 1 0
By purchase of tenants fixtures at the Woodford Wells Gate	1 15 0	Duck Lane box and iron bars	2 10 0
Balance in hand carried to the General Account of the Treasurer	827 5 6	Epping gates and fencing	8 3 0
		Woodford Wells gates and fencing	1 2 0
	£957 0 0		£957 0 0

The general statement of account, consisting of receipts
and disbursements, to be certified by the Chairman, and a copy
sent to the Home Office, was made to the end of June : it
includes the payment of the only remaining bond and interest,
£572 10s. The balance was ordered, at the adjourned meeting
of the Trustees held August 26th, after all the Trust's liabilities
had been satisfied, to be divided into two equal portions, one
portion to be equally divided between the clerk, treasurer, and
surveyor, and the other moiety between the several parishes
through which ran the road comprised within the Trust.

The following are the particulars of the final balance
sheet :—

	£ s. d.		£ s. d.
To balance due to the Treasurer as per his account	552 4 1	To balance in hand on sale account	827 5 6
To composition awarded to Clerk, Treasurer, and Surveyor	142 10 9		
To balance for distribution amongst the respective parishes	142 10 8		
	£837 5 6		£837

The Woodford turnpike gate at the junction of the old road through Loughton and the new road through the forest has been removed, and a horse trough put in its place. But the Epping toll-house still remains. It has had a story added to it, and is known as Belle Vue Cottage. Standing opposite the road which leads to Theydon Bois it commands extensive views over Bell Common, the forest, along the high road in each direction, and down the road to Theydon that runs on one side of Bell Common, from which it was formerly separated by a ditch and bank having on it a fence to prevent travellers passing over the common, and so avoiding the turnpike, and the payment of tolls.

CHAPTER XI.

Accounts of the Trust.

The account book commences in 1805 with a balance brought forward from the previous year of £104 14s. 1d.

The items run on, and no balance is struck until the end of July, 1810.

The money received during the 5½ years, including the balance above mentioned, amounted to .. £8,332 5 3
and the expenditure to 7,867 6 4

leaving in the hands of the treasurer £464 18 11

The receipts were derived principally from tolls; a small sum came in for road sand, and occasionally there is mention made of a small fine, but what for is not stated. The accounts were again made up to the end of September. During the intervening two months there had been received from tolls £290 19s. 4d. and expended £47 4s. 7d.

The balance September 30th, the end of the financial year, in the treasurer's hands was £708 13s. 8d.

The expenditure had been, during the 5½ years, for

	£	s.	d.
Gravel	513	4	2
Cartage	738	11	0
Gravel and carting	684	11	8
,, labour	1,490	17	9
Labour	216	16	4
Interest on the money borrowed on the			
security of the toll	1,499	0	0

and £480 for incidental expenses, such as salaries, repairs to buildings, drains, &c. And in June, 1805, £8 was paid for land required to widen the road at Bobbingworth.

The accounts, during the next four years, were commenced in the October of one year and completed and balanced September 30th in the following year; they were audited and signed by the Trustees present. The balance commenced the next financial year.

For the sake of comparison it is thought to be advisable to arrange the account as follows. In the account book each item, both of receipt and expenditure, is recorded.

ACCOUNTS (showing the year in which they are audited and balanced).

—	Balance.	Money received.	Money expended.	Total, including balance.
	£ s. d.	£ s. d.	£ s. d.	£ s. d.
1811	708 13 8	1,983 12 8	1,958 16 4	2,692 6 4
1812	643 10 0	1,600 4 8	1,792 7 2	2,245 14 8
1813	453 7 6	1,775 16 8	1,980 10 3	2,299 4 2
1814	248 13 9	1,871 16 3	1,368 3 0	2,120 10 6
1815	752 7 6			

June, 1811.—There are the following entries forming part of the outlay :—

The Clerk of the House of Commons .. £213 18 4
The surveyor's expenses attending the
    Commons 7 0 0
Jessop's (the clerk) bill 134 6 8

After 1814 the accounts were made up at irregular intervals; and the balance not satisfactorily obtained, as appears by the following entry, November, 1816, in handwriting, differing from that of the keeper of the account books, and looking as if the writer had given up the attempt to obtain a correct balance as altogether hopeless.

" Treasurer debits by balance, reported to
    be in his hand £831 5 6
By 6 months receipt from the lessee of
    the tolls as on the other side .. 1,012 10 0"

The two items above mentioned commence the account for 1817, in April, leaving a balance £246 1s. 3d. The accounts are not again made up until September, 1819. When they are audited by the seven Trustees present and the balance, £911 14s. 7d., carried forward.

--	Balance.	Received.	Spent	Total and balance
	£ s. d.	£ s. d.	£ s. d.	£ s. d.
April 1817	231 5 6	1,864 1 10	2,450 2 0	2,695 5 11
	The balance is struck in February.			
1818	246 1 3	917 0 0	916 4 6	1,162 5 9

During the financial years, 1819-20, the accounts were made up and balanced in May, July, and November; the expenditure was £2,895 10s. 8d., and the balance £443 2s. 4d., carried forward to the next year's account. The expenditure seems large, but the sum, £526, was repaid to a bondholder.

The account for 1820-21 commences November 6th, 1820, and ends September 3rd, 1821.

—	Balance	Received.	Spent.	Total, including balance
	£ s. d.	£ s. d.	£ s. d.	£ s. d.
1820-1	443 2 4	1,838 5 0	1,662 14 0	2,281 7 4
1821-2	618 13 4	2,530 4 3	2,355 7 0	

The accounts run on without a balance, having been arrived at until January 30th, 1823. But the above figures appear at the end of September, 1822, in the body of the account; not breaking the continuity of entries, and apparently due to the necessity there was for the clerk to have the figures to enable him to fill in the forms, in compliance with the Parliamentary Order.

January 30th, 1823.—The figures are as follows:—

Balance.	Received.	Expended.	Total.
£ s. d. 618 13 4	£ s. d. 3,296 16 1	£ s. d. 2,865 16 8	£ s. d. 3,814 14 1

The expenditure included payments to bondholders, who had lent money on the security of the tolls.

Repayment of Money Borrowed.

In August, 1810, there is entered a payment made the previous December to Lord Henniker:—" Principal and interest due on mortgage of tolls, £201 13s. 4d."

							£	s.	d.
Jan. 17th.	1812	Payment off bond	....	....	....		200	0	0
	1813	,,	principal	....	....		200	0	0
	1814	,,	,,	and interest	....		304	0	0
	1817	,,	,,	,,	....		300	0	0
	1819	,,	,,	,,	....		300	0	0
	1820	,,	,,	,,	....		226	5	9
	1820	,,	,,	,,	....		200	0	0
	1821	,,	,,	,,	....		502	10	0
Jan. —	1822	,,	,,	,,	....		200	0	0
							£2,634	9	1

There is mention made of £300 paid to one of the bondholders, but there being no memorandum for what purpose the money was paid, it is omitted in the above list of payments

The financial year, 1822-23, commenced with an indebtedness on account of money borrowed of £3,500.

Until the year 1822-23 the accounts of the Trustees have been, at times, irregularly kept. It seems, however, as if similar irregularity was to be met with in the accounts of other trusts. For, in the Act 3 George IV., cap. 126, August 6th, 1822, there is a clause giving instructions as to the compilation and rendering of accounts. Clause 78 directs, " That the Trustees or Commissioners of every turnpike road shall, at their general annual meeting in each year, examine and audit the accounts of the treasurer, clerk, and surveyor, in their employ, distinguishing

GENERAL STATEMENT OF THE INCOME AND EXPENDITURE

OF THE

EPPING AND ONGAR TURNPIKE ROADS,

Between Michaelmas 1822, and Michaelmas 1823.

Expenditure.	£.	s.	d.	Income.				£.	s.	d.
To Surveyor's Account of Day Labor, between Michaelmas 1822, and Michaelmas 1823, for Maintenance or Repair of Roads	198	15	9	By Balance in the Treasurer's Hands				756	0	7
To Surveyor's Account of Team Labor, between same time	266	17	3	By Amount of Tolls received from the Gatekeeper, between Michaelmas 1822, and Michaelmas 1823, as follows :—						
Ditto, for Work executed by Contract, being for 11 miles on Ongar Road, including Stones and Labor	310	0	0		Stag Gate	1125	14	0		
Ditto for Repair or Maintenance, or Building of Houses, Gates or Bridges	161	7	5		Epping Gate	275	8	0		
Ditto for Rents of Quarries, and Costs of Stones	235	2	1		Thornwood Gate	324	0		
Ditto for Salaries and other Payments to Clerks, Surveyors, or other Officers	143	14	11		Ongar Gates	218	12	6		
Ditto for Printing, Advertising and Stationary	20	3	6		Duck and Bink's Lane	6	9	0	1950	7	6
Ditto for Interest of Debt	102	10	0	By Incidental Receipts for Road Scrapings				32	11	0
Ditto for Incidental Charges	10	8	9							
Ditto Bond Debt paid off	300	0	0							
Ditto Balance in Hands of Treasurer	929	19	5							
£	2738	19	1				£	2738		

GENERAL STATEMENT OF DEBTS AND CREDITS.

	£.	s.	d.		£.	s.	d.
An Account of the Amount of Debt bearing Interest	3200	0	0	On Account of Incidental Receipts, for Road Scrapings	14	0	0
Account of interest due up to Michaelmas, 1823.	62	10	0	Nett Amount of Debt	3248	10	0
	3262	10	0		3262	10	0

[Signed]   DAVID POWELL, CHAIRMAN.

6th October, 1823.

[Signed]   NICH. PEARSE, TREASURER.

FARM-HILL HOUSE, WALTHAM ABBEY,
November, 1823.

DEAR SIR,

Agreeable to the Directions of the Statute 3 Geo. IV. Ch. 126. I herewith send you a Copy of the Accounts and Statements of the Treasurers, as Signed and Settled at the General Meeting held for that purpose, on the 6th day of October last.

The next Meeting of the Trustees will be held at EPPING PLACE, on Monday, the 5th day of January next, at 12 at noon.

I am, Dear Sir,
Your very Humble Servant,
JOHN JESSOPP,

CLERK TO THE TRUSTEES.

bond from other debts," and when found to be correct, the Chairman had to sign them. The accounts, &c., so certified were to be made out in accordance with a form appended to the Act of Parliament, and a copy transmitted to the Clerk of the Peace of the county in which the roads, or the major part, were situated. The Clerk of the Peace was to cause the accounts to be produced to the justices assembled at Quarter Sessions, and then to be registered, and kept amongst the records of the Quarter Session. The statement was to be printed, and a copy sent to each acting Trustee or Commissioner of the road.

The introduction of forms in which the accounts were to be rendered, secured uniformity in the highway accounts throughout the kingdom. But it does not appear that there was any idea of transmitting copies to a central office until the 3rd and 4th William IV., cap. 80, required copies of the annual statements of highway accounts to be forwarded to the Secretary of State.

The object is explained in the Turnpike Act of 1869 to be, "To enable the principal Secretary of State to elucidate said statements, and to make abstracts thereof to be laid before Parliament."

It is, however, due to the Act of 1822, that the following accounts of the receipt and expenditure of the Epping and Ongar Trust have been kept in a manner allowing them to be readily tabulated.

A copy of each year's account made out on the form ordered by Parliament was pasted in a book kept for that purpose. One of them has been reproduced by photo-lithography, and it is, therefore, a facsimile; a copy faces this page.

The amounts were made up at Michaelmas, and, therefore, include the last quarter of the previous year.

Statement of Income and Account of Interest on account of Loans

—	1830.	1831.	1832.	1833.
	£ s. d.	£ s. d.	£ s. d.	£ s. d.
Account of day labour for maintenance and repair of road	305 10 0	406 10 5	302 13 0	358 17 11
To amount for team labour	220 15 6	132 6 8	209 2 11	184 7 10
Or of work done by contract	541 17 4	555 11 4	01 0 1	544 1 1
To repair of buildings, houses, gates and bridges	81 1 10	89 1 7	153 18 2	88 18 7
To rent of quarries and cost of stones	91 5 0	184 18 1	102 16 1	153 11 5
Salaries and other payments to Clerk, Surveyor, and other Officers	197 10 0	28 8 0	284 5 1	114 1 0
Printing, advertising and stationery	13 5 8	72 15 0	42 10 0	7 0 0
To interest on debt	95 5 0	315 5 0	309 0 0	350 0 0
To incidental expenses	95 12 0	63 6 2	4 2 0	55 11 6
Outlay on new roads	291 8 5	2,075 5 3	5,643 1 0	142 12 5
Exchequer Bills		1,000 0 0		
Purchase of exchequer bills		500 10 0	2,201 1 0	
Balance due to Treasurer			501 4 5	452 15 7
Balance in hand of Treasurer	121 5 3			
	1,911 10 0	42 5 18 6	7,379 15 7	5,091 12 11

Statement of Income and Amount of Debt on account of Loans.

—	1830.	1831.	1832.	1833.
	£ s. d.	£ s. d.	£ s. d.	£ s. d.
Balance in the Treasurer's hands	121 4 1	121 5 3	...	...
Tolls received :—				
Stag Gate	207 1 0	81 10 10	...	...
Epping Gate	239 13 0	13 4 0	...	...
Thornwood Gate	254 6 0	...	...	...
Ongar Gate	193 10 0	7 10 0	...	...
Duck Lane Gate	4 15 0	...	...	...
Fines and penalties	17 7 2	14 15 0	52 15 0	11 12 0
Received from the Lessees of the tolls	...	2,420 0 0	2,420 0 0	2,420 0 0
			Cash by sale of Exchequer bills.	Cash by sale of Exchequer bills.
Cash borrowed on security of the tolls	...	7,000 0 0	4,578 4 0	511 8 9
Balance due to Treasurer	...	271 4 5	252 13 7	146 5 2
	1,095 16 0	9,839 16 6	7,729 15 7	3,042 12 11
Amount of debt bearing interest	1,500 0 0	7,000 0 0	7,000 0 0	7,000 0 0
Exchequer bill in			...	

The form in which the accounts were to be kept, as ordered by 3 and 4 William IV.

GENERAL STATEMENT of the Income and Expenditure of the Epping and Ongar Turnpike Trust, in the County of Essex, between the Twenty-ninth day of September, 1833, and the Thirty-first day of December, 1833.

INCOME.	£ s. d.	EXPENDITURE.	£ s. d.
Balance in Treasurer's hands brought forward	[illegible]	Balance due to Treasurer brought forward	[illegible]
Revenue received from tolls	[illegible] 15 [illegible]	Manual labour	[illegible]
Parish composition in lieu of duty	[illegible]	Team labour and carriage of materials ...	[illegible] 7 1
Estimated value of statute duty performed	[illegible]	Materials for surface repair	[illegible]
Received from fines	[illegible]	Land purchased	[illegible]
from incidental expenses ...	4 [illegible]	Damage done in obtaining materials ...	[illegible]
Amount of money borrowed on the security of the tolls	[illegible]	Tradesmen's bills	[illegible] 4 [illegible]
		Salaries—Treasurer	[illegible]
		Clerk	7 17 [illegible]
		Surveyor	[illegible]
		Law charges	[illegible]
		Interest of debt	111 [illegible] 8
		Improvements	[illegible]
		Debt paid off	[illegible]
		Incidental expenses	4 [illegible]
		Statute duty performed—estimated value	[illegible]
		Balance due to Trust...	[illegible]
Balance due to Treasurer	[illegible]		
	£[illegible] 15 [illegible]		£[illegible]

	£ s. d.	Rate of Interest per cent. £ s. d.		£ s. d.	Insert the Name and Place of Abode of the Treasurer, Clerk, General and Superintending Surveyor hereof.
Bonded or mortgage debt... ...	[illegible]	[illegible]	Arrears of tolls for current year ...	[illegible]	Treasurer, Ralph Doubleday, Epping.
Floating ...	0 0 0	0 0 0	Arrears of parish composition for current year ...	[illegible]	Clerk, John Windus, Epping.
Unpaid interest ...	0 0 0	0 0 0	Arrears of any other receipt for current year	[illegible]	General Surveyor, James McAdam, London.
Balance due to Treasurer	0 0 0	0 0 0	Arrears of former years	[illegible]	Superintending Surveyor, James Weeks, Stanstead, Essex.
	[illegible]	0 0 0		[illegible]	

The above account is for one quarter only, from Michaelmas to Christmas, 1833.

Statement of Yearly Accounts commencing January 1st and terminating December 31st

INCOME ACCOUNTS.

—	1834.	1835.	1836.	1837.	1838.	1839.	1840.
	£ s. d.	£ s. d.	£ s. d.	£ s. d.	£ s. d.	£ s. d.	£ s. d.
Balance in Treasurer's hands brought forward	387 13 11	...	...	...	...	...	...
Revenue received from tolls	2,355 0 0	2,371 15 0	2,549 9 6	2,410 0 0	3,156 0 0	3,224 10 0	3,152 10 0
Parish composition in lieu of statute duty	...	...	...	...	...	...	...
Revenue from fines	1 6 0	36 0 0	...	0 2 6	0 15 0	...	...
... from incidental receipts	27 15 0	41 5 0	4 0 0	30 14 0	6 10 0	23 0 0	22 10 0
Amount of money borrowed on security of the tolls	1,800 0 0	1,800 0 0	...	500 0 0	...	...	...
Balance due to Treasurer	325 2 4	781 0 8	1,289 4 2	645 8 2	332 15 9	211 11 10	64 0 3
	5,... 3	4,820 19 3	3,833 13 8	4,101 4 2	3,641 3 0	3,459 7 10	3,247 0 3

EXPENDITURE.

—	1834.	1835.	1836.	1837.	1838.	1839.	1840.
Balance due to Treasurer	...	325 2 4	781 0 8	1,289 4 2	645 8 2	332 15 9	211 11 10
Manual labour	251 1 6	273 1 1	351 6 0	592 5 0	557 12 8	672 5 5	755 5 3
Teaming	3 2 7 10	437 0 0	373 11 0	313 5 0	655 6 6	441 5 0	653 10 7
Materials for sundry line repairs	273 5 5	259 3 5	355 1 2	456 1 4	454 1 0	353 13 2	385 2 0
Land purchased	...	...	...				
Damage done in obtaining materials, &c.	...	...	...	...	...		
Travelling expenses	356 14 0	72 11 0	126 10 0	74 7 0	135 7 0	...	...
Salaries — Treasurer	12 0 0	50 0 0					
Clerk	52 10 0	50 0 0	As the salaries were the same each year, the total is given				
Surveyor	100 0 0	100 0 0	151 10 0	151 10 0	151 10 0	151 10 0	151 10 0
Law charges	67 10 4	45 3 6	31 15 6	20 6 0	... 3 4	...	25 10 0
Interest on debts	455 0 0	370 3 10	497 0 0	497 0 0	530 2 0	537 0 0	...
Debt paid off	...	...	...	...	500 0 0	... 0 0 0	
Improvements	2,755 14 4	1,311 14 0	733 10 0	41 12 0	111 0 0		
Statute duty performed, estimated value	...	...	(Expenses of to new sidle of statute duty at Act 115 17 10)				
Incidental expenses	12 13 10	75 5 10	(16 15 0, new toll gate 128 9 6)	40 15 10	...	...	...
	5,277 13 3	4,209 16 8	3,512 13 8	4,111 4 0	...	... 7 10	3,... 0 3

DEBTS — Interest, 5 per cent.

—	1834.	1835.	1836.	1837.	1838.	1839.	1840.
Bonded or mortgage debt	10,500 0 0	11,500 0 0	11,500 0 0	12,000 0 0	12,000 0 0	11,500 0 0	11,500 0 0
Floating debt	...	...	...	...	...	...	...
Unpaid interest	...	...	...	...	...	...	...
Balance due to the Treasurer	805 5 4	708 16 0	1,289 4 2	645 8 2	332 15 9	211 11 10	64 0 3
	11,305 5 4	12,208 16 0	12,789 4 2	12,645 8 2	12,332 16 0	11,711 11 10	11,564 ...

INCOME ACCOUNTS.

—	1841.	1842.	1843.	1844.	1845.
	£ s. d.	£ s. d.	£ s. d.	£ s. d.	£ s. d.
Balance in Treasurer's hands brought forward	...	...	...	45 18 6	233 10 4
Revenue received from tolls	2,989 11 9½	2,561 8 3	2,208 6 8	2,231 5 0	2,277 1 8
Parish composition in lieu of statute duty	...	...	...	...	...
Revenue from fines	3 7 9	...	...	...	...
Revenue from incidental receipts ..	45 18 0	29 10 0	33 19 0	45 18 0	55 15 10
Amount of money borrowed on the security of the tolls	...	...	...	...	...
Balance due to Treasurer	22 2 0½	357 12 1	...	...	...
	3,060 19 7	2,948 10 4	2,242 5 8	2,323 1 6	2,566 7 10

EXPENDITURE.

	1841.	1842.	1843.	1844.	1845.
Balance due to Treasurer	94 0 3	22 2 0	357 12 1	...	...
Manual labour	655 10 3	543 7 4	408 6 2	360 18 0	338 14 4
Team labour	546 2 0	553 1 0	412 2 8	326 14 7	279 6 9
Materials for surface repairs	393 2 6	390 2 5	290 6 0	163 2 9	139 13 4
Land purchased...	...	...	...	...	...
Damage done in obtaining materials	...	...	...	...	...
Tradesmen's bill	143 18 3	140 15 11	44 6 7	71 2 2	82 0 0
Salaries— Treasurer ... ... Clerk .. .. Surveyor	181 10 0	181 10 0	151 10 0	151 10 0	151 10 0
Law charges	3 13 4	29 12 2	29 8 8	26 5 0	25 10 6
Interest on debts	537 10 0	525 0 0	500 0 0	483 6 9	453 5 5
Debt paid off	500 0 0	500 0 0	...	500 0 0	1,000 0 0
Improvements	...	...	...	...	...
Statute duty performed, estimated value	...	...	...	...	...
Incidental expenses	5 13 0	57 10 6	2 15 0	6 12 0	49 2 4
Balance in the hands of Treasurer ..	...	...	45 18 6	233 10 4	46 15 2
	3,060 19 7	2,948 10 4	2,242 5 8	2,323 1 6	2,566 7 10

DEBTS—INTEREST.

	1841.	1842.	1843.	1844.	1845.
Bonded or mortgage debt	5 per cent. 10,500 0 0	5 per cent. 10,000 0 0	5 per cent. 10,000 0 0	5 per cent. 9,500 0 0	5 per cent. 8,500 0 0
Floating debt	...	...	...	...	...
Unpaid interest...	...	...	...	...	...
Balance due to Treasurer	22 2 0½	357 12 1	...	...	...
	10,522 2 0½	10,357 12 1	10,000 0 0	9,500 0 0	8,500 0 0

INCOME ACCOUNTS.

1846.	1847.	1848.	1849.	1850.	1851.	1852.
£ s. d.	£ s. d.	£ s. d.	£ s. d.	£ s. d.	£ s. d.	£ s. d.
40 15 3	72 4 7	...	...	171 7 11	108 11 4½	174 0 4
1,075 0 0	1,556 13 11½	1,511 0 4½	1,519 3 4	1,554 14 4	1,274 7 8	1,554 15 4
...	...	...	...	...	...	...
...	...	...	...	...	...	...
11 13 0	25 3 7	43 5 0	17 17 0	8 5 0	63 17 6	22 10 0
} Property tax returned 11 13 4	...	5 9 4½	...	10 0 0½	{ 6 13 4 omitted 1841 5 0 1	6 10 1½
	139 4 1	172 11 0	...			
2,045 6 6	1,533 11 2½	2,034 0 3	1,567 0 10	1,855 14 3½	1,100 0 11½	2,085 2 0

EXPENDITURE.

...	...	159 4 1	172 17 0	...	...	...
277 17 3	231 7 1	372 9 11	344 5 0	21 9 8	312 17 0	42 14 4
} 334 14 7½	273 13 11½	277 9 7	141 7 11	225 3 0	112 14 0	112 1 0½
	133 17 11½	115 14 11	98 4 3	112 14 3	5 17 1½	107 0 0½
...	...	...	...	...	...	...
...	...	...	...	...	...	...
42 15 3	112 1 5½	114 1 0½	...	6 11 11½	112 8 4	18 9 7
131 10 0	151 10 0	136 10 0	131 1 0	130 10 0	131 10 0	131 10
25 10 6	4 7 6	36 10 0	25 11 6			...
415 17 1	314 10 0	322 10 0	252 1 0	347 10 0	311 0 0	277 10 0
500 0 0	500 0 0	5 0 0	...	500 0 0	500 0 0	500 0 0
...	...	...	...	...	...	...
Property tax 13 11 10	...	5 7 4½	...			6 19 0½
6 5 0	33 1 3	5 13 6	0 0 0	22 0 0	...	4 0 0
72 4 7	...	...	...	175 11 4½	224 0 1	44 0 0
2,045 6 6	1,953 11 1½	0 0 0	0 0 0	0 0 0	1,100 0 0	...

DEBTS—INTEREST.

5 per cent.	5 per cent.	5 per cent.	5 per cent.	5 per cent.	5 per cent.	4½ per cent.
8,000 0 0	7,500 0 0	7,000 0 0	7,000 0 0	6,000 0 0	6,000 0 0	5,000 0 0
...	...	...	...	...	...	...
...	...	...	...	...	...	...
...	...	172 11 6	...	...	...	...
8,000 0 0	7,500 0 0	7,172 11 6	7,000 0 0	6,000 0 0	6,000 0 0	5,000 0 0

* Called income tax in some returns, and property tax in others.

† After 1847 the accounts are not entered in the minute book, but a copy made out on the form shown and pasted in a book. Where in the above copies "0" is placed, it is to denote that the figure has perished.

INCOME ACCOUNTS.

	1853.	1854.	1855.	1856.	1857.
	£ s. d.	£ s. d.	£ s. d.	£ s. d.	£ s. d.
Balance in Treasurer's hands brought forward	435 9 8	502 19 2	61 7 3½	126 19 2½	107 6 7½
Revenue received from tolls	1,655 16 8	1,772 10 0	1,661 5 0	1,615 0 0	1,466 5 0
Parish composition in lieu of statute duty	...	...	...	...	...
Revenue from fines	...	...	...	...	...
Revenue from incidental receipts ..	59 12 6	25 4 0	43 6 0	20 9 0	86 4 0
Amount of money borrowed on the security of the tolls	6 11 3	8 10 7	10 17 6	10 10 0	7 8 9
Balance due to Treasurer	...	...	...	...	31 6 8½
	2,157 10 1	2,309 3 9	1,776 15 9½	1,772 18 2½	1,698 11 1

EXPENDITURE.

	1853	1854	1855	1856	1857
Balance due to Treasurer	0 0 0	0 0 0	0 0 0	0 0 0	0 0 0
Manual labour	348 6 10	387 5 2	381 10 0	324 3 8	368 2 4
Team labour	229 3 1	267 9 4	234 3 2	144 10 0	145 12 0
Materials for surface repairs	114 11 7	133 14 8	117 1 6	292 14 0	296 12 0
Land purchased...	...	...	...	...	...
Damage done in obtaining materials	...	...	...	...	...
Tradesmen's bills	85 1 4	116 16 8½	95 6 11	94 1 4½	98 5
Salaries— Treasurer ... ... Clerk .. .. Surveyor	136 10 0	136 10 0	136 10 0	136 10 0	136 10 0
Law charges	...	...	...	80 0 0	...
Interest on debts	232 9 10	197 10 0	168 15 0	163 0 0	0 0 0
Debt paid off	500 0 0	1,000 0 0	505 12 6	500 0 0	500 0 0
Improvements	...	...	...	...	...
Statute duty performed, estimated value	6 11 3	8 10 7	10 17 6	0 0 0	...
Incidental expenses	1 17 0	...	...	0 0 0	0 0 0
Balance in the hands of Treasurer ...	502 19 2	61 7 3½	126 19 2½	106 6 7½	...
	2,157 10 1	2,309 3 9	1,776 15 9½	000 0 0	000 0 0

DEBTS—INTEREST.

	4 per cent.	4 per cent.	4½ per cent.	5 per cent.	5 per cent.
Bonded or mortgage debt	5,000 0 0	4,000 0 0	3,500 0 0	3,000 0 0	2,500 0 0
Floating debt	...	...	...	...	...
Unpaid interest...	...	..	...	...	...
Balance due to Treasurer	...	...	...	...	31 6 8½
	5,000 0 0	4,000 0 0	3,500 0 0	3,000 0 0	2,531 6 8½

The following form differs from the others in having a line for the money received from the sale of road sand; in the others it is included in "incidental receipts."

INCOME.

	1868.	185.	185.	186.	186.	186.	186.	186.	1862.*
	£ s. d.	£ s. d.	£ s. d.	£ s. d.	£ s. d.	£ s. d.	£ s. d.	£ s. d.	£ s. d.
Balance in Treasurer's hands, brought forward.	...	...	...	...	...	...	...	...	...
Revenue received from tolls ...									1,285 13 4
Revenue received from road sand									27 2 9
Parish compensation in lieu of statute duty.									*Received from Great Eastern Railway for Sale of Waste Land :— 42 4 0*
Estimated value of statute duty not formed									
Revenue from fines									
Revenue from incidental receipts									...
Amount of money borrowed on the security of the tolls									...
Income tax recovered									0 6 3
Balance due to Treasurer									4 7 9

* The account for the years 1861 and 1867 are not to be found.

Expenditure.

	1858. £ s. d.	1859. £ s. d.	1860. £ s. d.	1861. £ s. d.	1862. £ s. d.	1863. £ s. d.	1864. £ s. d.	1865. £ s. d.	1868. £ s. d.
Balance due to Treasurer brought forward.	31 0 8	103 17 4½	33 7 6½	...	...	...	...	...	10 7 2
Manual Labour	339 19 6	316 17 0	349 18 0	322 4 6	374 3 8	355 18 4	356 14 0	409 16 4	435 2 4
Team Labour	140 0 0	306 5 4	171 18 0	254 17 6	263 14 9	33 17 7	256 1 11	295 0 0	241 9 8
Materials for surface repairs	308 0 1	153 1 6	363 0 11	500 0 0	681 11 6	802 18 1	768 5 9	641 2 0	642 3 0
Land purchase	...	...	...	...	...	32 0 0	...	...	...
Tradesmen's bills	122 0 6	115 12 2	438 4 5	145 14 9	120 14 2	203 18 6	113 14 9	160 0 11	169 5 8
Salaries	136 10 0	136 10 0	136 10 0	136 10 0	136 10 0	136 10 0	180 0 0	180 0 0	160 0 0
Law charges	6 0 0	6 0 0	...	...	...	9 16 4	...	...	...
Interest of debt	...	...	...	75 0 0	73 8 9	50 0 0	75 0 0	25 0 0	25 0 0
Improvements	...	...	...	...	...	...	...	...	...
Debts paid off	500 0 0	...	...	...	500 0 0	500 0 0	...	...	...
Incidental expenses	...	...	...	...	...	...	...	...	...
Income tax	...	...	...	...	...	...	1 5 0	...	0 6 3
Balance due in the Treasurer's hands	...	...	292 15 11	474 1 1	...	162 8 6	231 11 2	...	...
									1,690 14 1

Rate of Interest—5 per cent. per Annum.

	1858. £ s. d.	1859. £ s. d.	1860. £ s. d.	1861. £ s. d.	1862. £ s. d.	1863. £ s. d.	1864. £ s. d.	1865. £ s. d.	1868. £ s. d.
Mortgage debt	2,000 0 0	1,500 0 0	1,500 0 0	1,500 0 0	1,000 0 0	500 0 0	500 0 0	500 0 0	500 0 0
Floating debt	...	...	...	...	...	...	...	...	250 16 8
Unpaid interest	...	...	...	...	...	...	...	...	...
Balance due to Treasurer	...	...	...	...	...	...	...	...	4 7 9
	2,000 0 0	1,500 0 0	1,500 0 0	1,500 0 0	1,000 0 0	500 0 0	500 0 0	500 0 0	755 4 5

Several of the columns are not added up because they are imperfect, the paper and the figures having perished.

Gravel.

In the account book the cost of labour and materials appears each year, under their separate headings, but no mention is made of the prices charged for gravel per load. In June, 1828, three contracts were entered into by three persons to cart gravel for three years, and put it by the side of the road, as instructed by the surveyor, at the following prices :—

> From the " Bald-face Stag " to the 15th milestone, at 1*s.* 3*d.* per load.
>
> From the 15th milestone to 17th milestone, at 1*s.* 6*d.* per load.
>
> From the 17th milestone to 19th milestone, at 2*s.* per load.
>
> And to obtain the gravel, and cart it from 19th milestone to Harlow Bush Common, at 4*s.* per load.

July, 1831.—The contract having expired there were fresh tenders offered by four contractors, and accepted, as follows :—

> From Woodford to the 14th milestone, 1*s.* per load.
>
> From the 14th milestone to the 17th milestone, at 1*s.* per load.
>
> From the 17th milestone to the 19th milestone, at 1*s.* 4*d.* per load.
>
> And for obtaining the gravel, and carting it from the 19th milestone to Harlow Bush Common, at 3*s.* per load.

The contract was for one year.

In 1832 Mr. McAdam was empowered to make the contract, subject to the approval of a Committee appointed for that purpose, but the prices were not named.

April, 1834.—There was a special contract for the supply of gravel to the New Road. The contract was for 5,000 loads of gravel and flints delivered on the New Road, between

T

Woodford and the "Wake Arms," at 2s. 6d. per load.   But the
contractor was paid, in January the year following, £788 6s. 4½d.,
as follows :—

£600 1s. 3d. for 4,800½ cubic yards, or loads, of gravel,
    at 2s. 6d. per yard, as per contract ; and
£108 5s. 1½d., for 1,158½ loads of flints at 3s. 3d. per
    load.

The contract for the old roads, entered into June, 1834,
shows a great reduction in price for carting.   The prices
being—

From Woodford to the 14th milestone, at 1s. per load.
From the 14th milestone to the 17th milestone, at 7d.
    per load.
From the 17th milestone to the 19th milestone, at 10d.
    per load.
From the 19th milestone to Harlow Bush Common, for
    the gravel and carting, at 2s. 11d. per load.

August, 1835, shows a further reduction—

Woodford to the 13th milestone, 10d. per load.
From the 13th milestone to the 16th milestone, 7d. per
    load.
From the 16th milestone to the 18th milestone, 10d.
    per load.
And obtaining the gravel, and carting it from the
    18th milestone to Harlow Bush Common, 2s. 10d.
    per load.

The New Road through the Forest having shortened
the distance from London by one mile, the 14th milestone
by the "Wake Arms" had become the 13th milestone, and
the other distances mentioned shortened one mile. (*See*
page 143.)
    1836.—The previous contracts for carting were renewed

at previous prices, excepting that from the 16th to the 18th milestone, which was reduced to 9d. per load.

Although the accounts show each year an outlay for materials and carting, there is no entry in the Minute book of any fresh contract having been made, until 1842; it may, therefore, be concluded that the contracts had been continued from year to year during that time.

December 20th, 1842.—On the recommendation of Sir James McAdam it was ordered that 200 loads of stones and gravel should be supplied each year for every mile of the road. There was also an advertisement for tenders; and in reply to it there was one offer to supply stones for the first six miles, and another for the remainder. They were both accepted, but the amounts are not mentioned. The contracts were continued through the following years, with the exception of only half the quantity being sufficient on the old Loughton Road. In 1846-7 the contract was for the supply of 1,722 loads each year.

It is quite clear that the Trustees did not adhere to the advice given by Sir James McAdam as to quantity, for in February, 1848, the tender accepted was for 725 loads of stones and gravel, at 2s. 7d. per load for the first six miles, and 1,000 loads for the remainder of the road at 2s. 2d. per load.

1849.—The contracts were for 1,000 loads of gravel and stones to be laid upon the road between the "Wake Arms" and the end of the Trust at Woodford, and 1,400 loads for the remainder of the road.

1850.—There was only one contractor; he agreed to supply 1,700 loads of gravel, to be placed where the Surveyors directed, at 2s. per load. The next year's contract was for 800 loads, at 2s. per load, and 530 at 2s. 7d.

1852.—1,100 loads were supplied at 2s. per load, and 600 at 2s. 7d.

1853.—1,300 loads at 2s., and 600 at 2s. 7d. per load.

After 1853 the price for gravel and stone delivered rose very considerably.

                                                      Per load.

1854.—The tender was for 1,400 loads at 2s. 4d.

	,,	,,	750	,,	3s.
1855	,,	,,	1,100	,,	2s. 4d.
	,,	,,	650	,,	3s.
1856	,,	,,	1,400	,,	2s. 6d.
	,,	,,	750	,,	3s.
1857	,,	,,	1,200	,,	2s. 6d.
	,,	,,	750	,,	3s.
	,,	,,	150	,,	3s. 6d.
1858	,,	,,	1,350	,,	2s. 6d.
	,,	,,	600	,,	3s.
	,,	,,	200	,,	3s. 6d.
1859	,,	,,	500	,,	2s. 6d.
	,,	,,	150	,,	3s.
	,,	,,	650	,,	3s. 6d.
1860	,,	,,	200	,,	2s. 6d.
	,,	,,	1,200	,,	3s.
	,,	,,	850	,,	3s. 6d.

Cubic yards.		s.	d.	Cubic yards.		s.	d.
1861.— 300	at	3	6	600	at	4	10
1,200	,,	3	10	550	,,	3	9

1862.—Quantity the same, price not mentioned.

1863.— 400	at	3	6	1,600	at	3	10
300	,,	3	9	600	,,	4	0
800	,,	4	10				
1864.— 400	,,	3	6	1,200	,,	3	10
300	,,	3	9	600	,,	4	0

1,000 for Ongar Division at 3s. 6d.

1865.— 250	at	3	6	300	at	4	6
600	,,	3	11	800	,,	4	6
Ongar Road.— 550	,,	3	11	250	,,	3	10

July, 1865.—The surveyor was to prepare a detailed report setting forth the quantity of gravel, or stuff intended to represent gravel, procured by the Trust labourers and placed upon that portion of the New Road near the Woodford Wells Gate. The cost per cubic yard of such gravel, the royalty, the cost of sifting, the number of times sifted, and the net quantity remaining after such sifting as compared with the quantity originally placed by the sides of the roads, and from which the cartage per yard has been paid.

August, 1865.—It is entered that, "No report was furnished by the surveyor as instructed by the Trustees at the previous meeting."

1866.—It is stated that the contracts for gravel were accepted, but there is no mention made of price or quantity.

CHAPTER XII

CONCLUSION.

IN the Minutes of July 21st, 1868, it is stated that the proposed new Bill was laid before the Trustees, and its further consideration postponed. At the meeting held the following month mention is made of a letter having been received from the Home Secretary, and that the Trustees were unanimous in expressing an opinion the tolls could not be abolished until 1870; there is no abstract of the letter sent by the Home Secretary entered in the Minute Book affording any clue to its purport; the opinion, however, of the Trustees, as recorded, shows that it related to the times when the Trust should cease.

The Act under consideration must have been the Annual Turnpike Act Continuance Act of 1868.

As the framers of the Act considered it advisable to continue some of the existing Highway Acts and to repeal others, schedules were attached, and it was ordered as follows :—"The Acts specified in the first schedule are to be repealed on and after the 31st day of December, 1868."

The Acts specified in the second schedule were to expire at the time mentioned in the Annual Turnpike Continuance Act, 1867.

"The Acts specified in the third and fourth schedules were to continue until the 30th day of June, 1870, 'unless Parliament in the meantime otherwise provides;'" the next clause orders "that all Turnpike Acts now in force in Great Britain, which will expire at or before the end of the next Session of Parliament, shall continue until the 1st day of November, 1869, and to the end of the next Session of Parliament"; the Act also gave permission to the Trustees, under certain conditions, if they thought fit, out of the balance remaining in their hands after all debts had been paid, to award any person whose office expired with the Trust, a sum of money, if he had held the office for not less than ten preceding years; the gratuity was not "to exceed in any case the amount of three years' salary."

An Act of George IV., chap. 95, permitted the Trustees to sell only the materials of the toll houses, but not the ground on which they stood. But the Annual Turnpike Acts Continuance Act, 1866, gave the Trustees power, subject to the right of pre-emption, to sell the toll houses as freehold, or to pull them down and add the land on which they stood to the highway, as may be thought best. These Acts conferred on the Trustees the powers they exercised in selling the toll houses, and dividing some of the proceeds amongst the officers of the Trust.

The Epping and Ongar Trust not being out of debt, appears in the fourth schedule of the Act of 1868, under the heading—

Turnpike Acts nearly out of debt and continued by the Annual Turnpike Acts Continuance Act—as follows :—

—	Toll in 1866.	Debt in 1866.	Per cent.	No. of Act.
Epping and Ongar	£1,413	£500	5	37

The Annual Turnpike Continuance Act of 1869 included the Epping and Ongar Trust, in the second schedule : "Acts which are to expire at the date (30th June, 1870) mentioned, 31 and 32 Victoria, Chap. 99;" the entry appears in the schedule as under :—

DATE OF ACT.	TITLE OF ACT.
6—W. IV. C. xl. 14.	50. An Act for more effectually repairing the roads from Harlow Bush Common, to and into the Parish of Woodford, and the road from Epping to Writtle, and other roads therein mentioned, all in the County of Essex.

It is, perhaps, outside the limits of subjects relating to the Epping and Ongar Highway Trust to mention the changes which have taken place during its existence. Commencing in 1769 and terminating in 1870, it lasted for one hundred years. Alterations, however, which have been made during that period and since in the management of parish affairs, as well as in the mode and rapidity of travelling, both by land and water, have an interest to those whose attention has been directed to what may be termed the domestic transactions of the country, and merit some notice.

In the earlier period of the Trust the speed of travelling by road reached its height. An average rate of ten miles an hour by fast coaches, including stoppages, was looked upon as rapid travelling; the Brighton coaches made the journey from London, of fifty miles, in five hours; but railway trains have superseded coaches, and run the distance in a quarter of the time. Passenger sailing vessels have been replaced by steamships, and the time occupied by voyages has been reduced from months to weeks, and from weeks to a few days.

Great changes have also taken place in the management of parish matters.

When Government substituted unions for parish workhouses, it gave to the Poor Law Board the supervision of the transactions of the Guardians and the control of all matters relating to parish relief; the management of the local endowed charities has been placed under Charity Commissioners; the education of the parish children has to be carried out in accordance with the orders of the Educational Commission, whose inspectors, by examination and reports, keep them informed of the progress made by the children, and the condition of the school house in which they are instructed; the Board of Health looks after sanitary condition of towns and villages; the sanitary authorities, through their inspectors, can interfere in the domestic arrangements of dwelling-houses, and, when required, order the landlord to make what alterations are thought necessary for the maintenance of the health of the inmates. The inhabitants of towns and villages have no choice, but must provide an adequate means of drainage, and obtain a supply of pure water if there is a deficiency, or the old supply has become contaminated and unsuitable for domestic use.

So that not only has there disappeared the fast stage coach, post-horses, and gaily-dressed post-boys, heavily laden carriers' broad-wheel waggons, turnpike gates, and highway trust, but also the management of parish affairs as existing when the maintenance of the road from Woodford to Harlow Bush Common was handed over to the highway Trustees. The controlling power exercised for so many years by Clergymen, Landlords, and Landowners, has now been transferred from local authority to Government officials at Whitehall.

Sciant presentes et futuri quod ego Hunfridus de Hasting miles concessi et hac presenti carta mea confirmavi pro me et heredibus
meis Rogero de Paris civi London et heredibus suis et suis assignatis pro homagio et servicio suo omnes terras et tenementa que tenet de feodo meo cum suis pertinentiis in Northwalde Hasting et in mesuagiis terris boscis pratis pasturis homagiis redditibus wardis releviis eschaetis et omnibus aliis pertinentiis suis Habendum et tenendum de me et heredibus meis predicto Rogero et heredibus suis et suis assignatis et eorum heredibus bene et in pace libere quiete integre et heredetarie imperpetuum Reddendo inde annuatim michi et heredibus meis ad festum Nativitatis sancti Johannis Baptiste unum denarium Pro omnibus serviciis auxiliis consuetudinibus sectis curie et omnibus secularibus demandis salvo tamen michi et heredibus meis toto forinseco servicio scilicet scutagium domini Regis quando evenit tantum quantum pertinet ad feodum unius militis Et faciendo inde annuatim per me et heredibus meis Radulpho Kayareschal et heredibus suis viginti solidos ad duos anni terminos scilicet ad festum sancti Michaelis decem solidos et ad festum pasche decem solidos et ad festum penthecostes unum par calcarium deauratorum vel sex denarios pro omnibus serviciis homagiis foditarum wardis releviis eschaetis auxiliis et omnibus secularibus demandis idem Radulphus vel heredes suos pertinentibus Et ego predictus Hunfridus et heredes mei warantizabimus defendemus et acquietabimus predicto Rogero et heredibus suis et suis assignatis omnes predictas terras et predicta tenementa cum omnibus suis pertinentiis per predictum servicium contra omnes homines et feminas tam judeos quam christianos imperpetuum In cuius rei testimonium presenti carte mee sigillum meum apposui Hiis testibus domino Ricardo de Tonbrigge Ricardo de Suthamcle Henrico filio Ancheri Reginaldo de Ginges Johanne de la Gare Galfrido de Portgate et militibus Willelmo Karasse Johanne de Ry Willelmo de Ayayeny Rogero de Tayrden Ghiloino de Pellam Alvredo Ghinges scriptis dicto et multis aliis Datum London die dominica proxima post festum sancti Michaelis Anno regni Regis Edwardi filii Regis Henrici Nono

S' VMFRIDI DE HASTING

APPENDIX.

DEEDS RELATING TO EPPING FOREST, THEYDON GERNON, THEYDON ATTE MOUNT AND THEYDON BOYS, &c.

I.

TRANSLATION OF THE GRANT BY HUMPHREY DE HASTINGS TO ROGER DE PARIS, CITIZEN OF LONDON, OF HIS TENEMENT, NORTH WEALD, 1280.

Let present and future men know that I, Humphrey de Hastings, Knight, have granted and by this my present charter have confirmed, for me and my heirs to Roger de Paris, Citizen of London, and his heirs and his assigns, for his homage and service, all the lands and tenements which he holds of my fee, with their appurtenances, in Northwalde Hasting, as in messuages, lands, woods, meadows, pastures, homages, rents, wards, reliefs, escheats, and all other their appurtenances; To have and to hold of me and my heirs to the aforesaid Roger and his heirs and his assigns and their heirs, well and in peace, freely, quietly, wholly, and hereditarily for ever; Yielding, therefore, yearly to me and my heirs at the feast of the Nativity of St. John the Baptist one penny: For all services, aids customs, suits of Court, and all secular demands; Saving, however, to me and my heirs the whole foreign service, to wit, the scutage of the Lord King whenever it shall happen, so much as appertains to the fee of one knight; And making, therefore, yearly for me and my heirs to Ralph Le Mareschal and his heirs, twenty shillings at the two terms of the year, to wit, at the feast of Saint Michael ten shillings, and at the feast of Easter ten shillings, and at the feast of Pentecost one pair of gilded spurs or sixpence, for all services, homages, fees, wards, reliefs, escheats, aids, and all secular demands to the aforesaid Ralph or his heirs appertaining; And I, the aforesaid Humphrey, and my heirs will warrant, defend, and acquit to the aforesaid Roger and his heirs and his assigns all the aforesaid lands and aforesaid tenements with all their appurtenances by the aforesaid service against all men and women, as well Jews, as Christians for ever. In witness whereof to this, my present charter, I have appended my seal. These being the witnesses, the Lords Richard de

Tany, Richard de Suthchirche, Henry, son of Aucher, Reginald de Gynges, John de la Mare, Geoffrey de Rothinges, Knights, William le Masle, John de Ry, William de Mareng, Sayer de Teyden, Symon de Pelham, Alured Turgis, Stephen, the clerk, and many others. Given at London on the Sunday next after the feast of Saint Nicholas, in the ninth year of King Edward, the son of King Henry.

Endorsed: Charter of Humphrey de Hastinges of his tenements of Weld.

(margin: :ember. 8o.)

II.

Grant by Richard Gernun to Latton Priory of a Rent of Twelve Pence in the Demesne of Sawbridgworth.

Omnibus Christi fidelibus ad quos presens scriptum pervenerit Ricardus Gernun, salutem in domino.

Noverit universitas vestra, me pro salute mea et antecessorum et heredum meorum concessisse dedisse et hac presenti carta mea confirmasse Deo et ecclesie Sancti Johannis de Latton et Canonicis ibidem Deo servientibus duodecim denariatas redditus in puram et perpetuam elemosinam percipiendas de dominico meo de Sabrichteswrthe per annum ad duos terminos scilicet ad festum Sancti Michaelis. vj. d. et ad pascha vj. d. Ita quod ego vel heredes mei ad terminos statutos ipsum redditum predictis canonicis sine difficultate mitti faciemus. Et ego et heredes mei warantizabimus predictis canonicis totum predictum redditum versus omnes gentes. In hujus rei testimonium hanc meam cartam eis feci et sigilli mei appositione roboravi. Hiis Testibus. Ricardo de Taney, Petro de Taney, Magistro Waltero de Taney, Petro de Goldintone, Willelmo, persona de Estwike, Rogero de Tothame, et aliis.

(Brit. Mus. Harl. Ch. 50, G. 18.)

Early 13th century.

Translation of the Grant to Latton Priory.

To all the faithful of Christ to whom the present writing shall have come, Richard Gernun greeting in the Lord.

Know all of ye that I, for the health of my soul and the souls of my ancestors and heirs have granted, given, and by this, my present charter, confirmed to God and the Church of St. John of Latton and to the canons therein, serving God twelve pence worth of rent in pure and perpetual almoigne, to be received out of my demesne of Sawbridgeworth by the year, at the two terms, to wit, at the feast of St. Michael sixpence and at Easter sixpence. So that I, or my heirs, shall cause that rent to be sent at the appointed terms to the aforesaid canons without difficulty. And I and my heirs will warrant to the aforesaid canons the whole rent aforesaid against all people. In witness hereof I have made this, my charter, to them, and I have corroborated it by the appending of my seal. Witnesses, Richard de Taney, Peter de Taney, Master Walter de Taney, Peter de Godintone, William, the parson of Estwike, Roger de Totham, and others.

III

Taxation of Pope Nicholas IV., about a.d. 1291.

p. 15 *b.*—Goods of the Prior of Latton in Storteford, rent 2s. 0d., Lond. temp.

    ,,   ,,   ,, in Gedeleston, ,,   2s. 0d.

      Sum 4s. Decime 4¾d.

p. 16 *b.*—   ,,   ,,   ,, in Macching, ,,   4s. 0d.

    ,,   ,,   ,, in Latton, lands,

  rents, customs, young of animals, &c. ... 2 li. 11s. 6d.

Goods of the Prior of Latton in Reyndon, rent   0s. 5d.

    Sum 2 li. 15s. 11d. Decime 5s. 7d.

p. 25 *b.*—Deanery of Aungre, 2s. 7d. rent ; Alta Laverne, 1s. rent ; Morton, &c., 5s. rent : North Welds, 3s. 6d. rent.

p. 26.—Deanery of Chelmsford. Chelmsford, Prior of Latton, 4s. rent ; Molesham, Prior of Latton, 4s rent.

IV.

xxvii. Hen. viii. 12.

Rex per certam manucapcionem comisit Johanni Wentworth, armigero, et P. aliis custodiam scitus circuitus et precinctus Monasterii sive prioratus de Latton, in comitatu Essex, Necnon custodiam ducentarum acrarum et cet. Habendum a tempore capcionis inde usque finem sancti Michaelis tunc proxime sequentis, juxta formam statuam, et cet. Rotulo predicto (*i.e.*, xi *to.*).

(Brit. Mus. Add. MS. 6364, f. 131.)

The King, by a certain mainprise, has committed to John Wentworth, esquire, and others, the custody of the site, circuit, and precinct of the Monastery or Priory of Latton, in the county of Essex ; also the custody of two hundred acres, et cetera. To hold for the time of the prise thereof to the end of St. Michael then next ensuing, according to the form of the Statute, etc. (In Roll aforesaid.)

V.

xxviii. Hen. viii. *vo.*

Rex primo die Aprilis concessit Henrico Parker, Militi, scitum nuper Monasterii sive prioratus de Latton ac omnia terras, et cet. Habendum ei et heredibus suis imperpetuum. Rotulo predicto (*i.e.*, xlv.*to.*).

(Brit. Mus. Add. MS. 6364, f. 145*b*.)

The King, on the first day of April, has granted to Henry Parker, Knight, the site of the late Monastery or Priory of Latton, and all the lands, etc. To have and hold to him and his heirs for ever.

VI.

xxxiii. Hen. viii. Prima Parte.

De homagio Willelmi Morres, pro scitu, et cet., Monasterii de Latton, in comitatu Essex, ac pro omnibus terris advocacionibus, et cet., nuper Monasterio spectantibus in comitatibus Essex, Hertford, London, et Middlesex. Rotulo predicto (*i.e.*, iiii.^{xx}iii.).

(Brit. Mus. Add. MS. 6365, f. 157 *b*.)

Concerning the homage of William Morres for the site, et cetera, of the Monastery of Latton, in the county of Essex, and for all the lands advowsons, et cetera, belonging to the late Monastery in the counties of Essex, Hertford, London and Middlesex.

VII.

ii. et iii. Phil. et. Mar.

De scitu et precinctu nuper Prioratus Sancti Augustini in Latton, alias Lacton, cum diversis terris et tenementis ibidem spectantibus in comitatibus Essex, Hertford, et Middlesex, Johanni Tytley et heredibus suis alienandis. Rotulo xxxii.

(Brit. Mus. Add. MS., 6369, f. 98.)

Concerning the alienation of the site and precinct of the Priory of St. Augustine in Latton, otherwise Lacton, with divers lands and tenements thereto belonging, in the counties of Essex, Hertford, and Middlesex, to John Tytley and his heirs.

VIII

In the Lord Treasurer's Remembro Office

Concerning the King's letters patent Here Pickering his patent Prest of Lands

(Signature date)

M of R

Concerning James Wilson

The architecture of the chapel—early English—is that which prevailed during the end of the twelfth and the greater part of the thirteenth century; and the grant of land by Richard Gernon shows that the Priory was in existence early in the thirteenth century, so that it is a very ancient building. The clustered columns are light and elegant. Its preservation is no doubt due to its being of value as an addition to the buildings required by the occupier of the farm; but it is to be regretted that no more appropriate use can be found for it.

One of the duties of the monastic orders was hospitality, and many a traveller along the road from Waltham Abbey (*see* page 5), over the dreary waste on which the Priory was built must have rejoiced when he came within sight of its walls, for there he knew he would find both food and shelter.

The Augustine monks followed the rules of St. Benedict, by which they were required to give each day eight hours to labour. The rough, hard work was, however, done by laymen, or "conversi," who were an order, from an ecclesiastical point of view, much inferior to the canons, or monks proper, and occupied in the monasteries, and also in the chapel, portions set apart for them, distinct and separate from those occupied by the monks. By the Cistercians they were subjected to strict rules, and only those could be admitted who could give the equivalent of a hired labourer's work. Under the "Majester Conversorum," who was a professed monk, they went to work at sunrise, and were exempted from many of the religious services of the monks proper.[*] The land in the district still remaining uncultivated—Rye Hill, Harlow Bush, and Hazlewood Commons; and (within the last fifty years) Thornwood Common, beyond it Wintry Wood, and miles of forest—afford evidence of the loneliness of the situation of the Priory, and also of the wildness of the country by which it was surrounded. The perseverance of the monks and the labour of the Conversi, must, however, soon have surrounded it with cultivated land, since at the end of the thirteenth century it was able, as appears by the deed quoted, to contribute to the wants of the Pope, to the value of £2 11s. 6d. When surrendered in 1536 it possessed 200 acres of arable land, 200 acres of pasture, 30 acres of meadow, and 10 acres of wood.—(Morant's "History of Essex.")

J. and Greig Storer's "Antiquarian and Topographical Cabinet" (1809, vol. vi.), has an article on Latton Priory, from which the accompanying two illustrations are copied. On the change of ownership, the names of the families are mentioned to which the property passed; and in addition particulars respecting the Priory are given; as they appear to be the result of personal examination, it is thought desirable to add them to the foregoing description.

The ground supposed to be the site of the Priory was surrounded by a moat. Outside the moat, on the south side of the present buildings, there appears to have been the Priory burial grounds, as bones have been frequently dug up. To the east of the Church, and a little way from the moat, there were remains of a low embankment, enclosing ground which the peasantry in the neighbourhood are said to have called the Monk's Bowling Green.

---

[*] Strata Florida, by S. W. Williams, page 163.

X.

An indented charter whereby Walter Waltham, John Peruyle, Richard Peruyle and Edward Milys sell to Johanna, late wife of Edward Herde, a tenement, with all the lands, tenements, etc., thereunto belonging, called "Colman's Tenement," in the town of Theydone atte Mounte, in co. Essex, for her life, with remainder to John Herde, brother of Edward Herde, for his life, and afterwards to John, son of the said John Herde.

Witnesses:—Thomas Lampet, Edward Halstede, Robert Smythe, Thomas Parker, Thomas Wrattyng.

Dated at Theydone atte Mounte, Monday after the Feast of St. Thomas the Apostle (21 December), 1st year of Henry IV. (A.D. 1399).

Four seals.

(British Museum : Add. Ch. 28,800.)

Latin.

The counterpart of the same deed.

Two seals.

(British Museum, Add. Ch. 28,801.)

Latin.

XI.

Lease for her life by Johanna, late wife of Edward Herde of Theydone atte Monte in co. Essex, to John Herde, junior, of Theydone aforesaid, of the tenement anciently called "Colmanes" in Theydone atte Monte, at a yearly rent of twenty-six shillings and eight-pence. And the said John Herde shall receive from the said Johanna of live-stock four cows, price of each nine shillings, and ten ewe sheep, price of each sixteen pence, to be accounted for at her death.

Dated at Theydone atte Monte, Friday before the feast of St. Peter ad Vincula (1 Augt.) 7th year of Henry IV. (A.D. 1406).

Broken seal.

(British Museum : Add. Ch. 28,809.)

Latin.

XII.

Power of Attorney by Thomas Hierde of Theydone atte Mounte in co. Essex to Robert Bakere of Theydone atte Mounte aforesaid to give seisin to John Pake of Theydone Garnone, Edmund Aldahm of Theydone atte Mounte aforesaid, John Hierde, brother of the above Thomas, and Hugh Rodynge, of all his lands and tenements in Theydon atte Mounte aforesaid.

Dated at Theydone atte Mounte aforesaid, the twentieth day of February, 11th year of Henry IV. (A.D. 1410).

Broken seal.

(British Museum : Add. Ch. 28,821.)

Latin.

XIII.

Grant by Edmund Hierde of Theydone atte Monte in co. Essex, to John Chamberleyn, William Bette and Henry Bette, of all his lands and tenements, etc., in the town of Theydone aforesaid, and also the reversion of all those lands and tenements which he will inherit from Alice Bette, his mother, in the same town.

Witnesses :—Reginald Malyns, esquire, John Hierde, Edmund Aldeham, John Smythe, Walter Hierde, Robert Smythe, John Whitebred.

Dated at Theydone aforesaid, the tenth day of April, 9th year of Henry V. (A.D. 1421).

Seal.

(British Museum : Add. Ch. 28,832).

Latin.

XIV.

Power of Attorney by Edmund Hierde of Theydone atte Monte, in co. Essex, to Edmund Aldeham and Simon Baker to deliver seisin to John Chamberleyn, William Bette, and Henry Bette, of all his lands in the town of Theydone, aforesaid, and of the reversion of the lands which he will inherit from his mother, Alice Bette, in the same town.

Dated :—the tenth day of April, 9th year of Henry V. (A.D. 1421).

Broken seal

(British Museum : Add. Ch. 28,833)

Latin.

XV

Grant by John Chamberlayn of Theydone atte Mounte, William Bette and Henry Bette of Navestoke, feoffees of Edmund Herde son of Thomas Herde of Theydone aforesaid, to Simon Archer, William Stonherd, and William Pecok, of Theydone Gernone, of all their lands in Theydone atte Mounte aforesaid called "Warynes," with a cottage in Colemanestrete, the reversion of lands and tenements in the same town called "Skynners" after death of Alice, mother of the aforesaid Edmund, on condition of a payment by the said Simon and the others to Johanna eldest daughter of the aforesaid Thomas Herde of 40*s.* and to Johanna Wolfeld 13*sh.* 4*d.* and to each of the feoffees, 6*sh.* 8*d.* on their taking possession. The said Simon and the others to find a priest to pray for the souls of the said Thomas and Edmund for two years in the church of Theydone atte Mounte at a stipend of 10*l.* 13*sh.* 4*d.* Also 40*sh.* each to Alice and Johanna daughters of the aforesaid Thomas, at marriage ; 26*sh.* 8*d.* to Johanna daughter of Christina Rothyng when she comes of age ; 13*sh.* 4*d.* for repairing the bridge called "ffulwellebregge ;" and 40*sh.* for repair of the road between this bridge and heyfeld. With a bond for performance of these conditions.

Dated at Theydone atte Mounte aforesaid, on the Vigil of St. Katherine the Virgin (24th Novr.) 9th year of Henry V. (A.D. 1421).

Seal.

(British Museum : Add. Ch. 28,836.)

Latin.

XVI.

Grant by John Chaumberlayn of Theydon atte Mounte, William Bette, and Henry Bette of Navestoke, to Simon Archer, William Stonherst, and William Pecok of Theydone Gernone of the lands and reversions which are set forth in the previous deed.

Witness :—Reginald Malyns, Esquire, John Lambherde, Robert Smyzthe, John Smyzthe, Walter Herde.

Dated at Theydone atte Mounte aforesaid, on the feast of St. Katherine the Virgin (25th Nov.) 9th year of Henry V. (A.D. 1421).

One seal.

(British Museum : Add. Ch. 28,837.)

Latin.

XVII.

Grant by Hugh Roger and William Pecok of Theydone Garnone, and John Rokke of Navestok in co. Essex, to Sir Ralph Botiller, Knight, Ralph de Lee, gentleman, Thomas Scargill, Valet of the Crown of the Lord King, and John Ferne, yeoman, of all their lands, tenements, rents, and services which the said Hugh, William, and John, together with William Pykeman and Henry Bette ately held of the gift of John Pake, in the towns of Theydone Garnone and Theydone atte Mounte in co. Essex.

Witnesses :—John atte ffelde, John Archer, Simon Baker, John Roger, Richard Herde.

Dated at Theydone Garnone, twenty-fifth day of June, sixteenth year of Henry VI. (A.D. 1438).

Three seals.

(British Museum : Add. Ch. 28,852.)

Latin.

XVIII

Grant by John Herde and Richard ffreman to William fielde, Thomas Smythe citizen and carpenter of London, Richard Turnour, Peter Smythe, William Herde, and John ffelde, of all their lands, tenements, rents, and services in the town of Theydone atte Mounte in co. Essex, which they the said John and Richard lately held of the gift of John Pake and Hugh Roger of Theydone Gernone.

Witnesses:—John Hampden, esquire ; Richard Cok, William Pecok.

Dated at Theydone atte Mounte, the second day of November, the seventeenth year of Henry VI. (A.D. 1438).

Two seals.

(British Museum : Add. Ch. 28,853)

Latin.

XIX.

Quitclaim by William Pykeman and Henry Bette, to Sir Ralph Botiller knight : Ralphe Atte Lee, gentleman ; Thomas Scargill, valet of the Crown of the Lord King ; and John Ferne, yeoman, of their right in lands, tenements, rents, and services in the towns of Theydone Gernone and Theydone atte Mounte, in co. Essex, which they hold by the confirmation of Hugh Roger and William Pecok, of Theydone Gernone, and John Rokke, of Navestoke (see Add. Ch. 28,852), and which they formerly held conjointly with the aforesaid Hugh William, and John, by the gift of John Pake.

Witnesses :—William Pecok, John Prestone, John Archer, John Roger Walter Bakere.

Dated at Theydone Gernone, the tenth day of September, the twenty-fifth year of Henry VI. (A.D. 1446).

Two seals.

(British Museum : Add. Ch. 28,360.)

Latin.

XX.

Quitclaim by John Pake, senior, of Theydone Gernone, in co. Essex, to John Verne, late parker of Haveryng-park, in the same county, of his right in lands, tenements, rents and services in the towns of Theydone Gernone and Theydone atte Mounte, in the same county, which the said John Verne and John Pake formerly held conjointly with Simon Campe, esquire, John Boomhale, esquire, William Beauchampe, esquire, and William Dacris, esquire, of the demise of Hugh Roger, of Theydone Gernone ; William Pecok, of the same ; William Pykeman, of Lambourne ; Henry Bette, of Navestoke, and John Rokke, of the same.

Witnesses : — William Pecok, John Preston, John Archer, John Roger Walter Bakere.

Dated at Theydone Gernone, the twelfth day of September, the twenty-fifth year of Henry VI. (A.D. 1446).

Seal.

(British Museum : Add. Ch. 28,861.)

Latin.

XXI.—XXII.

Indented grant by John Verne, late parker of Haveryng-park, in co. Essex, to John Pake, senior, of Theydone Gernone, and Johanna, his wife, of lands in the towns of Theydone Gernone and Theydone atte Mounte, which the said John Pake and John Verne held with Simon Campe and others, of the gift of Hugh Roger and others (see Add. Ch. 28,861), and afterwards the said John Pake quitclaimed the same to the said John Verne (Add. Ch. 28,861). To have and to hold for their lives, with remainder to Richard Pake, son of the said John and Johanna, and his right heirs, with reversion to John Pake, citizen and clothier, of London, junior, son of the said John and Johanna.

Witnesses :—William Pecok, John Prestone, John Archer, John atte ffelde, William ffoster.

Dated at Theydone Gernone, the sixteenth day of September, the twenty-fifth year of Henry VI. (A.D. 1446).

One seal.

(British Museum : Add. Ch. 28,862.)

The counterpart of the same deed.

One seal.

(British Museum : Add. Ch. 28,863.)

Latin.

XXIII.

Power of Attorney by Sir Ralph Botiller, knight, Ralph atte Lee, gentleman, and Thomas Scargill, Valet of the Crown of the Lord King, to John iferne, yeoman, to deliver seisin to John Pake, senior, of Theydone Gernone, and Johanna, his wife, of all the lands, tenements, etc., in Theydone Gernone and Theydone atte Mounte, in co. Essex, which they lately held conjointly with the said John fferne, of the gift of Hugh Roger and others (see Add. Ch. 28,852), excepting one field called Wedynsfeld, two crofts called Gulventescroft and Schapecotecroft, and a meadow called Edwynesmede. To have and to hold to the said John and Johanna for life, with remainder to John Pake, citizen and clothier, of London, senior, son of the said John and Johanna, and to William Pake, son of the same, and the right heirs of the said John Pake, citizen, with reversion to the next of kin.

Dated at Theydone Gernone, the twenty-sixth day of September, the twenty-fifth year of Henry VI. (A.D. 1446).

Three broken seals.

(British Museum : Add Ch. 28,864.)

Latin.

XXIV.

A Grant by John Newman, son of Thomas Newman, of Theydone Gernone, in co. Essex, to William Pecok, senior, William Pecok, junior, William Archer, and John atte Ree, of a messuage called Badegorishache, with two crofts of land called Badegoriscroftes, in Theydone Gernor, between the highway leading from Coupereshale to le Strode, on the east, and a lane called Sonnoures lane, on the west, whereof one head abuts on the land of John Archer, called le Stone, on the south, and the other head abuts on the highway leading from Coupereshale to Eppynghethe, on the north. Formerly held of Thomas Newman aforesaid, conjointly with Simon Archer and William Martyn, late of Theydon Gernon, deceased.

Witnesses :—John Prestone, Richard Martyn, John Archer, Thomas Hierde, William ffoster.

Dated at Theydon Gernon, first day of March, in the thirtieth year of Henry VI. (A.D 1452).

Seal in red wax.

(British Museum : Add. Ch. 9,255)

Latin

XXV.

Grant by S. Ralph Botiller, knight, Ralph atte Lee, gentleman, Thomas Scargill, esquire, and John fferne, yeoman, to John Pake, citizen and clothier, of the City of London, younger son of John Pake of Theydon Gernone, and Johanna his wife, John Stokker, clothier, John Shopman, upholder, and Thomas Elys, clothier, all of the said city, of one field called Wedynsfeld, two crofts called Gulwentescrofte and Shepecotecrofte, and a meadow called Edewynesmede, in the towns of Theydon Garnone and Theydon atte Mounte, in co. Essex, which the grantors held of Hugh Roger and other (see Add. Ch. 28,852).

Witnesses :—John Roger, John Archer, William Pecok, John ffeld, William fforster.

Dated the third day of March, in the thirty-sixth year of Henry VI. (A.D. 1458).

Four seals.

(British Museum : Add. Ch. 28,874.)

Latin.

XXVI.

Power of attorney by Sir Ralph Botiller, knight, Ralph atte Lee, gentleman, and Thomas Scargill, esquire, to John fferne, yeoman, to deliver seisin to John Pake, citizen and clothier, of the City of London, and others, of the field, closes and meadow in Theydon Garnone and Theydon atte Mounte (as in Add. Ch. 28,874).

Dated the third day of March, in the thirty-sixth year of Henry VI. (A.D. 1458).

Three seals.

(British Museum : Add. Ch. 28,875.)

Latin.

XXVII.

Grant by Richard Bette, Richard Janyne, and John Heierde, of Stanford Revers, in co. Essex, to William Bette, son of Richard Bette aforesaid, Robert Metyngham, son of Walter Metyngham, of Westminster, gentleman, and John ffaukener, of Northe Weld, in the said county, of all the lands, tenements, rents, and services called " Warynes " and Skynners in Theydon atte Mont, in the said county, which they lately held of the gift of William Bette, of Navistocke and Thomas Skargill and William Smyth, of Stapilford Taney, in the said county.

Witnesses :—Thomas Edward, Thomas Baker, junior, Richard Smythe, John Edward, junior, Thomas Baker, senior.

Dated at Theydone atte Mont, the tenth day of May, in the sixth year of Edward IV. (A.D. 1466).

Two fragmentary seals.

(British Museum : Add. Ch. 28,883.)

Latin.

XXVIII.

Defeasance by Catherine [Howard] Duchess of Norfolk [daughter of William, Lord Molines, and wife of Sir John Howard, Earl of Norfolk], of a bond for a hundred and sixty-six pounds, thirteen shillings, and fourpence, in the statute staple by Sir George Nevile, knt., Lord Bergevenny; Thomas Ormonde, esquire; William Scot, of Theydone Mounte, in co. Essex, esquire, and Robert ffenne, of London, gentleman, for the yearly payment to her of six pounds, fifteen shillings, and sevenpence, in the church of St. Paul's, London, at the altar, near the image of the crucifix, called "the Rode of the North dore," on the Vigil of All Saints, between the hours of eight and eleven in the forenoon, and a like sum on the Vigil of Pentecost at the same place.

Dated the fifteenth day of July, in the eighteenth year of Edward IV (A.D. 1478).

No seal. Signature (initials) of the Countess.

(British Museum: Add. Ch. 28,905.)

Latin.

XXIX.

Acquittance by Katherine [Howard] Duchess of Norfolk, to Sir George Nevile, knt., Thomas Ormond, esquire, William Scot, esquire, and Robert ffenne, gentleman, for six pounds, fifteen shillings, and sevenpence sterling, payable on the Vigil of All Saints, next ensuing, in the cathedral church of St. Paul, within the City of London.

Dated the twenty-seventh day of October, the nineteenth year of Edward IV. (A.D. 1479).

No seal. Signature of William Lord Berkeley.

(British Museum: Add. Ch. 26,908.)

Latin.

XXX

Grant by Richard Pake, son and heir of John Pake, senior, late citizen and clothier of London, to Robert Cobbe, Thomas Englisshe, clerk, William Brystowe, chaplain, Richard Bruer, and Richard Godfrey, of all the lands, tenements, rents, etc., lying in the parishes of Theydone Garnone and Theydone atte Mounte in co. Essex which descended to him at the death of his father aforesaid. With power of attorney to William Coo of London, haberdasher, to take possession and deliver seisin.

Dated the sixth day of April, in the twentieth year of Edward IV. (A.D. 1480).

Broken seal.

(British Museum: Add. Ch. 28,909.)

Latin.

XXXI.

Quitclaim by Robert Cobbe, Thomas Englisshe, Richard Bruer, and Richard Godfrey, to Richard Pake, son and heir of John Pake, senior, late citizen and clothier of London, of their right in lands, tenements, etc., in the parishes of Theydone Garnone and Theydone atte Mounte in co. Essex, which they lately held together with William Brystowe, chaplain, of the gift of the said Richard Pake.

Dated the third day of March, in the twentieth year of Edward IV. (A.D. 1481).

Four seals.

(British Museum : Add. Ch. 28,916.)

Latin.

XXXII.

Quitclaim by William Isaac and Richard Isaac, citizens and clothiers of London, to Richard Pake, son and heir of John Pake, senior, late citizen and clothier of London, of their right in lands and tenements, etc., in the parishes of Theydone Garnone and Theydone atte Mount in co. Essex, which lately descended to the said Richard by the decease of the said John Pake.

Dated the fifth day of March, in the twenty-first year of Edward IV. (A.D. 1481).

Two seals, one fragmentary.

(British Museum : Add. Ch. 28,917.)

Latin.

XXXIII.

Grant by Robert ffabyan, citizen and clothier, of London, and Elizabeth, his wife, daughter and heir of John Pake, junior, late citizen and clothier of London, deceased, to John Tuttesham, John Jakes, William Spark, clothiers ; William Martyn, ffuller, citizens of London, of all their lands in the towns of Theydone Gernoun and Theydon atte Mounte, in co. Essex, late in possession of John Pake, senior, of Theydon Gernoun, grandfather of the aforesaid Elizabeth, and afterwards of John Pake, father of the aforesaid Elizabeth, and whereof he died solely in fee "Also all that parcel of our land called Oxspitilhellys," in the town of Theydon Boys, in the said county, lying between the land formerly of William ffoster on the north, and the highway from Affebrigge towards Newchepyng on the south, one head whereof abuts on land called Millefeld on the west, and the other upon land late of John ffelde on the east, of which land the same John Pake, junior, died solely seized. Also a certain croft called Modelond, in Theydone Boys, lying between the highway leading from Affebrigge to Newchepyng on the north, and the land of the Abbot of Waltham on the south, whereof one head abuts on land formerly belonging to William: ffoster Colyer on the west, and the other on land formerly belonging to John ffelde on the east, of which land the same John Pake, junior, died solely seized. Also a field called Wedynsfeld, two crofts called Gulwentescroft and Shepecotecroft, and a meadow called Edwynesmede, in Theydone Gernoune and Theydone atte Mounte, whereof the said John Pake, junior, died solely seized. Also a loft called Bollys, with a garden and croft adjacent, in Theydone Gernoun, viz., in length between the highway from Brettes Brygge to "le welde Golet" on the south, and a field called "le Brodefeld" on the north, one head whereof abuts on "le Mersshfeld." Also another croft with a meadow of two acres, in Theydone atte Mounte, the croft lying between "le Mersshfeld" on the south, and the Brodefeld on the north, one head whereof abuts on "le Pethopes" to the north, and the other head on the common marsh to the west, and extends along the marsh, held as above. Also five and a half acres of land in Olyvet Brome, in Upton ffelde, in the parish of Westhamme, co. Essex, which the said John Pake and Henry Pake, his son, held conjointly of the gift of Hugh, Abbot of Stratford Langthorn, whereof the said John Pake died solely seized. Also all the lands and tenements in Esthamme, held as above. Also a croft called Howfeld, in Affebrigge, alias Abridge, in the parish of Lamburn, co. Essex, lying between the highway towards Rumford on the east, and land of John Pykeman, called Longlond, to the west, whereof one head abuts on the land of William Hurt to the north, and the other on our croft, called Hancotfeld, to the south, acquired of John Tramps, of Lamburn, husbandman.

Witnesses:—John Pykeman, William Pykeman, William Baker, Richard Lye, John Symme, Robert Jacob, Robert Lye.

Dated the twenty-fourth day of May, in the second year of Richard III. (A.D. 1485).

One seal.

(British Museum: Add. Ch. 28,925.)

Latin.

XXXIV

Indenture by which it is covenanted that William Fitz-William, alderman, of London, shall at his own costs pursue, out of the King's hands, the Manor of Gaynes Park Hall, Hemnalls and Madells, with lands, etc., in Theydon Garnon, Ippyng, Theydon Boys, Theydon Mount, and Northweld, co. Essex, purchased by him of Sir William Willoughby, Lord Willoughby and Eresby, but held of the King by Act of Parliament for ten years after the death of Cicely (ob. 24 Aug., 1507), daughter of King Edward IV., late wife of Viscount Welles (John,

1st Viscount, *ob.* 1498); the said Lord Willoughby to make an abatement in the purchase money.

Dated eighth day of June, the twenty-third year of Henry VII. (A.D. 1508).

Signature and fragment of seal of William Fitz-William.

(British Museum : Harley Ch. 55 H., 28.)

English.

XXXV.

Indented Lease by William ffitzwilliam, of Gaynes Parke, in co. Essex, Esquire, and Anne, his wife, to William Clerke, of Cowpersale, in the parish of Theydon Garnon, in the said county, of two "closes in the Hoke, called the Hovelles and the Herbage of the Grove hoke, called the Hovelles and the Herbage of the Grove, aforesaid," from the feast of the Annunciation of the Virgin last past, for the term of Twenty-one years, at a yearly rent of Twenty-one shillings and eight pence. The lessee to "take sufficient hedgeboote and carteboote of and uppon the woodes and underwoodes growing and being on the premises duringe the terme aforesaid, withoute makinge or doinge any stripe or waste." The lessors reserving power to sell the woods, etc.

Dated the twenty-sixth day of May, in the thirty-eighth year of Henry VIII. (A.D. 1546).

One seal.

(British Museum : Add. Ch. 28,950.)

English.

XXXVI.

An Indenture, whereby Henry Denny, of Dalonce, in the parish of Waltham Holy Cross, co. Essex, esquire, covenants with Robert Hall and John Dodyngton, gentleman, that they shall recover against him, lands in Waltham aforesaid, Nasyng, Epping, and elsewhere in co. Essex, to the use of the said Henry Denny.

Dated the twenty-ninth day of November, in the third year of Queen Elizabeth (A.D. 1560).

Signature and seal of Henry Denny.

(British Museum : Harley Ch. 77 F., 27.)

English.

The exemplification in the Court of Common Pleas of a Plea wherein John Dodyngton and William Nele, gentlemen, recover against Henry Denny, esquire, lands, etc., in Nasyng, Waltham St. Cross, Upshere, Eppyng, etc., in Essex.

Dated the twenty-eighth day of November, in the fourth year of Queen Elizabeth (A.D. 1561).

Fragment of the Queen's seal for the Court of Common Pleas.

(British Museum : Harley Ch. 75 E., 36.)

Latin.

XXXVII.

Royal Letters Patent of Queen Elizabeth, whereby licence is granted to Henry Denny, esquire, and Honora, his wife, to alienate to John and Richard Savage, the Manors of Claverhambury and Hallyfelde, with lands and messuages in Waltham St. Cross, Nosynge, Eppynge, etc., in co. Essex, which are held of the Queen in chief.

Dated the first day of January, in the third year of Queen Elizabeth (A.D. 1561).

With the first great seal of the Queen.

(British Museum : Harley Ch. 75 H., 8.)

Latin.

XXXVIII.

A Final Concord, whereby Henry Denny, esquire, and Honora, his wife, assure to John Savage and Richard Savage, the Manors of Claverhambury and Hallyfelde, with messuages and lands in Waltham Holy Cross, Nasynge, and Eppyng, co. Essex.

Dated the Octave of St. Hilary, the third year of Queen Elizabeth (A.D. 1561).

(British Museum : Harley Ch. 80 C., 35, 36.)

Latin.

XXXIX.

The Exemplification, in the Court of Common Pleas, of a Plea wherein Robert Hall and John Dodyngton recover against Henry Denny, esquire, the Manors of Claverham Bury, and Hallyfeld's Hall, with messuages, rents, etc., in Waltham Holy Cross, Nazing, Epping, and other places in co. Essex.

Dated the twelfth day of February, in the third year of Queen Elizabeth (A.D. 1561).

Fragment of the Queen's seal of the Court of Common Pleas.

(British Museum : Harley Ch. 75 E., 34.)

Latin.

XL.

Royal Letters Patent of Queen Elizabeth, whereby licence is granted to Henry Denny, esquire, and Honora, his wife, to alienate to John Dodyngton and William Nele, gentlemen, lands in Nazing, Waltham St. Cross, Eppynge, and elsewhere in co. Essex, which they hold of the Queen in chief.

Dated the seventh day of September, in the third year of Queen Elizabeth (A.D. 1561).

First great seal of the Queen.

(British Museum : Harley Ch. 75 H., 10.)

Latin.

XLI.

An Indenture quinquepartite between Henry Dennye, and Honor, his wife of the first part ; John Dodington and William Nele, gentlemen, of the second part ; John Tamworth, of London, one of the Grooms of the Chamber, of the third part , William ffenscliffe, gentleman, of the fourth part ; and Robert Hall, of Nasinge, co. Essex, gentleman, of the fifth part, concerning the division of lands in the Manor of Waltham Holy Cross, and among them Nasing Wood, containing by estimation six hundred acres in the parishes of Nasing and Eppinge.

Dated the seventh day of October, in the third year of Queen Elizabeth (A.D. 1561).

Six seals, and the signatures of the parties.

(British Museum : Harley Ch. 79 F., 13.)

English.

XLII.

An Indenture, by which John Tamworth, of London, esquire, sells to John Searle, of Epping, co. Essex, yeoman, the underwood, crops, lops, etc, in Wyntrie Park and Wyntrie Common, lately belonging to the Monastery of Waltham Holy Cross, co. Essex, which said underwood, etc., the said John Tamworth held on lease for thirty-one years of the Duchy of Lancaster.

Dated the nineteenth day of May, in the seventh year of Queen Elizabeth (A.D. 1565).

Seal in red wax.

(British Museum: Harley Ch. 80 F., 24.)

English.

This Indenture made the nynetenth daie of Maye in the Seaventh yere of the Regne of our Soueraigne lady Elizabeth by the grace of God Quene of England ffraunce and Irelond Defendour of the faithe, etc., Betwene John Tamworth of london esquier one of the Chief Gromes of the quenes hignes prvaye Chamber on the one partie, And John Searle of Epping in the Countie of Essex yoman on the other partie, WITNESSETH that whereas our saide soueraigne ladye quene Elizabeth by Indenture under the seale of her duchie of lancaster made betwene her hignes on the one partie, and the saide John Tamworth by the name of John Tamworth Esquier one of the chief Gromes of her hignes prvuye Chamber on the other partie bearing date the Twelveth daie of Maye in the fyveth yere of her hignes Reigne for the consideracion therin specified by thadvise and Counsell of her Chauncellour and councell of her saide Duche dyd bargayne sell gave and graunte absolutely to the saide John Tamworth his Executours and assignes all the vsuall and fallable woods and vnderwoodes cropps lopps Busshes and all olde storven hornebeames growing within and vpon the woodes called Wyntrie parke and Wyntrie comon otherwise called Wyntrie wood with thappurtenaunces and of in or vpon every or any parte or parcell of the same to be cutt felled shredd lopped or cropped in seasonable tyme within Thirtie and one yeres next after the feast of Seynt mighell tharchaungell next ensuyng the date of the saide Indenture, which saide woodes and premisses lately dyd apperteyne and belonge to the late dissolved monastery of Waltham holy crosse in the saide Countie and by force of a certeyne acte of pariyament amonges other thinges to the saide Duchie were lately vnyted and annexed and now are parcell of the saide Duchie in the saide Countie of Essex and also do conteyne in the hole one Hundreth and Threescore acres more or lesse besydes the wayes and voide grounde within the same. AND ALSO the saide quenes hignes by the saide Indenture dyd dymyse graunte and to ferme Iett to the saide John Tamworth all maner of proffittes and advauntages of the agistment and grasse growing within and vppon the aforesaid Wyntrie parke during the terme hereafter expressed Excepte and alwayes reserued to the saide quenes majestie her heires and Successours Syx score Oken Stathelles somtyme Doble merked called Oke Stathelles. The bodyes of all horne beames that be not Storven which be there standing and growing at the date of the saide Indenture To

HAVE HOLD TAKE and enioye as well the saide vnderwoodes loppes croppes and Shreadinges before by the saide former Indenture bargayned and solde, To be felled cut downe and taken within the saide woodes and either of them Excepte before excepted, As also the saide agistment and grasse growing within the saide wyntrie parke to the saide John Tamworth and his assignes from the feast of Saint Mighell Tharchaungell next ensuyng the date of the saide Indenture vnto the full end and terme of one and Thirtie yeres from thence next folowinge and fully to be complete and ended, YELDING AND PAIENG therefore yerely to the saide quenes majestie her heires and successours the Some of ffortie shillinges of good and lawfull money of England at the feastes of Easter and of Seynt Mighell tharchaungell by even porcons to be payde during the saide terme As by the saide Indenture thereof made amonges dyvers other covenauntes grauntes rehersalles and clauses ther in comprised more playnely at large it doth and maye appeare, THE SAIDE John Tamworth for and in consideracõn of the some of Three hundreth poundes of lawfull money of England to him by the saide John Searle in hand at thensealling of thies presentes paide whereof the saide John Tamworth knowlegeth him selfe well and truely contented and paide, And thereof and of euery parcell thereof dothe clerely acquite and discharge the saide John Searle his Executours and adminstratours by thies presentes HATH bargayned solde aliened Assigned and sett over. And by thies presentes doth fully and clerely bargayne sell aliene assigne and sett over vnto the saide John Searle as well the saide Indenture vnder the seale aforesaid, As also all the estate right title interest demaunde possession benefite and terme of yeres which the saide John Tamworth hath should ought or myght have of in and to the saide woodes vnderwoodes loppes croppes Shreadinges agistment and grasse and all other thinge and thinges to him the saide John Tamworth bargayned solde or graunted by the saide former Indenture by force of the saide Indenture or otherwise To HAVE HOLDE TAKE and enioye the saide former Indenture and terme of yeres and all the saide estate right title interest and demaunde yetto come of the saide John Tamworth and all the premises with thappurtenaunces Excepte before excepted vnto the saide John Searle his Executours and assignes from the daie of the date hereof during all the Resydue of the yeres which be yetto come of the said terme of Thirtie and one yeres comprised in the saide former Indenture in like and in as large ample and beneficiall maner and forme to all intentes respectes and purposes in every thing as the saide John Tamwoith his Executours or assignes or any of them shoulde or ought to have had taken or enioyed the premises by vertue of the saide former Indenture or any thinge ther in conteyned or otherwise by any meanes yf thies presentes had never bene had ne made AND THE SAID John Tamworth for him his Executours and Administratours Covenaunteth and graunteth to and with the saide John Searle his Executours and assignes by thes presentes, that the saide Indenture of leasse and terme of yeres and the saide woodes vnderwoodes and all and singuler other the premises to him the saide John Tamworth bargayned sold or graunted by the saide former Indenture and euery parte and parcell there of be the daie of the date hereof and at thensealling and delyuerye of thies presentes shalbe clerely discharged and exonerated of and from all former bargaynes sales leasses giftes grauntes arrerages of rentes reentries forfaitures and of and from all other charges and encombraunces whatsoever had made or don by the saide John

Tamworth or any other for him or in his name. The rent covenauntes and charges wherewith the premisses bene charged by force of the saide Indenture of lease due and hereafter to be due, paide and performed according to the tenour of the saide former Indenture onely excepte and foreprised, And that the saide John Searle his Executours and assignes paieng the saide yerely Rent of fforty shillings according to the tenour of the saide former Indenture, And doying and performyng the other covenauntes grauntes and clauses expressed in the same Indenture which on the partie of the saide John Tamworth his Executours or assignes are to be performed and kepte shall or may from hensforth peasably and quietly have holde take occupie and enioye all and singuler the premisses by thies presentes bargayned solde or graunted and every parte and parcell thereof according to the effecte and true meanyng of the saide former Indenture and thies presentes except in the saide former Indenture excepted withoute lett trouble interupcon or disturbaunce of the saide John Tamworth his Executours administratours or assignes or any of them or of any other persone or persones by his or their assent meanes or procurement in any wise. And that the saide John Tamworth from tyme to tyme vpon request to him made by the saide John Searle his Executours or assignes shal shewe his lawfull favour in that he maye lawfully do withoute his preindise towardes the saide John Searle his Executours or assignes touching the quiett having and enioyeing the premisses according to the tenour of thies presentes yf any suche nede require during the saide terme without frawde or covyn, AND FURTHER the saide John Searle for him his heires Executours and assignes covenaunteth and graunteth to and with the saide John Tamworth his Executours and administratours by thies presentes, That he the saide John Searle his executours and assignes at his and there owne proper costes and charges shall clerely acquite discharg or otherwise save harmeles the saide John Tamworth his heires Executours administratours landes Tenementes goodes and Cattelles agaynst the quenes majestie her heires and successors and all other persone or persones as well of and for all suche Rent covenauntes grauntes and charges as be conteyned in the saide former Indenture which on the partie of the saide John Tamworth his Executours or assignes were or are to be performed paide or kepte according to the tenour of the saide former Indenture, IN WITNES whereof the saide parties to thies Indentures interchaungeably have setto their sealles yoven the daie and yere first above written.

Endorsed :—"John Searle for Wyntry Park."

(British Museum : Harley Ch. 85 F., 24.)

XLIII.

IN THE YEAR 1683.—THE MANOR OF EPPING.

The counterpart of the Indenture Quadripartite between Ford Grey, Lord Grey Baron of Warke, Richard Neville, of Billingbere, co. Berks, and Henry Ireton, of Gray's Inn, of the first part : the Hon. Ralph Gray, of the second part ; Sir Henry Johnson, of Blackwall, knight, of the third part ; and the Hon. Roger North, of the Middle Temple, Sir Michael Heneage, of St. Giles in the

Fields, and Andrew Harrington, of Gosfield, co. Essex, of the fourth part, whereby Sir Henry Johnson mortgages to the fourth parties the Manors of Epping and Gosfield, co. Essex, and of Wooller and Doddington, cos. Northumberland and Durham.

Dated the third day of March, in the thirth-fifth year of Charles II. A.D 1682 (1683).

Signatures of Lord Grey and R. Grey.

(British Museum: Add. Ch. 13,731.)

English.

EXTRACT FROM THE MINUTES OF LINDSEY STREET CONGREGATIONAL CHAPEL, EPPING.

April, 1890.

"The old meeting house at Epping, in the county of Essex, being very much decayed, it was thought proper to take it down and to erect a new one. A committee was appointed; according to their agreement the old meeting house was begun to be pulled down on Monday, the fourteenth day of March, 1774; and the Rev. Samuel Saunders, minister at Epping, being appointed sole manager and director in ordering the building and overseeing the workmen, the first brick of the New Meeting house was laid by the said Samuel Saunders on Thursday, the 24th day of March, in the year of our Lord 1774, and what is scarce credible to relate, tho' at such a time of the year when unsettled weather is to be expected—yet from the laying of the first brick to the finishing of the superstructure and striking the scaffolding, the workmen were not hindered half an hour. So that the whole building was completed in one month and one day, being begun on the 24th of March, 1774, and the scaffolding was struck on the 25th of April following—the weather being so remarkably fine—for what rain did fall it was generally in the night, and there were no more than four trowe, men employed at one time, and mostly not above three."

Extracted by JAMES WINTER,

Hon. Secretary,

Lindsey Street Congregational Chapel, 1890.

COACHES.

THE following list of coaches at one time passing through the town of Epping and consequently along the highway from London, under the management of the Trustees of the Epping and Ongar Roads, is copied from the Almanac published in 1871, by Mr. Griffith, a printer and stationer in the town :—

To London.

The Fakenham	...	...	...	at	8 o'clock a.m.	
,, Norwich Coach...		...	..	,,	9 ,,	,,
,, Cambridge "Times"	...	...	,,	10 ,,	,,
,, ,, Coach	...	.	,,	2 ,,	p.m.
,, Bury Coach	...	...	...	,,	11 ,,	
,, Swaffham Coach	.	.	,,	8 ,,	,,
,, "Magnet"	..	. .	,,	4 ,,	a.m.
,, Norwich Mail	...	..	,,	5 ,,	,,
,, Walden Coach	..	.	.	,,	2 ,,	p.m.
,, Harlow	,,	. .	.	,,	9 ,,	a.m.
,, Thetford	..	.	...	,,	9 ,,	,,
,, Dunmow	..		..	,,	—	

From London.

,, Cambridge Coach	...		..	12 ,,	
,, Bury Coach	...		.	..	4 ,,	p.m.
,, Cambridge "Times"	...	..	..	5 ,,	,,
,, Norwich Coach ...		...	..	6 ,,	,,
,, "Magnet," to Norwich	..	.	..	8 ,,	,,
,, Swaffham	...	..	..	8 ,,	,,
,, Norwich Mail	..		..	10 ,,	,,
,, Walden Coach	..	.	..	12 ,,	
,, Harlow Coach	..		...	,,	6 ,,	p.m.
,, Stortford	..	.	.	..	5 ,,	,,
,, Dunmow	,,	...	..	—	

Besides these were the two Epping coaches, each performing two journeys a day, thus making the number of stage coaches to and from Epping twenty five daily. Each of these coaches had their respective inns of call where their horses were kept, and as each coach was driven four-in-hand, the number of horses in Epping could not have been less than two hundred. To these must be added the post horses. A large number were kept, and during the Newmarket races they were fully employed. At other times they were required for the yellow post-chaises then in use, and also for the travelling carriages kept by county families, which were strongly built, and arranged to carry a good deal of luggage, so that they were very heavy, and were usually drawn by four horses.

INDEX.

INDEX TO APPENDIX.

LONDON :
HARRISON AND SONS, PRINTERS IN ORDINARY TO HER MAJESTY,
ST. MARTIN'S LANE.

CPSIA information can be obtained at www.ICGtesting.com
Printed in the USA
BVOW07s1459140214

344961BV00007B/370/P